*"Under current laws a man has to be
functionally insane to marry and a drooling
idiot to sire a child."*
Dr Charles. E. Corry

*"A Man is like a Panda, he eats shoots and
leaves."*
Aristotle O'Connor-Murphy

*"Life is about choices, the one's we make
and not the ones that are made for us."*
Sam Butt

*"Ignorance is a choice and not the
only reason for life's failures."*
Sam Butt

First published in Great Britain by Sohail Butt 2012.

© Sohail Butt
All rights reserved.

The moral rights of the author have been asserted.

Printed in England by MPG Books Ltd, Cornwall.

Preview available on www.deadbeatdadbook.com
Book available on Amazon.co.uk

A DEADBEAT DAD
and the bloody pandas

Sam Butt

My compliments to Alexithymia

'Failure of men to express feelings with words.'

CONTENTS

Introduction

It is year 2004 and I am sitting here in a counselling session listening intently to what is unfolding in front of my eyes. You see my wife has been in counselling for six sessions already and I have been invited to the counselling process because our marriage has been through some turbulent times for the past sixteen years. She chose a female counsellor because somehow male counsellors are never on her wavelength nor do they understand her. Her words not mine.

Somehow, as soon as I walked in an uncomfortable feeling went through me. The counsellor's eyes and body language made me feel unwelcome. My wife of the past sixteen years sat down with her eyes firmly focused on the floor. An eerie silence prevailed and a feeling of discomfort is what I recall. The only definite was the expectation of the unexpected. I knew my wife well or so I thought!

I have known this person for the best part of sixteen years and only now, it is beginning to dawn upon me that I hardly know her. Vows we took to love, adore, cherish, for richer or for poorer, in sickness and in health seem hollow right now. Why do I believe that these vows only applied to me and not to Sarah? Poor and sickness have been to the forefront of my life since our second daughter was born.

I can feel knots in the pit of my stomach and nausea begins to rise. A sense of déjà vu, maybe. The goodness of my health has not been on the horizon for a very long time and this is not the first counselling session we have attended. Third, time actually. At each of the previous encounters, Sarah went in, built a rapport with the counsellor and then I was invited. The whole shebang would turn on its head and as soon as the finger of change was pointed at Sarah, she would dismiss counselling process or the counsellor as useless and flee. Sarah change, no way Hosé. This was Murphy's Law, jurisprudence et al. and she was never wrong.

Suddenly a stray thought enters my head; is this what life is all about? A lifetime of work and I am feeling a pit full of desolation, sadness, confusion, anger and feelings I have yet to decipher. An awful lot of thoughts and I wish my mind would stop. I felt dizzy with emotion. What a rollercoaster. It was time to get off but I could not, would not, and did not know how and always felt like I had no control. It was lost a long time ago when my battle for survival first began. I had two beautiful little daughters and a sick wife and time waits for no one yet my life had stood still and I was lost.

The counsellor is talking; I am listening but cannot comprehend a word being said. My soul has left the body and I feel nothing but emptiness and a sense of loss. I desperately want to be out of here and the words echo repeatedly in my mind. I feel like crying but cannot find a reason. I can feel the intensity of my pain yet it seems alien. A sensation of choking surfaces and I find it hard to breathe. I have hidden this pain for so long that it has no shape, no meaning or face but appears unbearable as it pierces my whole being.

The reality begins to settle and I can see the room, its surroundings and the people that are present. Now the counsellor is staring at me but there is confusion in her eyes, a hint of sadness and probably a little kindness. Sarah has moved further away from me. She is staring at the wall. At times there appears a blank stare that seems full of rage. I wonder if she is angry with me, again. This has been the norm for a long time but with reasons, I still do not comprehend.

My mind wanders again as I hear someone talking. The counsellor is looking for Sarah's attention and I can sense an impending confrontation. Her tone sounds stern and demanding. I am confused as I cannot believe what I am hearing. So Sarah, now that Sam is here why not start by telling him what you see wrong with him, I hear the counsellor speak. She does not answer.

The counsellor moves a little closer to Sarah. Her legs are crossed and I notice that one of her tights has laddered. It looks a little strange as it runs from the knee down to the side of her ankle. My wandering mind returns to hear voices and the two women are talking. Now Sarah what do you mean you cannot think of anything. If I asked a woman to make a list of grievances, she would have a list as long as her arm, I hear the counsellor speak. Well I cannot think of anything right now, Sarah replies.

The counsellor seems angry and I think I noted a frown. Surely, counsellors do not get angry with their clients; another stray thought meanders through my head. Sarah we have talked for seven weeks and discussed many things. Now surely Sam deserves an answer, the counsellor sounds exasperated.

Sarah stares at me. Her eyes appear full of hatred, venom and much more as she looks straight through me. I can smell trouble brewing and hear Britney Spears singing inside my head. Oops, I did it again! I am always at fault no matter what. Boy you gonna get it now, my loopy brain whispers and yes I do; because it is always my fault.

Jesus Christ have I gone cuckoo because I sure am beginning to sound like one. I thank god that it's only my thoughts and no one can hear me. My head is spinning, sanity is long gone and I tend to lose arguments even inside my head. Someone should bring in the strait jacket and at last I shall find peace amongst my fellow intellectuals. Hopefully there I will belong! Then my train of thoughts comes to a shuddering halt. Did I hear it right?

I ask of myself. It is all his fault, I hear Sarah thunder as she glares at the counsellor.

Hey, did I miss something as I look around me sheepishly. Once left, then right and my gaze settles on the tip of my shoe which I realise needs to be cleaned and polished. Well it was drizzling outside and I had to navigate the puddles. At last we are getting somewhere, I hear the counsellor exhale. Not me sister, I hear my loopy brain whisper as my train of thoughts goes choo choo. Shit I just realised that I cannot even control my thoughts never mind the wife. It's all his fault! Sarah reiterates. He spoilt me. He did everything for me. He is good at everything. Because of him I have low self-esteem.

She is crystal clear folks and I told ya. It is always my fault. Hey wait a minute. Isn't she supposed to tell her what's wrong with me? A stray thought appears but I decide to keep my wisdom to myself.

I hear the train of sisterhood derailing and the carriages are coming off track one at a time. By now they are glaring at each other and this is definitely not the way it is supposed to proceed. The counsellor seems a little bemused and asks; What do you mean your self-esteem is low because of him? What has he done? What is it that he does which is not acceptable to you? He is good with children, cooking, cleaning, ironing, sewing and everything else. He makes me feel small, Sarah bemoans.

By now the counsellor is definitely not enjoying this session. She looks thoroughly confused. God love her! Now she may help find the answer to all my confusions. What else does he do? She asks with her eyes wide open. He does the girls hair, their homework and everything else, Sarah replies. And this is wrong? The counsellor asks, looking more confused and ventures further. And I presume he goes to work as well, she asks in bewilderment.

Of course says Sarah, we have to pay the bills. Oh, yes when it comes to bills, I am part of her life and it is we. Then it's possible that it could be the royal we? Just like Maggie Thatcher. I did not say it loud, I admit sheepishly. What do you expect? I am not that stupid you know!

I think the counsellor is about to tear the hair out of her head and little beads of sweat begin to appear on the brow of her forehead. This is not going according to plan sister, I quietly muse. For the umpteenth time Sarah has managed to gain the sympathy of a professional before shooting herself in the foot.

Even I am part of this panto now as I listen. I feel glad to be here and I want to be here. I sense vindication at last and almost break into a chorus of glory, glory hallelujah before restraining myself and I am very good at restraining myself. It has taken years of practice. Three cheers for deadbeat dads, Hip hip hooray, I celebrate, quietly. Well exuberation is justified even if it is just one compliment and comes once in a blue moon. I think I can live with that and it is definitely a cause for celebration.

The leprechauns inside my head sound the bugle and then I hear the sound of pipes and bodhrans. One thing for sure this celebration is short lived as all will return to normal as soon as we leave this office? Such is guaranteed!

The session is deemed over and the counsellor looks at me, confused, bemused yet sympathetic, and utters a command, Sam, can you please get up. I obey as I mostly do and Sarah looks confused. She does not like this at all. The counsellor looks at Sarah and states; we women have been looking for a man like this for hundreds of years and you have no respect or regard for him. It's your loss not his. He needs nothing from anyone but sure could do with a hug and the counsellor proceeds to hug me.

This is all you need from anyone she assures me. The rest you can do better than anyone else, she states matter of factly. Shall I say something, anything? And then my mind decides to go walkies, again. It's totally blank and not a thinking leprechaun in sight. Even the little feckers desert me when I need them most. Sheepishly, only the word thanks comes out.

In the meantime we are asked to return with our daughters for a session of family therapy. I and Sarah agree as she gets up, turns around and without a word leaves the office. I thank the counsellor and follow Sarah out. The mind is still stupefied and searches for words to comprehend what has just transpired. There is no script and it is time to go home and face reality.

We did return for one session of family therapy. Aisha remained calm and composed without saying much and Rihana said nothing. Sarah was withdrawn and cautious. She probably did not wish to reveal anything in front of the girls. I answered relevant questions if and when asked but the session was eerie and uncomfortable.

When asked, Aisha described it as ok, Rihana did not like the counsellor, Sarah said nothing and the counsellor revealed that none of them had any respect for me and I really should learn to look after myself. It only took me six more years to concur.

Chapter One

It was the summer of 1985. London in the eighties was full of life. Work was good, money was plentiful and life had never been better. The Irish in London were hard working and lived life to the full. Thursday was payday and by Sunday, pennies were being counted. Between lame nags and the pubs, money flew out of their pockets.

Most of the friends I grew up with were Irish or of Irish descent. Lo behold even my favourite lecturer in college Mr Docherty, an absolute genius at maths, claimed to be Irish as did my driving instructor and yes he helped me pass my driving test at the first attempt after less than ten lessons.

It seems a paradox of cultures, as I did not drink nor had much time for nightlife, which was plentiful in London. One Saturday afternoon when the sky was grey and drizzle was persistent, Brentford were playing at home. Two of my friends John and Tommy, brothers in law, called to see if I would come over for a game of pool at Bricklayers Arms, right next door to Brentford football club.

The landlord and his wife were the most hospitable of couples. They treated us all like family especially when Tommy would become legless and fall asleep on one of the couches and breakfast was served every Sunday morning. Tommy was a fantastic block layer, made plenty of money and flushed most of it down pub urinals.

The football game was on and the pub was quiet, almost empty. We were taking turns in playing pool when young Johnny walked in. Now young Johnny was a character. Aged twenty-one and a bit, inhabited a slightly warped world and mostly seemed a little alienated from reality. His favourite pastimes were losing money on the horses and borrowing more for a drink. A tenner promised to be returned tomorrow had never seen the light of day. To add spice to life, he was well under the wings of an Irish mammy. Parents had separated and lived in their own houses. Johnny occupied both homes at his convenience. Mammy, Bridget had a roving eye for anyone with money, a pulse and time for a bit of craic. Her other hobbies included working full time in the civil service, part time in a pub while doing bed and breakfast from home whenever the occasion arose.

In later years I learned that most of her prey was her male lodgers. Dad, John senior used to work on the building sites but through injury had retired and was now a full time drinks connoisseur. Johnny has an older brother Michael who was an officer in the British army and twice did the tour of duty in Northern Ireland. Why the emphasis on the British Army, you may ask. Well the family was a staunch republican clan, tri colour, Danny boy, Fields of Athenry and all. A few drinks and the songs would pour; consistently loud and almost always out of key. Well fair play to the Murphy's.

Michael was also a keen shot at anything female who was ready and willing, yet he was a devoted husband and a father of two. His wife was from a good, upstanding English family, always kind, polite, and well mannered and like a good wife had learned early in marriage to ignore her husband's minor misdemeanours. It was a vision of a perfect, happy family.

Now young Johnny used to have perfect flights of fancy and often it was hard to tell the truth from fantasy. This afternoon looking dapper, prim and proper, he marched in with a beautiful girl on his arm wearing a blue figure hugging dress with big white spots and a scattering of light freckles on her face. Her hair seemed auburn with a hint of colour.

We could not help but notice. Introductions were made and decorum was held even though Tommy looked flush and poor

14

John lost his voice during introductions. The three of us could easily be mistaken for nuns rather than men in early twenties and female company always seemed to have an adverse affect on us. What a collection of male pride and misfits. Amongst all this is Mr MaGoo, that is, I, was scared shitless of the emancipated female and always tried to act cool while the butterflies somersaulted in my stomach. Not knowing what else to do I held my peace and tried to portray an air of calmness and dignity.

Young Johnny introduced her as his girlfriend from Ireland and called her Sarah. She was nineteen years of age. Now this was a bit fancy even for poor Johnny, unless all his prayers had been answered in one and dreams had turned to reality. I suppose every little fecker deserves a break and this little fecker's dreams must have come true, all at the same time.

The best was yet to come when Johnny proud as a peacock offered to buy a round of drinks. Four drinks for us and one for him, dear god what had happened. I had a good look outside the window just in case I missed the flying pig or a whole shower of them. You could have knocked us over with a feather. Maybe there is a god after all but I was still dreading the immortal words, on the sly of course. Would you lend us a tenner? I'll give it back to you next week.

The drinks were bought and I had my usual. To this day, I honestly believe that there is no drink worse than draught coke. It takes half an hour to drink and makes you piss for the next forty-eight hours. At least there is a bright side because I have never been caught for being drunk while driving. Eventually the butterflies in my stomach had settled as did the rest of us gobshites. Between playing pool, throwing darts and the occasional visit to the loo the craic was mighty. For the non-Irish, craic means having fun. You have to be in the company of the Irish to know the true meaning of the word gobshite. God bless 'em. Sarah was making polite conversation and no one knew how or what kind of girl would be seen on good 'ol Johnny's arm. We were all on our best behaviour but sadly it did not last. Sarah was fun to talk to and full of beans and it quickly became obvious that she liked being the centre of attention. Then she let the cat out of bag. Johnny was her first cousin and his poor face became flaccid faster than a eunuch's willy.

Yee haw! The ball was in play and game on! Tommy became his charming self, John looked at Sarah like a newly born calf yearning to suckle the mother cow and MaGoo, that is I sat there stupefied not knowing what to do, where to look or what to say. Yes, that is I, Mr Cool. Better still I could have done with adult diapers and no one would have noticed.

For some ungodly reason Sarah began to focus her attention towards me. I found her rather charming and soon the conversation began to flow. Johnny sat there staring like a lovesick puppy with a droopy face. How I wish I had a camera. Tommy soon gave up and started talking football with John.

Somewhere, somehow the conversation turned to planning a night out. Well if there is one thing the Irish are blessed with, it is to think and make plans before the brain is engaged. Decisions were made yet no one knew where we were heading and my input was negligible.

I had plans for going home, putting on the wash, doing a bit of ironing and my stomach was screaming for food. I tried to hush the involuntary grumblings of my stomach. Let me give you a piece of advice, empty stomach and draught coke are a definite no, no. You will spend the day sounding like a rumbling volcano on two feet. Sarah turned to me and asked, where are we meeting? What the hell is this, we? I thought and then panic set in. I have plans, I muttered like an idiot and it sounded pathetic even inside my head. Sorry, I have to go home and have some things to do. To this day, I still shudder at the mere thought of my stupid reply. Sweet Jesus, how sad was I.

Oh come on, she said sweetly, it will be fun. Now Tommy and John joined in and it was mutually decided, without my consent, that we were all going out to have some craic. Poor Johnny still looked lost and forlorn. If the truth be told I was quite excited. This was all new and fascinating for me.

Please do not get me wrong. I had been on dates before but not of my asking. They were always arranged by friends and led to nowhere. By now, I was as scared of dates as a nun in a whorehouse. Not bad for a twenty six year old male living in London. How I missed my calling to the seminary, I often wonder.

It was agreed that I would first collect Johnny and Sarah and then Tommy and John, for a night of craic, Irish style. Then we all departed for home to spruce ourselves up for the big night. I still had butterflies in my stomach. Any thoughts of food were long gone and my mind was racing like a chicken on speed. So many plans and none made sense. I wonder if I am the only man who ever felt like this. This was not even a date and I was shitting bricks the size of boulders.

Surprise surprise, we ended up in the Forum in Kentish Town. It was 'THE' haunt, or at least this is what I had heard and often been told. Tommy and John were all spruced up and young Johnny wore his pointy well-polished shoes and looked like a proper choirboy dressed by his mammy. I often wonder what I looked like. Selective amnesia, I claim to this day. Sarah looked great, chirpy and happy. Overall, we were looking forward to this evening.

Forum was packed to the rafters and floor was wet with spilt drinks, I presume. The music was deafeningly loud and many a proud male was found floating around like a rudderless aeroplane. Wow is this what craic feels like? I thought as I landed on planet Dementia.

Sarah came over while the others went scouting for talent. Well it would be a bloody miracle to find some here, I whispered under my breath. Let us dance, she said softly and I could suddenly visualise myself dancing like Pinocchio with dry joints. The image did not appeal to me. Sheepishly I asked her if we could sit down for a while as she asked if I would like a drink. Yes please, orange, I replied like a moron. You want ice and lemon with that, she asked jokingly. Yes please, I said politely. I bet I was the only lemon among a thousand happy lunatics with a permanent smile etched on their faces looking into the beyond, as an Irishman would say or on the other hand, maybe not.

Then it happened. The DJ played careless whisper by 'Wham', the coolest band of the time. Honestly, it was before I found out that George Michael was gay. Hey, the girls used to think he was the coolest dude in town and the fecker had made a fool of all of us. Sarah asked me for a dance and it soon became a pleasure once the knees had stopped trembling. I sincerely hope that I was not holding on to her for dear life. Thankfully she was still smiling when the music stopped. I thanked god profusely and may be after all I had not made a complete ass of myself.

The atmosphere began to take its toll. The company was good but everything else seemed out of control. Young women, some in their early teens, heavily under the influence of alcohol were fluttering their eyelashes while the male pride was on display like gombeens gala. In between incomprehensible blabbering each was trying to outdo the other while trying their best to regain the long lost composure. It seemed like mating season for the Neanderthals.

Nature called and Sarah decided that she would accompany me to find the toilets. Not easy when one has to try and make his way through a herd of bodies in drunken stupor, oblivious of the world while leering with blank stares into empty space. As soon as I opened the door to the toilets, a strange mix of female screaming emanated which sounded like the howling of the banshees.

On the floor appeared a couple of young girls no more than sixteen or thereabouts, lifeless. One was frothing from the mouth and the other seemed unconscious, surrounded by a horde of over made up and under dressed females. Two male companions stood around looking demented and clueless. There appeared another half a dozen young women with their eyes closed and heads resting firmly on the toilet seats unaware of what occurred around them. These and indeed many more on the floor did not look like newcomers to the scene. It seemed quite the norm and they acted like veterans. Most seemed young, far too young with faces that looked no more than fifteen or sixteen years of age.

Do something, Sarah whispered. Now this is not a familiar territory for me. What do you want me do, I asked. She did not look amused. Just do something, she repeated. In a flock of hysterical and seemingly pre pubescent females what is a stranger to do, especially if he happens to be of the wrong colour and creed. I turned to one of the males and suggested that he and his female companions try turning the young women gently on their side, open their mouths and help them breathe.

One of them spluttered to life and threw a mouth full of vomit up in the air, which sprayed in all directions with some landing on her well-coiffured hair. Thank god, she was alive and stared blankly without uttering a word. The second young woman wretched and heaved before a mix of vegetables, remnants of a donner kebab and god knows what else proceeded to belch from her stomach. She promptly got sick in her lap. I slid away quietly as Sarah proceeded towards the ladies. The noise, the smell, the whole atmosphere seemed unnatural. All I can describe is a feeling of sadness, discomfort and being out of place while a knot appeared in the pit of my stomach.

I met Sarah back at the table. There was no sign of Tommy, John or young stud Johnny. I did not know what to say and sat there quietly until Sarah broke the silence. So sad, Sarah muttered. I thought this only happened in Ireland. Jesus every second door is a pub back home. Wait until you come to Ireland and see for yourself. Ah sure this is nothing new. Her nonchalant statement surprised me even though she seemed honest and innocent in the way she talked. Her jovial character, her smiles and laughter were sweet yet contagious. She was fun to be with but I wanted the hell out of there. In spite of my dislike of the surroundings I thoroughly enjoyed her company.

The stench of vomit was still fresh in my nostrils and I could feel my stomach heaving. Sarah was quite content to stay but I assured her that I had to leave. We managed to find the other stragglers and told them that we were leaving for home. Young Johnny wanted to come home with us and looked dejected. He ruefully stated that he had not managed to score. Tommy was hanging on to a young woman, leering at her lopsided mammoth bosoms and a huge smile on his face while John looked happy for no apparent reason. They were to take a cab home I was informed.

Sarah was in London for a week or two and staying with her aunt Bridget who often described Sarah as the daughter she never had. We met every day and spent most of our time together. She seemed happy in my company and I felt the same. We talked about anything and everything. She asked me about my family, religion and my religious beliefs. I gave her a brief overview of my family, warts and all. Dad was a retired air force officer, hell to live with, loving mother with a tongue sharp enough to cut a loaf of bread into thirty slices from ten paces and a beautiful loving baby sister I had not seen for years. I think the pain of my recollections was apparent and she did not pursue the matter any further. It is not easy for a seventeen year old to leave home for pastures afar, almost four thousand miles away and learn to survive. London can be uncaring and intimidating at the best of times.

There were other questions. Why I would not drink? What was wrong with pork? I told her that as a Muslim this was my way of life and alcohol and pork could never be part of it. She asked me about getting married and having children and my answer was always the same; the children will have to be brought up as Muslims. She seemed to acknowledge and respect my beliefs.

She told me about her two older brothers and two younger sisters. The brothers Jimmy and Charlie were hard working yet many a time came to blows when drink was taken. She described Jimmy as the apple of her mother's eye, a father of three who acted and behaved like a teenager while Charlie had a cleaning business, an entrepreneur with focus on money but a heart of gold.

The younger sister Mary six foot two, seventeen stone, cabbage for brains seemed full of wisdom from planet nincompoop but no formal education and the youngest sister Kate was the sensible one. It appeared that family was very important to Sarah, no matter how dysfunctional, comical or screwed up they appeared and she could not bear the thought of losing them.

Mother was a steamroller that flattened everything in her way while father was a quiet man who seldom spoke and often mumbled. He had little substance and even less importance within the family. The wife treated him more like an adopted

21

son than a husband and he seemed perfectly content in his allocated role. Then Sarah told me about a boyfriend back home in Galway. Boy, talk about throwing a damper on a man's emotional barbeque. Whenever I was shown his pictures, he seemed in a state of drunken abyss. Not bad for a young man of twenty-two. She described her relationship as on and off and many other events were narrated which seem inappropriate and far too intimate to disclose. Most of these events are quite the norm among the Irish youth as I learned during my years in Ireland. At the time it seemed mostly incomprehensible and confusing for me.

Then the day arrived when she had to leave for home. It broke my heart when she told me that she did not wish to go back to Ireland. At the coach station, she became very emotional and did not wish to let go of my hand. If it were in my power, I would never have let her go. For a man who considered himself intelligent, calm and composed, this was alien territory. My thoughts and emotions seemed out of control no matter how hard I tried. Teary eyed and reluctant she boarded the coach for home.

Somehow, I thought I would see her again. No, I was sure I would see her again and left the coach station with a heavy heart. Something within me had changed for good but what, I did not know. It can hardly be called puppy love for a man of twenty-six. Two weeks together and somehow I thought I had known her forever. I had felt happy and comfortable in her company. Somehow, I think it was much more than that but I was not sure.

Then the letters begin to arrive. Sometimes heartening and encouraging while at other times leaving me in a state of utter confusion. Long letters full of confused feelings and emotions. I could do nothing but open my own heart in return, always encouraging and coaxing.

She was consistently in my thoughts and was becoming the focal point of my life. She always made it clear that she wanted to be with me but could never leave her family. It would appear that her mother was the dominant factor in her fear of leaving. Not because of the love of her family but the fear of losing them. She made me happy and that is what mattered. At least she was communicating with me but somehow this did not seem enough. I wished and wanted her back in London. I shudder to think what moronic thoughts I may have put to paper. Then a letter arrived stating that she was coming over with her mother.

Whoopity do. My heart was doing somersaults. Excitement and longing became one extended emotion and I could not wait to see her. Just to see her and hold her occupied my thoughts. Whatever it takes, I wanted her next to me. I had to remind myself that I was a man of twenty-six. It is amazing to note that when hormones come marching, common sense takes flight.

The day came when I met Sarah and her mother at Victoria coach station. A huge hug and a smile greeted me. Behind her appeared the mother, a portly woman with a smiling face. Very politely, she greeted me and exuded warmth. In an instant, the fear of the presumed matriarchal monster evaporated. All I could see was Sarah's beaming smile, which seemed to amuse her mother no end. This looked good but felt even better. I dropped them at Sarah's aunt Bridget's house and decided to take leave with the promise to see her later, but Sarah wanted to spend some time with me. Her mum gave her approval and we went for a drive. She seemed happy and I felt elated without a care in the world. Somehow life seemed complete.

We talked and Sarah expressed her desire to stay in London and being with me. Her mother wisely decided that she would only agree if Sarah were to reside with her aunt Bridget. Soon it was settled and I believe everyone was happy, especially Sarah and me. After a short stay, her mother left for Ireland and we went to see her off at the coach station. We met every day and spent hours talking about life and things in general. Sarah respected my religious beliefs and personal sentiments that alcohol and pork could never be part of our household if we were ever to get married. I expressed my desire for our children to be brought up as Muslims so at least they would have some of my heritage while growing up in this free flowing society of anything goes. She always appeared supportive and free of doubt.

Bridget worked part time in a pub in Shepherds Bush, West London and Sarah got her first stint of paid work alongside her aunt. Bridget made it clear that she expected Sarah to pay for her upkeep. As time went on it became clear that money and Bridget went hand in hand and the only person of importance in her life was, Bridget. Sarah's working hours were sporadic and intermittent. I drove and collected her from work. The odd time I was invited in for a cuppa while auntie and niece ate their dinner.

It soon became apparent that Bridget did not like me spending time with Sarah. Some of the things she said could be construed as racist to the extreme were they not comical and farcical. People with joined eyebrows cannot be trusted and my kind of men are only after one thing were the common denominators. This got worse with time as she practised her craft with unabated passion. Bridget soon made it clear that she did not appreciate me turning up at her door despite Sarah's invitations. Young Johnny was her confidante and trusted with Sarah's well being. He had never held a proper job, was forever broke and scrounged off people, especially his mum who could see nothing wrong with him. She often supplemented and replaced his supply of condoms, just in case. It was revealed in later years that Johnny had repeatedly intimated his wish to take Sarah to bed. To make matters worse it later transpired that older brother, Captain Michael of the Royal Irish Guards had also tried to ride his pony up Sarah's valley of sin.

This appears ludicrous but all I could think was Sarah and I loved her, deeply. She revealed that during one of her earlier stints with Bridget, one night a family friend had several times crept into her bed but she had managed to get rid of him. She was barely fifteen. Only God knows what else occurred in this house of fun. I would get angry and upset but Sarah always assured me that everything was under control.

Still the odd time, as planned I would visit Sarah but at the last minute would be told that Bridget had made other plans to my exclusion. There were times when Sarah seemed distressed but would placate that Bridget was being protective and thought of her as a daughter. Not only was this becoming irritating but driving me around the bend. Sarah promised that she loved me and things will soon work their way out.

Bridget upped the ante with daily lectures on cultural differences, religious background, women being second-class citizens and having to walk two feet behind their husbands. Her limited knowledge and bias were on a high and getting even higher. Not once did I try to entice or convince Sarah to leave her aunt's house. I told her that it would have to be her decision and she was aware of her mother's relationship with her sister and she could not dream of upsetting her mum.

Bridget blamed me for everything. I was the cause of arguments between Sarah and her and not a healthy influence. According to her, the conflict occurred because I could not be expected to understand the Irish way of life. In her wisdom even the English and indeed the western social and cultural habits were alien to me. I was different, too young to have gained the necessary understanding and even if it wasn't my behaviour and demeanour, it was the subtle defiance of their culture and ways of life. She wanted Sarah to spend more time with her Young Johnny. To this day only god knows what this woman was up to. It was not long before aunt and niece began to have arguments, which seemed to distress Sarah. Often she seemed upset and tearful and one-day things came to a head. I went to collect Sarah from work. It was around seven in the evening. We had planned to go out, get a bite to eat and spend the evening watching TV. As per usual, I was there twenty minutes or so early. Never feeling comfortable in a pub, I walked to the far side of the bar.

There were two men and a woman sitting two tables away from me. I had noticed their stare the moment I walked through the door. The odd time one would turn around to look at me with a strange smile or so I recall and the woman's repeated stares accompanied hoots of laughter. This was eerie as I had never seen or met these people before.

Sarah informed me that she would soon be ready but we may have to wait a while because Bridget wished to discuss something with her. They were both working the same shift. Sarah seemed around nervous and on edge. I asked her if she were ok. Yeah fine, I will be fine was all she said. I had no idea what that meant. The woman at the other table seemed familiar with Sarah and called her over to the bar where they spoke intently. I could not make head or tail of the proceedings. Sarah returned to my table as the woman went back to her companions.

Half an hour had passed when Bridget walked over to us and told me that she was not happy with my presence and Sarah and she had plans while Sarah looked extremely nervous. First, she asked me to go, then paused, and asked me to wait a while as she walked over to Bridget. Only god knows what transpired but she returned and said, let's go now. Bridget walked away and sat down with the strange trio and if looks could kill I would not be around today. I was none the wiser as Sarah pulled at my arm and walked away hastily. As we approached the car, she asked me to hold on as she had something to tell me. She explained that Bridget had fancied the older of the two men for ages. Eventually he had agreed to go out with her only if she could persuade Sarah to go out with his younger brother. This man had a reputation for screwing anything with or without a pulse. Those are Sarah's words not mine. The two brothers were regulars at the pub and the woman she spoke to at the bar had told her that the man is dynamite in bed and she had been with him several times. Sarah should make excuses with me and have the time of her life by accompanying her aunt and the two men.

This was an opportunity of a lifetime and she won't regret it. She was telling her from her own experience. When Sarah would not agree, she told her to do it for Bridget's sake as she was like a mother to her and all she had done for her. When Bridget heard that Sarah would not budge, she went into a rage and promised to have a word with her, later.

We went back to my flat in Hanwell, which I shared with my friend Charlie who had the lease to the premises. It was a small two bedroom flat, which was nice, cosy and comfortable. He had prepared the dinner and we sat down to eat. We had almost finished eating when the doorbell rang repeatedly.

I went to answer the door and there was Bridget with a face to curdle milk. She walked straight past me without uttering a word. She asked, no told Charlie to leave the room, as there was something private to be discussed. He looked gobsmacked and enraged. I asked him to do it for my sake. He was very fond of Sarah and left reluctantly. Knowing him, he probably would have kicked her out of his flat, physically if he had to. He was a black and white kind of person with little in airs and graces.

27

Straight away Bridget thundered into Sarah accusing her of ruining her evening after all that she had done for her. She blurted out how she had compromised her independence by allowing Sarah to stay with her and how she repaid by doing whatever she liked and when she liked.

She was rambling with rage and called Sarah thoughtless, selfish and ungrateful. She told me to stay out of it for this was a family matter and no one else's concern. Eventually the spouting and frothing stopped. She was sitting on the edge of the sofa as she ordered Sarah to get up right there and then to salvage the evening and her self-esteem in front of her friends. For the first time I saw Sarah stand up to her aunt and refuse to budge. Bridget gave Sarah an ultimatum to get up, leave with her and finish with me or else give her back the front door key.

Sarah asked me if she could stay and without hesitation, I said yes. It was a relief to know that I would not have to face poisoned insults on a daily basis. Bridget was enraged as Sarah handed the front door key back to her. Without uttering another word, she got up and left.

Then Charlie walked in looking sheepish to enquire about the pantomime as he put it. Thank god that he has a sense of humour. I briefly explained the events of the evening and he was most agreeable with Sarah's stay as long as I contributed towards the rental and monthly bills. Well each has his own priorities.

Now we were co habiting and I asked Sarah to marry me. She said that in good time she would give me an answer but not right then. Let us just be happy for now, was her reply. The news had been relayed to Sarah's mother and she went on the war path. To this day only god knows what was said and done between the sisters. She was livid and ordered Sarah to return home. When Sarah refused the Irish inquisition began; why could Sarah not find her own apartment? Why would she not return home? And there were plenty more why's to follow. One saga ends and another begins. Eventually her mother's rage subsided and she wanted to know about and plan the wedding.

Questions arrived thick and fast; when are you getting married? Make sure it is a Catholic church and find a good priest. Sarah dealt with these matters, her own way. By now I had learned not to interfere in the family affairs no matter how comical or farcical they appeared. Somehow mammy was always right and not in the habit of being questioned. The family way was the right way, never to be questioned, criticised or corrected.

Her dad was not happy with Sarah's decision to leave Bridget's house and stay in London. This sentiment was conveyed in later years! Good to know at least the man was permitted and could form an opinion. Were it not for me Bridget would never have been forced to kick her daughter out the matriarch had stated repeatedly. Worse still if Sarah had not met me, she would have returned home to Galway.

Since that eventful evening more stories began to emerge about Sarah's stays with her darling aunt. One story recounted Sarah's stay in Bridget's house when she was thirteen. While asleep in her room, one night she woke up to find a man in her bed trying to have sex with her. She managed to push him out of the bed and her room. In the morning she told her aunt but Bridget brushed it aside as if nothing had happened. The episode was never to be repeated.

It also came to fore that self respect and dignity were traits alien to this family. Young Johnny though living with his father would often bring girls to his mother's house. The older son was more discreet but did the same. Would you not think this was too much for a thirteen year old girl to handle?

I occasionally came across Bridget while playing pool in one of the pubs in Acton where young Johnny and his father were regulars. Johnny was still scrounging for a bob or two but he was harmless, gods bless him. I never got any of my fivers or tenners back though. It was amusing to see Bridget shouting for Johnny whenever he played pool with me. She looked animated, agitated and literally jumping out of her bloomers. She wanted to see me beaten.

That was the first time I saw Johnny look and feel embarrassed. It was worse if he lost to me. Winner stayed so we had to play good and usually I won. It was not so good for poor Bridget. Most of her time was spent chastising poor Johnny for losing to me. Small wonder he turned out the way he was. A mother like Bridget and an alcoholic father, the cards were stacked against him from the day he was born. I felt sorry for him.

Chapter Two

Now a new chapter began to dawn. I had an inkling of Sarah's intertwined, rather complex and at times paradoxical relationship with her family. The contradictions in her family values, sense of family and social norms were becoming apparent. There were rules for others and yet there were none for her family to conform.

Boundaries were rigid yet flexible; the family were loving yet full of venom and conflict. All in all rules were there for others to obey but not applicable to her family. The matriarch held the supreme power of wisdom and justice. It was a little paradoxical like our family law courts. I do not want to upset my family, I do not want to lose my family became Sarah's mantra that was repeated time and again in later years.

As Bridget began to fade Sarah's family began to appear like the Munster's family in High Definition to the accompaniment of fiddles, bodhrans and pipes. If and when they appeared in London, I was at their beck and call. The words Catholicism and Irishness were at their disposal to use as and when they wished to do so. Family jurisprudence allowed such behaviours because it was in the best interests of the family. I guess I was a bit of a novelty that created confusion, challenges or a perceived threat and could not be swept under the carpet.

Sarah had been visiting our general practitioner on a regular basis. She had often complained of her highs and lows which were a constant source of distress to her. Repeatedly she suffered glandular fever, thyroid problems and bouts of tiredness, headaches and restlessness. When she was good life felt great and the rest soon became the norm.

One day I asked her the reason for not agreeing to marry me. At first she appeared hesitant but said that she did not know for

31

sure. I was confused but left the matter alone. Knowing my own family and her's, it was always at the forefront of my thoughts that the appropriate thing for two people to do before co habitation is to get married. Her parents were strongly influenced by the black and white of the Catholic Church and my family, I was not so sure. In many ways they may as well be Irish. They have their own amusing habits and beliefs, which most of the time cause nothing but grief. All through my life they have been a conundrum too but right now I had new challenges to face.

One day Sarah returned from the doctor and asked me to sit down as she had something important to tell me. She appeared in a state of distress and found it difficult to put her thoughts into words. Unbeknown to me she had been undergoing some tests at the doctor's surgery.

The doctor told her that she could not have children hence she saw no point in getting married. Things were fine the way they were and what was the point in getting married when she could bear no children. This was Sarah's decision and not open for discussion.

Slowly more details began to emerge. The doctor had told her about her womb being inverted and her inability to conceive while there were problems with her ovaries and fallopian tubes. She looked drained, distant and detached. I reassured her that we will do everything possible and no matter what she will always be the most important person in my life. Anything else would be a welcome bonus.

This was pre IVF and she was put on a waiting list for Hammersmith Hospital where IVF tests and experiments were being conducted and researched by Dr Winston and his team. Over the following days she slowly returned to her normal happy self. Life was good and it felt great.

We went for drives around the country, visited friends, one or two that I had left, played sport, and watched TV, just the simple things in life. One aspect of Sarah's personality was quickly coming to the fore, her individuality. If her interests did not become common interests she soon got bored. She was still visiting doctors and awaited an appointment from the IVF clinic at Hammersmith Hospital. I quietly suffered alongside her. I love children and absolutely adore these little rascals. Being the eldest in my family I had helped raise many a cousin and sibling in my time.

By now Sarah had left the pub and got a job in the local dry cleaners. Initially she was thrilled to get the job and had great stories to tell of clients and fellow employees. Life was wonderful till she began to nitpick on the way her boss ran the business. Niggling little things started to take a life of their own and misery snowballed.

Many a day she literally dragged herself to work, looking tired and miserable. It was always the same, boss is an idiot and he does not know how to run a business and before long even the co workers were portrayed as idiots. What do they say before you marry your sweetheart, have a good look at the future mother in law. Well I never did lay claim to the crown of wisdom.

All I could do was listen or suggest finding another job. I advised her that as long as her boss was not criticising her, to leave him alone. She was getting paid and mostly happy. Soon finding faults with her co workers became her favourite pastime. Everything sounded and felt negative. She began to miss days without offering an explanation and often chose to stay in bed. Cooking, cleaning and paid work were my responsibilities.

After months of moaning and groaning she announced that she had found a new job at a newsagent in West Ealing. She liked the owner and the atmosphere. Straight away her moods improved and things were better. She was working hard and full time till the same pattern began to emerge, he does not appreciate me; I am being taken for granted.

It was becoming a full time saga with Sarah and her working life. My feelings and work were neither interesting nor important. At the time I was working for a courier company and thankfully earning more than my doctor, hence there were no money worries. My utopia was looking flawed but I did nothing. I love her, was the only rational thought that I could muster.

Then came our first Christmas together and I had left the joy of buying her a present till the last minute. I had to work Christmas Eve as the office had plenty of work to clear. I looked at the watch and it was five thirty. Now panic set in which only a male would understand having forgotten to buy something special for their sweetheart. I rushed to Roches Store on Ealing Broadway with the intention of finding something special, something nice, something that says something but I did not know what. After running around like a headless chicken for fifteen minutes which felt like eternity, I found a friendly face at the makeup counter.

Gentlemen, here is a piece of worldly advice. Every time your brain goes numb when thinking of buying a present for your loved one, run to the makeup counter. The women there will be most helpful in relieving you of your cash while telling you profusely about the joy your present will help deliver. I believed this prophet of joy, caked in foundation, thick coat of mascara, a liberal coating of polyfilla and put my faith in her capable hands. My apologies, I forgot to mention the well painted false nails, false eyelashes and hair extensions covering the bleached blonde hair. Can I please have one of this, one of that and can I have one of that yoke with a mirror in it and how much, I enquired with abated breath.

34

Ninety five Sterling was the total for a little vanity case, lip stick and mascara thingy. I counted, ninety in cash including all the change in my pockets. It was most embarrassing as I was fishing for money in every pocket that I could find and recounting the change that I had already counted.

I soon returned to my senses with the sweet sound of the prophet announcing that maybe she could find me something in my price range. My apologies, I said in the most cultured and gentlemanly tone I could muster. I'll be back in two minutes. I have some more money in the car. Sure, she said. It's not what she said, it's what she did not say and the way she said what she did say. This schmuck ain't coming back and there goes my commission. Ten minutes later I appeared with change to spare and less than a fiver left to carry me through Christmas.

I don't think she had believed me because when I returned she had put the items back in the showcase. What was this shit, made of gold? I thought sarcastically. Years later Sarah told me that the damn make up kit was coated in gold. She was curious and had taken the items to a goldsmith for valuation. She wasn't a fool after all.

I was working from seven till seven, six and at times seven days a week. Sarah had a notion that we needed a place of our own so I had to earn more and save money. My cooking was improving by the day and now I had to cook for three. Charlie admired my cooking so much that he had abdicated his duties in the kitchen. Sarah thought cooking was the equivalent of open heart surgery hence she did not qualify as a cook.

Someone had to cook or we would all starve. Sarah's culinary skills were limited to frying an egg or making a toast. Her menu stated that if hungry make a sandwich or a bowl of cereal. This almost sounds Irish but it was always anything for peace and we weren't even married yet.

Now Sarah was working part time because full time was too tiring for her, may gods bless her. Her leisure time was spent sleeping or watching TV. She was always tired. Eventually the medical tests showed that she was anaemic and had problems with her thyroid but nothing definite, yet. There were more tests to be conducted and different prescriptions were being tried.

In hindsight my life was dictated by Sarah's mood of the day and not knowing what tomorrow may bring. Communication from Ireland would further add drama to our lives and this communication always superseded the Ten Commandments.

Now I was repeatedly being asked the same questions over and again. Who do you love more, me or your mother? Who would you choose first, me or your family? You dear and my answer was always the same. It was rather confusing that I showered all my love and affection on her and the nincompoops of my family were nowhere to be seen then why the competition. If I loved them so much, I would be living with the dumbasses.

My monologues had begun which were to accompany me for the foreseeable future. These were the only conversations I could have or else it was Sarah and her family. She could not bear the thought of not being able to conceive. It was getting her down as she tried several doctors for a second opinion. The answer was always the same. Sorry, no chance of conception and no children. By now she had stopped taking the contraception.

One day I received a call at work to call home and it was urgent. I asked about this urgency but they had no details. They were well used to these emergencies and as per usual I dropped everything and went home. Sarah looked pensive, eerily quiet and in deep thought. It did not seem a good omen. I had a headache and was feeling really tired. I did not need a drama. I

36

waited patiently till she announced very slowly and deliberately, 'I think I am pregnant'. What do you mean you think you are pregnant? Either you are or you aren't? I exclaimed like a jackass. You are pregnant, aren't you? Well that's wonderful isn't it; I asked many a question in one breath and she nodded. I wanted to jump with joy. I felt elated. I felt like screaming excellent, fan dobeedoozeee, whatever! The feeling of ecstasy was indescribable. The worried look on Sarah's face put a damper on my jubilation and no words of wisdom came to mind. All I remember asking is, are you OK? What a numbskull I must have looked like.

I don't know how to break the news to my family, she said. The dreaded words had come to the fore once again. I hugged and kissed her only God knows how many times. I simply wanted to reassure her. We were gonna have a baby and that was all I could think. We had to make plans as life had changed forever. The mind was racing and creating plans in my head. What I was going to do with this baby? What games, how much fun, how to spoil this child, I wanted to give this child the world. Plans to ruin this poor child and its future were being conceived at the time of its conception.

Crazy as it sounds I wanted this child there and then, to see it, to hold it, to love it, to cherish it and whatever else that would come to mind. Hell I was excited. Mine. My child is all I could think. Then my train of dreams came to a shuddering halt. Sarah was talking. I have to visit my family and discuss this with them, I heard her say. I don't know how they are going to take this news. I don't want to see them upset. I am nervous and scared.

There was a miracle in the making and she was afraid of telling a bunch of gobshites that she was going to be a Mum. She had done much worse while under their roof and with their blessing. Now she was afraid of telling them that her greatest wish had been granted and yet her happiness needed their approval.

A thought of God being married to an Irish woman wandered through my head. No wonder this world didn't make much sense to me. When I finished talking inside my head, we talked. Let's get married, as soon as possible was my contribution to this conversation. Wow Mr Magoo and his wisdom and I really did surpass myself. Well now there was no excuse for not getting married. The only reason ever given was, if she could not have children, she would never get married.

My life with Sarah seemed a bit like the Irish constitution. There were clauses and sub clauses of which I was becoming aware but got little in clarity. We must get married otherwise this won't be acceptable to my family and I don't want to upset them or lose them. I want to talk to my dad. This is what I recall Sarah saying repeatedly.

I loved the sound of getting married, having a baby, being a family, not realising that there would be a huge extension to my expected family with unintelligible and indecipherable clauses attached to my future happiness. She went to Ireland and broke the news to her family. They told her that if I did not want the baby or was going to abandon her, she could come home and they will help her raise the baby.

The echo of this recall is making me nauseous and I just realised that they must have their heads buried deep up their holes for not to see and hear reality. Their daughter was telling them that she was going to have a baby with the man she loves and is going to marry while the gobshites were planning to have their daughter bring the unborn to them. Over my dead body! I thought. (If I knew then about family law what I know now, this prophecy may have been fulfilled).

Then she explained that they had misunderstood. Well how can any gobshite misunderstand simple English? Now it seems that the more respect I gave them, the less was being returned.

The most important thing was the baby, Sarah and me. On occasions I did try and discuss her family's behaviour which Sarah agreed was unacceptable but they were her family and she did not want to lose them. Any way we will only be seeing them occasionally so stop worrying, I was told.

I had never seen a prophecy go so wrong. Future had many a surprise in stock for us, especially me. I had to plan. A house, a home, a family and money worries were firmly allocated to me. She was planning shopping, wedding, guests, invitations and there were talks about money. The last one on her list was my responsibility to worry about.

During a brief conversation with a distant relative it transpired that he had a market stall in Kilburn for a Saturday market and he made more money in a day than most people earned in a week. His wife had a baby to look after and was not able to help him with the business anymore. He was finding it hard to cope with the market stall. The truth be told, it was the wife who did all the work while he was the pretty face on the stall. If I were interested he was willing to sell the stall and stock to me.

There was a snag in this wonderful venture. I would have to get up at three in the morning, set up the stall and move the van before other market stall holders arrived. It had to be all set by four and the task seemed daunting to say the least. I had no wish to get up for my funeral that early never mind a bloody market stall. I was finding it difficult to comprehend waking up at three on a cold winter's morning. Also, there was a small matter of having to raise cash for the van and the stock.

I asked him to hold on till I consulted with a friend. This friend was poor Charlie, a snail in human form who had a single gear for brain and half a gear to the pace at which he worked. Still if nothing else, he was reliable. We agreed to buy the stall, after consultation with Sarah, of course. After everything was agreed, the business venture took shape and our first morning of work on a freezing winter's morning arrived.

I swear I don't know what was rattling more, my teeth or the nuts. The good thing is eventually I could feel neither. With brains barely functioning and limbs reluctant to move we set about setting the stall. Charlie in his winter's attire looked bigger in the girth than in height. He looked like a brown Michelin man, five foot two in his high heels and the poor fecker was frozen solid. He appeared to don his entire wardrobe and the eyes were barely visible through the woolly hat and his scarf. Still he could see nothing for they were watering profusely. We must have looked like a couple of twats.

Putting up a stall is no easy job. Try putting together a camping tent, framing tubes and canopy with frozen fingers and an absent brain. We did not know our arse from our elbow. Two blind eejits fumbling around and fitting poles in every hole we could find till the frame looked more like spaghetti junction than a market stall. Eventually we managed to get the stall upright with a lot of rods to spare. Honestly if a passing bee farted the whole structure would have collapsed. Charlie spent most of the day holding onto one upright or the other.

We managed to survive and made good money which made the day's adventure worthwhile. I must not forget that soon after 10 am Sarah had arrived to help looking demure in the tightest pair of jeans and full make up. Shame I was too tired to notice but still complimented her on her appearance.

She was good at serving customers and taking the money. Well we were all finding our strengths that day! What I forgot to mention was our merchandise, ladies and gentlemen's underwear, lingerie and socks. We made over two hundred and fifty sterling profit, in 1987 London. Our best sellers and best customers were XXXl in ladies underwear, bras and knickers

40

which catered for the voluptuous amongst the Afro Caribbean while men's y fronts, socks and baby dolls were mostly bought by Irish males in their twenties and thirties. They were all great customers and the craic was mighty. Women were loud and did their shopping with gusto while the Irish men looked sheepish and suspicious as if planning a million dollar heist. I think they are born looking guilty.

Eventually we got home and sat down which was a bad move. Neither Charlie nor I were able to get up and yes we were starving. Somehow I managed to lift my sorry ass up and went cooking. Suddenly a thought occurred to me that poor Charlie had been dying to go for a leak since the morning but could not manage to open his flies due to frozen fingers, thermal pyjamas, a pair of trousers and waterproof pants plus the blanket over his shoulders didn't help.

When I reminded him at six in the evening, he said that he was too tired to relieve himself. I honestly thought the poor devil would lose his bladder and won't make it through the evening. Thankfully he proved me wrong and lived to become an asset in the long run.

The market carried on for over five months and with the consent of other traders we managed to convince the local council to extend the market into Sunday. The routine included going to the lock up garage, getting the van and stock to the market by three thirty in the morning, shovelling and sweeping the snow, getting a couple of cups of coffee that looked like tar and tasted like shit down Charlie's throat. This helped in jump starting him to life and then we would set up the market stall and eagerly wait for the punters.

Feet were kept off ground for fear of frost bite and even the moon boots offered little comfort against the frozen ground. Michelin man Charlie would get dressed like a Hobbit and was beginning to enjoy this lark. He and Sarah were at their happiest when counting the takings at the end of the day. Yes she still arrived late but was good company. She was beginning to interact with the customers especially men from Kerry whom she found rather amusing.

This was the first month of her pregnancy and the purchase of a house was always foremost in her thoughts. We were looking at houses but everything seemed out of our reach. Whatever I earned from my two jobs was never going to be enough but economics and common sense had never been strong in Sarah's forte.

Eventually we found a house in Southall, West London, which seemed within our budget but if I were to miss a week's work it would have left us in dire straits financially. By now fatigue was beginning to take its toll. I was forever feeling tired and headaches had begun to set in. The lower back pains were becoming more severe on a regular basis and yet I never consulted my doctor. There were more important things to take care of.

We put down the deposit for our house while a friend of mine managed to organise a mortgage within forty eight hours and soon we became house owners. It was our first foot on the property ladder and my first step towards an early grave. New baby, new house and I thought life would be wonderful. An exhausted body with an even more exhausted mind was surviving on happy thoughts. It felt wonderful in this fool's Utopia!

Now a new side to Sarah emerged as an old friend from the past appeared on the scene. Naseem and I were friends from our teenage years in Pakistan. He was a good person, a dear friend and always available and willing to help as he proved repeatedly in later years.

To their face, Sarah was polite and charming to Charlie and Naseem but slowly she started to tell me that she did not want anyone to know our new address and our date of moving. This seemed strange but she explained that she wanted the house free from intrusions and would invite them when we had settled in the new house. I did not feel comfortable with this idea and told her so, repeatedly. It felt impolite, unethical, immoral, improper, and whatever other words I could find in the English dictionary were utilised.

Apparently these words were missing in her vocabulary. As the day for moving got closer so did Sarah's repeated rant of telling no one, especially Charlie and Naseem. To this day I am ashamed to say that eventually I caved into her demands. Sarah had given up smoking while I was still addicted to nicotine. On the day of move, everything was planned quietly and we told no one. One minute we were there and next we had vanished without a trace.

Now we had a roof over our head and there was so much cleaning, painting and wall papering to do. Previous owners had cats for pets and the house was infested with millions of fleas. Now I had two extended families to take care of, Sarah's and the bloody fleas.

Sarah was second month into her pregnancy and feeling more pre occupied than usual. I was working all day and painting and wallpapering late into the night while she made the shopping lists. Every time I reminded her about our financial situation she chose not to hear me. One day I came home and there appeared a new washing machine alongside a tumble dryer. It wasn't long before a cooker arrived soon to be followed by bedroom furniture. Exasperated I asked her who was going to pay for all this. We'll manage was always her answer. In reality this meant that I had to find the money. My migraines were getting worse and the lower back pain was so bad that I often drove with one hand clenched in a fist resting at the base of my spine to relieve pain. I was barely managing the bills and we were only two months into mortgage. She was going head first into all her plans without giving much thought to reality.

Now another aspect of her personality began to develop. Pugilism! This began as an odd thump or two, in the back because she felt frustrated. Then she progressed face to face with the odd thump to the chest or the shoulder. I could see the rage in her eyes and I still don't know why. The reasons were always the same, 'you don't understand me and I get flustered'.

One evening after a hard day's work I was getting ready for bed and felt more knackered than a hooker having serviced an entire shipyard. I was quiet and pensive when wham a punch landed on my right shoulder for no apparent reason. As I turned around one, two landed on my shoulder and chest.

They hurt. She was raging, because she felt ignored while I changed into my pyjamas. I remember warning her that if she ever punched me again I would hit her back and got into bed.

Next thing she jumped across the bed trying to scratch my face and I ended up getting a knee in the groin. The shooting pain brought tears to my eyes. As I pushed from under the quilt, she fell, bum first on the floor. She was surprised and looked astonished.

I never thought you would do this to me, she said and went quiet. I turned over in the bed nursing my crown jewels and eventually fell asleep. Sometime later she quietly slid into the bed and put her arm around me saying sorry, it won't happen again. For years it didn't but then it did. That's another chapter in this fascinating story of love, hate and relationships.

Now she was making plans for the wedding and a whole new Pandora's Box was about to open. She had invited her parents over and wanted the house ready before their impending arrival. Money was becoming invisible but her spending was there to be seen.

How are we going to cope was met with a new answer. I am expecting a baby and surely you don't expect me to get a job and feel stressed. It will affect the baby. Then she would start the other mantra about wanting to impress her parents and not wanting to upset her family. 'I want my parents to be happy' was her favourite line.

I went to Victoria coach station to pick them up and brought them home. From now on at every given opportunity our home was referred to as Sarah's house and my job was the handyman and the chauffeur. Everything went well, politeness was displayed and decorum was held. Her dad was a quiet man, not much to say and seemed very reserved. I believe a mutual respect was apparent and polite conversations were never a problem. Mother on the other hand was an out of control juggernaut that knew no boundaries. Why don't you do this? Why don't you do that? And this is how it should be done were repetitive instructions. Her favourite quote being, I have seen the gentry and worked in respectable houses so I know how things are done and should be done. Oh boy, this woman never shut up.

It transpired that she had worked as a cleaner in some middle class homes in Cricklewood and St John's wood where she learned the art of silver setting and only god knows what else. She had no formal education but a hard working woman who kept the family unit working while driving everyone demented. The functionality of a dysfunctional family was slowly beginning to emerge. This was new to me even though my own family had set the bar pretty high in fuck ups. The real characters were on stage and it seems I was allocated the role of a horse's backside in this panto for the rest of my life.

All new household toys were inspected by mother and daughter with a comment or two for everything on display. In between there were talks of wedding plans and shopping. While Sarah proudly showed her newly acquired possessions, Mr MaGoo, that is I, had to go to work. One day during a conversation I told Sarah that we could not afford a big wedding. I could barely manage to pay the bills and there was a baby on its way. How would we cope?

Her mother had her own plans. She wanted a Catholic Church wedding inclusive of all the family, wailing banshees and the dancing leprechauns! Sarah was busy visiting priests. They would only hold the wedding if I were a catholic and the children of the marriage were to be reared as Catholics, good Catholics. And I was beginning to get sick and tired of this unholy show.

One day I told her that I had no problems getting married in a Catholic church but no one was going to tell me how to raise my children. Eventually one priest said that he would marry us irrespective of my beliefs provided if just for the service I agreed to say that the children of this marriage would be brought up as Catholics. This was the last straw that broke this lame camel's back.

I sat down with Sarah and calmly told her that I loved her more than anything and would do the same if not more with the baby but, it will be us three and no one else in our family. The world could go to hell. Let's buy a wedding dress, book a date at the civil registry office, get two friends as witnesses and get married.

It was quietly obvious and often stated that she was sick and tired of her family's shenanigans but was too scared to say it loud. Yes, she did not want to fall out with her family but at the same time she did not want anyone of them at the wedding ceremony. She said at every event her family ended up in an argument or a fight and she did not want her day ruined. I managed to convince her that at least her parents should be there. After all they are her mum and dad. She said we'll see. A few days later her brother gave me a piece of advice, which to my detriment I chose to ignore.

Do not invite any member of our family to your wedding, especially the mother. Apparently she had ruined his wedding day and every other special event but details were scarce. I wish I had listened to his timely advice.

We went shopping everywhere. You name it we visited the shop and her mother had to have a say in everything. Eventually we ended up in Brent Cross shopping centre. I quietly slid away with Sarah's blessing and allowed her to endure her mother's company. I bought a suit and tie in ten minutes and met them as they were cruising around the ladies wear shops.

By now a little bump was beginning to appear and most of the dresses Sarah liked were tight fitting. Eventually in Harvey Nicholls we found a beautiful dress in cerise pink that fitted her perfectly and we both liked it. It looked fabulous on her.

The saleswoman suggested slight alteration to the dress for better fitting which Sarah agreed was appropriate and we left for home to our mutual relief. Her mother was still nattering away to Sarah's annoyance. It would be better if the dress was white, she said repeatedly, sometimes loud and at other times it was a muttering. A pen full of pubescent clucking hens would be no match for this woman. I was too tired to say anything. Most important thing was that Sarah was happy. At least I had one less thing to worry about.

One day after a twelve hour shift I opened the front door and was greeted with raised voices. Sarah rushed to the front door to tell me that her mother was on a war path. Her dad her called her a cacklin' hen and she was feckin' (Irish word!) anyone and everyone out of sight and wanted to return home. Her father was upstairs packing his suitcase.

She revealed that her mother was jealous that her nineteen year old daughter had a house and everything while she had worked hard all her life and got nothing. She relayed this in no uncertain terms to her husband. Mum is feeling very angry and jealous, Sarah confided, quietly. I went to talk with her dad and managed to calm things down. They left after a few more days of stay. All seemed well except mum. She was unusually quiet and her mind seemed elsewhere.

A month or so later I was informed of her younger sister Mary's impending visit to our public abode. She was two years younger than Sarah and worked as a childminder. No formal education and barely able to read or write. The fateful day came when we met. Six foot two, over seventeen stone, sharp as her mother and dumb as a horny mule but in possession of a smaller brain. Ability to think is not in her forte, never has been and nor will it ever be. God love her. Everything she said or did had a reference to the mother.

One day when I was cooking dinner, Sarah had a craving for chips. I peeled the potatoes, which Mary said is not the way mam did. I chopped the potatoes, which Mary said is not the way mam did. Then she walked over to Sarah and asked, are you going to let him cut the chips the way he is doing? This is not the way mam does chips, tell him. Sarah looked exasperated and I felt a strong urge to shove every spud up the tank's hole.

Then again one day when cooking curry, she walked into the kitchen and started talking. I would rather have my testicles crushed in a grinder than muster energy to have a conversation with her. Yes the experience could be that painful. Then she saw a handful of green chillies lying on the counter. What are these? Can I try some? She asked. I felt a sense of justice and vindication coming my way and the timing seemed perfect. Common sense and common decency had long flown my coot. Yeah sure, that's all I said.

She promptly picked one up and took a nibble as she walked back to the living room. Next I heard roaring and screaming which sounded like a stampede. It sounded like a herd of demented elephants was let loose and a poor gazelle was being crushed to a slow and painful death. It was Mary, holding her throat, eyes popping out of their sockets and gasping for air. For once she was unable to utter a word.

I profusely and repeatedly thanked God for small mercies. She had taken a big bite out of a green chilli and her mouth was on fire. I saw Sarah smiling and glaring at the same time.

This was a little taste of my life. Full of spice and bite alright.

Chapter Three

The wedding plans were made and the date was set. Sarah's mother and father were invited on my insistence but he chose to abstain. Two of our mutual friends were invited as witnesses and an Italian restaurant was booked for the meal. It catered for all tastes and was the favourite haunt of many a celebrity and business executive. Our unborn baby was the guest of honour.

On the big day Dee Singh, a friend of mine borrowed his boss's Mercedes limousine, which was a pleasant surprise and Del another close friend and best man arrived. I appeared calm, in control, happy yet on the inside felt a bundle of nerves. I had no close friends or relatives and the only uncle living less than five minutes away was not invited. He is another character about whom I can write a book. All the participants were screened and approved by Sarah. She looked happy and glowing and slowly it began to feel like perfect day.

The entourage arrived at Acton registry office. Dee and Del were the witnesses until mama threw a curve ball. She wanted Mary as a witness and unilaterally invited her sister Bridget and nephew Joe to the reception. Poor Sarah looked nervous while narrating the unfolding events to me. By now I knew well that her mother was devoid of any sense of shame or common decency.

Oh hell, do whatever you like and feel necessary was the only response I could muster. To my surprise the whole ceremony went without a hitch. Del took some pictures with his pocket camera and Dee drove us to the restaurant. Great ambience, Sarah looked happy and buzzing with excitement. I was happy and relieved to have survived the clan thus far. Not so, I am afraid. Another impromptu circus was about to begin. When circus comes to town its best not to fuck with the clowns and plenty were to surround me on the day.

We were led to our reserved table adorned with a surprise cake and candles. Sarah's mother got busy fussing and re organising the table which the restaurant had laid with precision. The staff retreated and looked bemused while Del looked cross and me, I was used to it by now.

The orders were being taken when Joe and the clan started asking for food that was not listed on the menu. It presented a perfect opportunity for matriarch to start finding holes in everything from food, to shopping, back to food then service and whatever else she could think of. The staff looked exasperated, Sarah looked embarrassed, and Del and Dee were looking at each other like Laurel and Hardy. I for a change chose to ignore their antics and alongside Sarah ordered my starters and the main course. It was our day and the hyenas were being kept at an arm's length.

Now it was Joe's turn to start nit picking on the choice of steak. This restaurant did the best steak this side of London but apparently not good enough for the Irish Clan. The feckers were fed on bacon and cabbage and now appeared full of airs and graces. Wine was served, as an exception for the day. Another bad move on my part it seems. The wine was not good enough and plenty of audible comments were made. Point to note that Joe is a reformed alcoholic and a former seminarian. It looked liked the staff had had enough by now. I got up quietly, made apologies, and asked them to be patient. By now there was definitely a damper put on the proceedings.

Thankfully the meal was soon over and the cake was cut. Some joy returned and the staff joined in the merriment. The cake tasted beautiful till Sarah's mother decided to tell anyone within earshot or willing to listen how she would have baked the cake. By then everyone was tired of her crap and chose to ignore her. She found solace in Mary's company.

It was time to pay the piper and go home. Del insisted that he pay for the meal but my stubbornness and false sense of pride would not hear of it. I gallantly went to pay the bill until I found myself short of money. I knew this place was exclusive but how expensive, I had no clue.

People use the word embarrassed loosely. I wished for someone to shoot me there and then. I felt like crying with embarrassment till I heard the words, thank you Del, see you again soon. Del had paid the bill while I stood in a state of suspended stupor. I reimbursed him later and he accepted my sentiment, graciously though reluctantly.

Sarah's mother had scored again and I was beginning to acknowledge that this woman would never let anything stand in the way of her idiosyncrasies, no matter what the cost. Yes, she always had to have her say and tried to get the last laugh as only time will tell. True to her nature she had already made every effort to fuck up her daughter's special day. I desperately wished for this bloody woman to grow wings, stick a feather up her backside and fly straight to hell.

We arrived home and Dee went home to collect some food his family were busy preparing since early in the morning. They were a very close knit, warm and caring family. This was their wedding gift to Sarah and me.

The matriarch had another card left to play and she never gives up on her tricks. This is not our kind of food, she piped. She and Bridget to the amusement of some and ire of others proceeded to make sandwiches. Now they wanted to get turkey and ham which horrified Sarah. She warned her mother that she would be killed if she did not behave and her mother thought that it was a hoot. This woman should be stuffed and declared a national monument by the Irish state. Where in the world would you find such a specimen?

Sometime later in the day Bridget's ex husband turned up. The matriarch had invited him without consulting Sarah or me. Then I had made another mistake. Sarah had asked me if we could serve drinks for the day and I had agreed. I had invited a few friends from work and one of them, gods bless fellow Pakistanis, decided to bring a friend to add merriment to the proceedings.

He seemed harmless until it transpired that when drunk he could be a real dickhead. I was uncomfortable around drinking and this clown was turning out to be a real pain in the ass. Del was not amused and decided to keep an eye on him. Sarah and others put the music on and everyone was having a good time until raised voices were heard from the front room as I was busy entertaining the clan in the dining room.

As I rushed towards the front room, Del was busy escorting this Pakistani clown out of the front door. Do not worry it is under control, he said. Dee was not far behind. What is under control, I asked. I will tell you in a minute they both replied in unison. Sarah appeared from the front room looking flush. She explained that he wanted to dance with her and while doing so had grabbed her behind in full view of the guests. Everyone looked embarrassed.

Sarah came over to calm me down as we all gathered in the dining room. All the friends slowly began to leave and I settled down with the clan. It was Sarah, mam, Mary, Bridget, Joe, Bridget's ex and me. Out of the blue another character had appeared, Willie McFly, Joe's older brother. Sarah told me later that they were both recovering alcoholics and raised by Sarah's mother. The cast of the panto was ever increasing and I should have known by now that I did not stand a chance in hell of retaining what little sanity I had left.

Drink was flowing freely and every empty glass was quickly refilled. Bridget looked animated, her ex looked on edge, and

Joe was talking. Willie sat in the background slurping away his cup of tea with six spoonfuls of sugar. This guy looked cagey and there was something very fishy about him. He reminded me of a sly fox about to strangle a chicken but could not decide which one. The matriarch and Mary were talking quietly while Sarah looked nervous. There felt an eerie atmosphere before all hell broke loose.

Bridget with the matriarch by her side flung a drink at her ex, and started screaming at him. Then she proceeded to slap him, repeatedly before sly fox Willy jumped out of his chair and started to shadow box around him. He was circling like a demented ass before proceeding to pull at his shirt which ripped and the buttons flew up in the air. Colourful language took all the shades of the rainbow. Sarah sat in a corner looking like a headless chicken while the matriarch tried to pacify these lunatics like a waffling diplomat. Mary, well she looked as she always did, completely blank and clueless.

You are never ever going to hit me again, Bridget screamed as she attacked him again while calling him every name under the sun. Willie aged fifty two and a bit looked comical hopping around shadow boxing, imitating the Ali shuffle and screaming obscenities of his own. You cripple now try and hit me with your stick, you feckin cripple, he sneered.

I got up and walked out to the back garden. I felt an urge to scream and cry at the same time. This scum had managed to lower the bar of common decency yet again. No matter how thick and ignorant a person this was beyond comprehension. Not the tiniest hint of common decency, apology or a sense of guilt. I was in a state of shock as I stood in the garden livid, angry, upset, feeling a mixture of emotions and torment, all at the same time.

Emotions were running up and down my whole being. The head felt light as it throbbed. Blood was gushing and my heart pumped as I felt ready to explode. Instead, I said nothing and did nothing while shaking with rage. With the darkness closing in I stood silently, staring into the abyss. This was around nine thirty in the evening and slowly I began to feel tired, drained and resigned. Then I sensed Sarah standing behind me. She gave me a hug and we held each other silently. She said sorry, repeatedly. 'Please don't do or say anything'. They are my family and I do not want to lose them. And then she started to cry. It was not her fault. The marriage had begun the way it was to end in 2008.

After a little while, we came back inside the house. All had quietened down. People were moving around, fixing furniture, wiping this that or the other. I decided to go upstairs when I heard Sarah's mother utter those immortal words; you will get used to the ways of the Irish. This is how we are. I stared at her, said nothing and went upstairs. I do not know who did what, said what and when they left the house. The garbage had left the building and that was good enough for me.

Chapter Four

The joyful journey of married bliss had started with a bang. At long last the clan departed and life began to take shape. Sarah found a job at a local hardware store and started to earn a wage, which took some pressure off me. In fact, she became quiet good at managing her money.

The store had newly opened and the staff was undergoing training in Southall and Edgware. Sarah seemed happy and found some social interaction. She would often meet with her work colleagues at a local pub. As far as I know, she did not drink. She had also given up smoking. I dearly wish I had too. There were seven months to go with her pregnancy. I would drop her on the way to work and collect her on the way home. My work schedule was dictated by her work practices.

Soon the previous pattern of behaviour at work began to emerge. In the beginning, she seemed animated and happy when talking about work and colleagues but soon they were being referred to as bitches and bastards. She went to their first staff get together party which was held a local hotel, ten minutes from our home. A day before the party I was informed that it will involve an overnight stay. Sarah would always do what she wanted and I had little or no say in the proceedings.

She returned late the next morning and was very quiet. I was a bit miffed but asked how the party went. It was good she said and no more information was forthcoming. A few days later, she disclosed that the newly appointed store manager was making her life difficult. I asked her if she would like to speak with the area manager whom she described as a very nice guy. She asked me to leave it alone for now.

A week or two later she said that she dreaded going to work because life was becoming unbearable. Yes, it was the store manager again. This time I told her that I would speak with the area manager as this matter needed to be sorted for the last time. After all, she was being harassed from what I had gathered.

There is more, she said. Now I was told that the store manager had propositioned to her on several occasions and on the night of the staff party wanted to have sex with her. I really did not know how to handle this newly disclosed information. She admitted to some playful and jovial flirting but no more. When asked about kissing, she said it was just a little kiss on the cheek, whatever that meant!

I felt that I had to take my wife's side and promptly rang the area manager the next day seeking an appointment. He was most polite and understanding and offered a meeting at a mutually agreeable time. I thanked him for his courtesy and rang him the next day. He seemed apprehensive and stated that there was more to the story. He had quizzed the staff who attended the party and all pointed the finger of blame at Sarah for her flirtatious behaviour. They had also disclosed that Sarah was not easy to get along with at work and was divisive and disruptive. He asked me to discuss the matter with Sarah before he took further action. Thus far, it was all off the record.

I was confused and did not know what to say. I thanked him for his time and asked him to put the matter on hold until further consultation with Sarah. When at home, I told Sarah what had transpired in the conversation with the area manager. I also told her that I was willing to take the matter further if she so wished. Her face was red and she went quiet. It was only a little horseplay, she said. It did not mean anything serious. I had little idea what this meant and it confused me even more.

Then she decided that she was going to pack up work and did not wish to return. She also asked me not to pursue the matter any further. I knew no better and let the matter rest. The next day I got a call at work, emergency at home, call a sap and I duly obliged. Sarah asked me to come home as she had something important to tell me. She had been fired from her job. Even though she insisted that the manager had it in for her, she did not wish to take her case to the job tribunal.

In the past, Sarah's flirting had also caused problems nearer to home. On Sarah's twenty first-birthday party, Bridget of all people approached me and asked me to put manners on her. What kind of a man was I to allow my girlfriend away with such outrageous behaviour? It transpired that Sarah and Bridget's son Johnny were openly flirting and people were talking. Things must have been bad if Bridget of all people felt indignant. Once again Sarah's explanation was it's only a bit of fun.

There was little said in the next few days until she started to complain that she was bored and had nothing to do. She also began to complain about my working hours even though we were living on the breadline. At times she wanted to go to work and then she wished to stay at home.

It was not long before she informed me that she had been offered a better job as wages clerk in another hardware store in South Ealing. It often felt like I was living with the daughter of Walter Mitty. Past was rarely mentioned and I began the same routine of dropping her off and collecting from work. Her new job was in an office and she had little contact with other employees or customers. This continued until two months prior to our darling daughter being born.

There were good days and bad days but somehow I was managing to survive. Some days she enjoyed her work so much that she regretted being pregnant. Other times she said that she would return to work after maternity leave. I had no clue whatsoever where I stood with her on a daily basis.

The clan members were not visible but ever present. Sarah was in constant communication with her family, especially her mother when it was revealed that Cousin Willie would soon be appearing in London. By her mother's decree, we should put the poor man up for a couple of days. Poor man Willie was fifty-two years of age, cagey, conniving, fraudster, liar and a manipulator as Sarah described him. He was a habitual liar and a crook yet her mother could never do enough for him and all her siblings despised him with passion.

So why was I being bestowed with such honour one may ask. After much discussion, I ceded to Sarah's request to allow him a stay with us for a couple of days. Just so, she could keep peace with her mother. In hindsight I should have asked what do a couple of days mean in Irish. Sweet Jesus, am I really this slow and soft in the head? Cousin Willie duly made an appearance and made himself comfortable. Charming as a one eyed hooker and did not have much else to offer. Every day I was told he would be gone in a couple of days.

He is looking for a place and work. He always finds work and will soon be gone. I often wondered where he was looking, hopefully not up his hole where he seemed to spend most of his time. I was getting sick and tired of the sight of him. A slimy liar who believed all he said as the gospel truth. He turned out to be a complete and utter shameless creature who could not tell the truth even if it bit him on his backside or his life depended on it.

Couple of days changed to a couple of weeks until one day I came home early to find a brown envelope with Willie's name on it. It was from the Social Welfare Department. For some ungodly reason I felt compelled to open the envelope and found a hefty cheque and a rent book as its contents. He had forged my signature as the landlord. Poor imitation but at least he had spelled my name correctly and got the address right.

I was livid and wanted to kill the bastard as I called Sarah at work. She had never heard me this angry. Please do not say anything when he returns, I will deal with him she said. I went to collect Sarah and returned home. Mr Willie McFly arrived soon thereafter and looked surprised to find us home. He duly asked Sarah if there was any post for him. I was upstairs clenching and unclenching my fists while Sarah's voice sounded calm. Why would there be any post for you here? Did you give anybody this address? She asked.

Ah sure only one or two people, he said. I did not think you would mind, was his reply. Then I heard Sarah's voice becoming angry. How dare you give our address to strangers? Mr McFly was indignant. He started giving out to Sarah. How dare she speak to him in that tone, he demanded to know.

She told him about the contents of the letter and now he was livid. Who gave me the right to open his post? Who the fuck did I think I was? He screamed. By now, I had had enough. Sarah must have heard me coming down the stairs. She was standing at the bottom of the stairs and looked nervous. The little fecker was standing there ready and willing to fight. Get the fuck out of my house; I screamed.

At the sound of my voice he backed off. This cheque and rent book is going to the cops and you, you little shit get the fuck out of my house right now, I roared again. He meekly asked for the cheque and then quickly scampered. His last words were that this was not the last of this matter and her mother would deal with her. I saw his skinny behind disappear into the dark as I stood there shaking with rage and for once Sarah did not say a word. The cheque was duly returned to the social welfare office the next day.

Literally two days later after collecting Sarah from work, I found Master Willy sitting in the dining room drinking coffee and watching TV. This time before I had the chance to do anything Sarah lay into him and told me to call the cops. The son of a bitch had managed to wriggle open the downstairs window and was lecturing me about the lack of security in the house. By now even I had realised that there seemed a genetic fuck up in this clan of intellectual dumbfucks.

Very calmly he stated that he had returned to ask nicely for the cheque. I called the cops and was prepared to strangle this slimy piece of shit while he tried to make polite conversation. All he would get today was his funeral and I had had enough of them all. Sarah was heavily pregnant and begged me to leave him alone. I could do nothing as Sarah stood between him and me and then the scumbag left.

Within two days Sarah received a letter from her mother admonishing her for her behaviour and letting me get away with mistreating and threatening poor Willie. He had done nothing wrong she had stated. How dare I throw him out of my house? Who the hell did I think I was? Oh, she had much more to say but Sarah would not let me read the rest. The letter was promptly destroyed and I never got a chance to know the rest of its contents. I reiterate that this woman should be declared a national treasure, stuffed and put on top of the spike in O'Connell Street.

Now another chapter in my life began. The youngest sister Kate aged almost fifteen was to visit us. Apparently, she was refusing to go to school and causing problems at home. Sarah was to impart wisdom and fix her errant ways. I was back to my chauffeuring duties but Kate turned out to be a well mannered quiet young woman of good manners and lovely personality. We got on well from the start and her stay was enjoyable to say the least. The only problem appeared to be with her mother and no one else. She hated the school just like all her older siblings but her mother would not let go of the matter. She stated tearfully that she was here to get a break from the lunatics. Her wish was to return if it was ok with me and she did return. She was most welcome but there appeared a problem as this time she had a boyfriend accompanying her. Even Sarah was surprised. It was decided that she would sleep upstairs in the spare bedroom and he was given the floor downstairs.

They spent most of their time downstairs and late in the night Kate would go upstairs to sleep. Every evening they visited the local pub which was strange as Kate was still under sixteen but Sarah saw no problem with that. Underage drinking in UK was not only frowned upon but also considered a serious offence.

One night when coming downstairs for a drink, I heard noises in the front room, loud ones. Even though groggy with sleep, it was loud and clear that mating season was in and bunny rabbits were busy humping. I quietly tiptoed back to bed feeling extremely uneasy and restless. Now underage sex could be added to this sorry saga. I spoke with Sarah about the night's events and she literally tore into me.

How dare I speak about her sister in such a way? She is an innocent child, she thundered. Why do I say such things? She demanded to know. What could I say but bite my tongue and get on with life. I had no choice, baby was on its way and I did not want Sarah stressed out! There were weekly pre natal classes to attend where I was shocked to see how little the newly expectant mothers knew about babies, their needs and aftercare. However, I remained a dutiful husband carrying bags and cushions, walking quietly behind my dear wife, minding my manners, opening doors and being polite.

By now, Sarah had stopped working, as the baby was due in five or six week's time. She had the option to return to work, which was her intent but that changed quickly once the baby was born. Every evening before going to sleep, I would talk to the baby. I talked to her before going to work; I talked to her as soon as I arrived home from work. I just could not wait to get my hands on her. Anything baby you can think of, I had it bought. Some of the necessities were bought twice over.

The cot was set right by our bed. I could visualise the baby in the cot. Hell I just wanted this baby so much, it used to make me cry. Sarah used to find this very amusing. By now I could see and feel the baby kicking against Sarah's protruding belly. Hell, I could feel her repeated kicks in my back every night. I honestly believe that this baby had it in for me from the onset.

One evening I woke up with a jolt. The bed was wet. Sarah, I called while trying to wake her up. She was groggy with sleep. What do you want? She asked. I think you have wet yourself, I said shitting bricks with excitement and nerves. I somehow knew her waters were about to break but she was in no rush. Go back to sleep. I am not due for another three days, she replied. I repeated that the bed sheet was wet. Oh it is only a little wet, now go back to sleep, she murmured. The waters broke, Sarah panicked and soon we were on our way to Perivale Maternity Hospital. All her bags were packed and ready for weeks; hence, no last minute preparations were required.

I was nervous but felt so excited with the thoughts of being able to hold my bundle of joy at last. My head felt more like Mills and Boon than Shakespeare. There are moments when I seriously worry about my cognitive mechanisms and the strangeness of my thought processes.

Sarah was admitted to the ward and panic dissipated. She was one centimetre dilated and there was some way to go. Then the contractions started and I soon realised that when my darling wife wished to hold my hand at this given moment, I should have had excuses ready, loads of them. My fingers were being crunched and I could hear the joints crack. Epidural, she screamed. Where is the bloody epidural? I felt I needed it more than her. She was killing me but I grimaced and went searching for the nurse. Epidural was duly delivered and I was allowed to soothe my aching wrists and badly mauled fingers.

For months this baby had been kicking my backside trying to get out and now she had decided to take it easy and rest. She seemed in no hurry as the labour went on and on. I talked to her, begged her to make a move but she was not budging. Twenty-four years later, she is still moody, stubborn as a mule and seldom listens to reason.

Nurse came; nurse went, only two centimetres dilated, some way to go yet and she informed us again that there was no need to panic. No need to panic, woman I needed valium as my head felt like a rollercoaster. This baby was doing my head in. Listen baby this is no time to mess around, no time for hide and seek, get a move on, pleeeeease! I begged her. This baby was not budging and taking her sweet time. I think Sarah was overtly amused by my shenanigans and forgot all about contractions. By now even she did not seem in any hurry. By now my bum had gone numb from all the sitting and waiting.

Eight hours later just when my patience had almost run out and I was ready to sing return to sender, something started to happen. Well one nurse came in, then another and then the midwife appeared and slowly things began to hasten.

Sarah was being wheeled to the theatre and I was asked to stay put. I would be told when the baby was born. What? I exclaimed. I am coming in with my wife, I declared indignantly. The midwife gave me a stern look and asked me to wait outside the theatre. She had picked a fine time for an argument. I was going into the theatre whatever it took and she was standing in my way. I wished to speak to the doctor on call and her stare told me that I was doing my very best to piss her off. Well she started it. Then Sarah said that she would like my presence in the theatre. You should have seen the look biddy midwife gave me and I seriously could not give a shit. Gown up and follow us in, she said in a matronly way.

Gown up, what in Christ's name does that mean I muttered which amused a junior nurse no end. She was doing her very best not to laugh but I could see and hear her snigger. Don't mind her she is always cranky and we have to put up with her every day, she said as she helped me into a gown followed by a face mask.

I walked in, knees turning to jelly, stomach churning and excitement oozing from every orifice in my body. The time had come. For whom the bell tolls! And I had heard the declaration. It was time to stand up and be counted. Shit the brain was beginning to go astray just when I needed the little fecker. I walked into the theatre and saw two nurses to the left flanking a doctor whose face I could not see and the battleaxe to my right. Sarah had her legs airborne and held in clamps while I stood there speechless, senseless and staring into, well nothing but a white sheet. Everything was appropriately covered.

I remember people were busy fiddling around and the friendly nurse found time to whisper a snippet of information to me. The man before you came into the theatre and fainted at the sight of childbirth, she said. The wife is walking around with the baby and daddy is lying in the ward resting with a bump on the back of his head. Now that was funny. I enjoyed that.

I swear either she was winding me up or she had a wager of kinds with the battle-axe. One thing for sure, she was enjoying herself at my expense. And then there appeared some problems. The baby was upside down and not shifting. The doctors decided to wait a while and then decided to try and move her around. Forceps were employed to get this trouble maker into the appropriate position for delivery and then the lazy ass moved. At last slowly but surely she made her way towards light and a little head began to appear covered in slimy white goo. My heart missed many a beat. Hand me some clamps please, I heard the doctor say.

Darling daughter had decided to make a pit stop. This baby was definitely grandstanding. Gently she was coaxed and coerced and then out she popped into the waiting hands of the battleaxe, sorry the midwife. The doctor cut the umbilical cord while one of the nurses clipped the belly button. The midwife looked at me and somehow knew that I wanted to hold my daughter. Let me wipe her clean she offered and then she looked at me.

She smiled and beckoned me to hold my baby daughter. Hell I was dying to hold her, slimy and all as she put a towel underneath and handed her to me. I was the tallest, proudest and the happiest Dad in the world. I kissed her slimy cheek which did not taste good but I didn't care. Surprises were coming tenfold. This baby looked so beautiful, the most gorgeous creature in the world. Then she decided to open her big brown eyes that twinkled as she stared at me.

I gently touched her hand and felt two of her fingers curl around the little finger of my left hand. It felt as if she would never let me go. Then I saw her smile. I swear to god my daughter smiled at me. I saw the midwife's plucked eyebrows go up an inch. She looked pleasantly surprised. Yes, she saw it too.

With the smile, I could see teeth. Look, she has four teeth, I said as the midwife looked closer and her face broke into another smile. By god, I would never! She exclaimed. I gently put my little finger into her mouth and she bit me. The little bitch bit me and smiled again. She had stolen my heart forever and somehow I think she knew it too.

66

They all saw it except Sarah. Then the baby's smile got even wider as I held her close to my chest. I had the world's most important and precious entity in my arms. Reluctantly I handed my darling daughter back to the matron to be cleaned and weighed. Then I placed her next to Sarah as mother and baby were wheeled back to the ward. After an hour or two I left them sleeping and went to work for a couple of hours. I badly needed some cash.

There was a little more drama to come as I received a call at work. Sarah was crying that they had taken the baby away and no one told her why. I left work immediately and returned to the hospital where I was informed that a nurse in passing had seen the baby having a fit. I wanted to see my daughter, right now, I demanded, politely of course. I was told to wait. Wait for what? I asked but got no reply.

Now I had everyone in a spiral and needed answers, now. Sarah was still emotional but much calmer. Soon my darling daughter was brought to me. She did not seem to have a care in the world. She looked so serene, sweet and beautiful as I handed her over to Sarah. The matron explained that for the benefit of the baby she would be kept under observation.

She also acknowledged that there should have been better communication with the mother. She duly and profusely apologised. Sarah seemed happy but I was happier to get another chance to play with my darling daughter. I wished that for the rest of my life I would never miss an opportunity to stay close to her.

My darling daughter was called Aisha. I was first to hold her, got the first smile, the first bite and Whoopity do I changed my daughter's first nappy, like a professional with aplomb. Poop it was not but a runny multi coloured goo. The real thing arrived three days later. Every day, every moment was spent playing with my daughter. Somehow work did not seem important anymore. I wanted to hold her, hug her and play with her. Every time she cried, my heart missed a beat. She had her father wrapped around her little finger from the moment she was born. Anyone who saw her fell in love with her. I bought her babygro's, little frocks, socks, booties, you name it and it was there at the beck and call of my little princess. There was so much pink, it would make you dizzy but I did not care. I wanted to capture every moment of her life.

I needed a camera and Sarah accompanied me to Dixon's in West Ealing where I bought the most expensive camera on display, a Chinon CP7M. It was the best camera on market and only the best for my daughter would do. I took hundreds of pictures, daily, weekly and at every given opportunity.

Life felt wonderful and every day I could not wait to get her home. A week later mother and daughter were allowed home with a clean bill of health. My life had changed for good. The day began with my daughter and ended when she went to bed. She sneezed I jumped, she cried I held her in my arms, she soiled a nappy, got a wash and massage in return.

Wherever I went, Aisha accompanied me. I showed her off to relations, friends, anyone I knew and expressed the least bit of interest. This was the dawn of silly season. I listened to her breathing while she slept. As she dreamt I would catch her smile. I often wonder if she was laughing at the old fool.

Those days SIDS (Sudden Death Infant Syndrome) was constantly in the media and became talk of the day. I believe that made me more scared and possessive of my darling daughter. It progressed to waking her up in the middle of the night. I wanted to talk to her and play with her. Twenty-four years later, I vividly remember the sleepy eyes, a little cry and a frown which she still owns. After her feed and now fully awake she was ready to play.

Dear god it was past midnight, every night and I must have driven the poor baby demented. Then it became our ritual. Just past midnight was daddy and daughter's playtime while Mummy enjoyed her beauty sleep. Then she would refuse to return to her cot and would fall asleep on my chest, while I lay awake, listening to the murmur of her little heart. It is the most beautiful sound you will ever hear.

After all this, it was not easy getting up for work at seven in the morning. Darling daughter would be awake at seven thirty while mum was still tired and wanted more sleep. I would feed Aisha; wash and massage her with baby oil, change the nappy, change her clothes and have her looking pretty as a picture and smelling divine. Then often she would fall asleep in the cot and I would reluctantly leave for work while Sarah slept blissfully.

Sarah was continuously tired and bored. I was repeatedly told that she had nothing to do, no friends and nowhere to go. She had unilaterally decided against return to work and became a stay at home mum. Even then there were times when I had to return home twice, maybe three times a day because there was a crisis.

It turned out she just wanted to see me, needed a break from looking after Aisha or wanted to go to bed. I still had to cook dinner after returning home from work. Once in a blue moon she would try and then give up. You know I am no good at cooking, was always her answer. Often I wonder if I managed to raise two children or three and for sure, she was definitely the more demanding.

In Southall of all the registered childminders over 98% were of Asian origin. She checked them out and then checked some more till one day she managed to find the only White/ Irish childminder and decided there and then that's where Aisha would go. Then she decided to go to college and enrolled on a Pitman's secretarial course. She made two friends, one Asian, other Spanish and thus began her social life. I would return home from work and often find her gone to her Asian friend's house. Worse still was Aisha's absence and life was not getting any better. This woman had borne three children, two with her husband and one with her lodger. They were all living under one roof in perfect harmony. Just to add spice to this curry, whenever I went to pick up Sarah, her friend openly flirted and made suggestive remarks alongside inappropriate propositions.

One day I told Sarah that I felt uncomfortable in that house and she would have to make her own way home. You just never want to see me happy, was her retort. When I told her about the ongoing events, she refused to accept that I was telling the truth or else responded by saying that her friend was just being friendly and I take things too seriously. Somehow I had forgotten that the blame always lay with me.

Money was getting tighter by the day. Her clan was coming and going and I felt more stressed than ever. To add icing on the cake, my mother started to write from Pakistan. My two younger brothers were at each other's throats and in their spare time dad was being dragged in. In her words it was hell to endure and there was non-stop mayhem at home. She wanted me to help save their future. What bloody future. This insanity had compelled me to flee home and run to England in the first place. She wanted me to help them set up in business.

With what? I had asked. Well it will not cost you a penny was their gift of wisdom. We will send you leatherwear and sports goods. You can sell them at a profit and then pay us. Everybody is doing it and making loads of money. Shit and I thought

Sarah's mother occupied the throne of queen Amazonia the stupid! And yet it's often stated that mother knows best.

Anytime a letter arrived from Pakistan Sarah wanted to know its contents. Now I had to translate stupidity to Madame stupid without pause or else I would be accused of hiding things from her. Then her incessant questioning about who do I love more, my mother or her was constantly driving me demented. This question was a daily routine but with the arrival of the letter, it would become more repetitive. I recited the contents of every letter and this time the ingenuity of my mother's proposal. In later years this was to become my second biggest mistake.

We mulled it over and discussed it further. Courier work and chauffeuring were facing competition and money was getting tighter while working hours were ever increasing. In the meantime, monetary affairs were getting worse. Naseem visited regularly and became a great source of support. Even Sarah was becoming fond of him. He really is a good person, a hard worker and was employed in a leather garments factory working all hours. The odd weekend he would visit.

This Saturday I was at the end of my tether. There were less than ten pounds in my pocket and I was staring at an empty fridge devoid of food, needed nappies for Aisha, mortgage had to be paid with no sign of money appearing from anywhere. I felt desolate and desperate. Thus far this was probably the lowest ever moment in my life.

Naseem appeared and went to the fridge to get a drink. It was empty. He looked at me quizzically and I quietly explained the situation, apologised and went to make some food. As I cooked we discussed Pakistan and the proposal on the table. Don't do it and don't go there was his solemn advice. I told him I was only going to do it for my mother's sake. It will be your funeral, he stated matter of factly. Now I wish I had more balls to stand up to my family, especially my mother and had listened to Naseem.

Then my thoughts returned to food. Thank god for Indian cooking. A meal can be cooked and enjoyed with little in cost and ingredients. At least I had some vegetables, flour and rice in the house. I made dinner, which was eaten in eerie silence. Every time I looked at Aisha, it broke my heart. I had wished and dreamt of giving her the world, not poverty.

The meal ended in silence and Naseem departed. I did not know what to do. For once, my brain had ceased functioning. Just when I needed the fecker to speak to me, it had decided to shut up. Sarah looked worried and I had no answers. A million thoughts of surviving the week raced through my head and my pay cheque was not due for another three days.

I needed baby food and it felt like hell, mentally and physically. I walked to the bottom of the stairs, sat down and began to cry. Yes, I broke down. Sarah quietly walked over to me and said she had found some money on top of the fridge. What money? I asked as she held fifty-pound notes in her hand. Then it dawned upon me, Naseem, it had to be him. It was always him. Sarah looked embarrassed and emotional. We had survived and life went its merry old way. I repaid the money in no time but the gratitude I felt was everlasting.

It was decided that we would visit Pakistan, stay a couple of months and assess the feasibility of the project. Pakistan was the largest exporter of leather and sports goods in the world but not everybody is born a businessman. At least I found out soon enough that I was not. Aisha was almost five months of age and Sarah had never been abroad. Sarah seemed excited, I felt nervous and Aisha did not seem to have a worry in the world. The journey was long, Sarah was tired and Aisha needed to be occupied. This job was allocated to me. Changing nappies, amusement and feeding while trying to take care of Sarah's needs was no easy task. Thankfully, the staff took a shine to Aisha and at every opportunity took her away to give me a break. I could see that they loved every minute of it and Aisha was in her element. She loved the attention.

After an arduous journey we landed in Karachi, Pakistan. It was hot and humidity hit us like a runaway train. The air was suffocating and corruption was rife. Passports with cash were being handed to customs officials and all the bad memories started to return. Not much had changed but at least now they had toilets with hand dryers and gun totting security was everywhere!

People were busy looking over their shoulders and everyone seemed nervous. One look at me said no money and I was quickly ushered through. They had money to make as a flight from Dubai had just landed and the connecting flight to Lahore was declared full. Our seats were probably allocated to well meaning and well paying passengers.

Sarah was tired while poor Aisha looked drained and exhausted. At the last minute, we were allowed to board the connecting flight. Aisha promptly fell asleep in my lap as I dreaded the journey to my family home. Somehow it seemed that time had stood still and the country felt just the same as I had left a decade and more ago. I was too tired to think but a strange and uncomfortable feeling hit me which was to last the duration of my two month stay.

I felt that I did not belong here and I guess I never did. My entire childhood was spent in fantasies of escape to somewhere, anywhere but here. Yes, escape was the word that had dominated my developmental years. Pain was always the dominant factor. There were some happy memories but they seemed lost for now. My younger brothers were there, waiting.

It was a strange and eerie feeling. There was little warmth or sense of closeness, but they greeted Sarah with respect and eagerly looked at Aisha who refused to leave her daddy.

They had a car waiting outside for the seventy-mile journey home. It feels strange calling it home because it had never felt like home. Fear and unease were the dominant feelings in my every day existence. Sarah looked comfortable while eventually Aisha decided to go to my younger brother and feel asleep in his lap. She was almost five months in age and looked gorgeous as she slept. My little fairy princess looked tired but peaceful and completely unaware of the thoughts occupying her father's head. Innocence is a wonderful thing.

The journey was quiet and barely a word was spoken. At last, we arrived. Mum was there, sitting quietly in her Buddha pose, as per her norm. She stared into empty space as her eyes welled with tears. All the past memories came rushing back. Oh yeah there were tears and lots of them. Then suddenly it hit me. This was the reason I had left in the first place. There were tears most of the time, hers and mine. A quiet lingering hug and then the floodgates opened. Poor Sarah stood there trying to take it all in. Aisha was being passed from one to the other but she only wanted Dada. She had started to say a few words by then.

I felt exhausted and needed sleep. News had travelled that I was home. People were coming to visit, friends, family, cousins, sports fans, former house servants and people who were children when I last played cricket in Pakistan. Oh heck! I was a child when I left home. How did these people remember me? Some of them I did not even recognise. I was there in body but not in mind and spirit. I felt alien to the proceedings and dearly wished to be somewhere else.

Then there stood Dad. The fearsome and frightening figure from my past looked lonely, forlorn and desolate. We shook hands and hugged. He was most polite to Sarah and proceeded to pick Aisha up. Poor darling looked like a chimp in a zoo, but an absolute delight. He handled her as gently as she was made of china. I had seldom seen that side of him. Terror and dread were my daily norms in his presence. She nervously kept looking at me but then settled down to enjoy the attention until dad brought her back, eventually. She had fallen asleep. A room was laid out and I had forgotten how spacious the house was. Compared to the pigeonhole we lived in the UK, this seemed massive. We made ourselves comfortable, had a shower and all three of us fell asleep in the same bed.

People were still coming and going. I could tell from the hushed sounds. There was so much to talk and catch up with the past. For some ungodly reason I could feel suspended fear hanging in the air. It was only a matter of time and then it happened. A couple of days into our stay and all hell broke loose. My two brothers were fighting as mum and dad stared from a distance. Poor Sarah with Aisha in her arms, rushed to try and separate them but the two lunatics could not care less as they lashed at each other.

See what you left behind, I heard my mother whimper. This is what I have had to deal with when you were gone and the memories began to return. Everything was always my responsibility and I was expected to take blame for all the fuck ups of this family. Dad was desperately trying to separate them as Sarah tried to pull one away from the other. I felt so guilty for bringing her into this hellhole. Feeling of guilt has always been a dominant factor in my life.

When I stepped in the older of the two, just stared at me and walked away. I feel loathe to using their names. The younger one was spouting filth and now I became his involuntary target. It was entirely my fault because I had fucked off; he shouted and then stomped off.

Mum the Buddha had her usual sniffles and Sarah looked lost. I felt so bad for her but she was extremely understanding and supportive. She told me not to worry as she had seen her brothers at it many a time. Well I suppose my clan was trying to live up to her clan's standards. So there were similarities at last. Maybe this is what attracted me to Sarah! Our families fuck ups. Thankfully, my baby sister was married and now living in the US. I had often wondered how she survived this abusive and painful, lunatic asylum. With extreme difficulty, a lot of abuse and shit load of daily pain, was the answer given in later years. And this is the baby sister who was the focus of my love and attention from the day she was born only for me to let her down in later years. This was just a glimpse of my painful past merging with my here and now.

Things started to settle down and Sarah became friends with my youngest aunt who is an absolute dear and the two went shopping. She was very comfortable in her company, even though their sign language and gibberish was fun to hear and watch while they understood each other perfectly. My aunt is five years older than me but more like an older sister and a wonderful and caring human being. When she heard of the episode at home, she asked Sarah to come stay with her. This would be seen as disrespectful to the family and what would the people think, my mother had stated repeatedly.

I was busy visiting factories, old friends who had become successful businessmen, doors were opened, wisdom imparted and I returned home late every afternoon. Sarah was feeling lonely. The odd time we went for a drive or visited my aunt Raheela. I forgot to mention that dad had bought a brand new car for his daughter in law's convenience.

One day Sarah and I took Aisha to a cricket match with when she was almost six months old. I had a blanket on the ground and Aisha was having a great time. As yet she had not learned to crawl and every time she tried, it was a foot backwards, not forward. Eventually she did learn to crawl at the ripe old age of eleven months. Right now she was looking at me, gurgling and smiling as she tried to stand up and fell on her pudgy little bum. She tried again and her knees started to wobble.

Dada she said softly while looking nervous and tearful. Knees began to collapse and then she stood upright and took a hesitant step towards me. Then another cautious one and then her face lit up as she took another and then she literally took a lunge and jumped into my arms. Her face looked a treat as Sarah watched. I think she felt a little put out. When she had tried hard to teach Aisha to say mama, the child repeated dada and now the first steps were towards dada too. Somehow life did not seem fair.

I turned Aisha towards Sarah and let go of her. She took tiny tentative steps and slowly reached her mum. They both looked so proud and happy. This was a most joyful moment. Now Aisha would not sit still. She had found her feet and wanted to walk, more wobble than walk but it was truly a sight to behold. When we got home, it became a circus. One minute poor Aisha was walking in one direction and then a call from another direction would catch her attention. She was like a learner driver doing a three-point turn. It was absolutely brilliant until she got dizzy and tired.

She was the belle of the ball and brought joy to an otherwise dreary and painful environment. One day we decided to visit my other aunt in Lahore. Her husband was a consultant anaesthetist who had been appointed the District Health officer. They had three sons, the eldest a doctor and the youngest was still at school. The one in the middle could speak English, was a handful and an absolute brat. Sarah got on well with him and they often went on his motorbike for a spin or two. My uncle in law had always been good to me and it was a pleasure to see him again. He could not do enough for us. His family treated Sarah extremely well and Aisha was herself, the centre of attention. These visits were most pleasant and memorable. Then it was back to hell at home with the odd moment of sanity thrown in for good measure. I wanted to be back at home in London. Eight weeks seemed too long a time to endure while Mum wanted Sarah and Aisha to stay a while longer.

My migraines had decided to return with vengeance. One day after enduring another episode in the house, my head felt ready to explode. I went to the corner shop to get some aspirins, returned home, took a couple and lay down in bed. Once the panto had ended my dad asked Sarah about my whereabouts. It is amazing how the bloody human mind worked, especially in our household. Fingers of accusation were pointed in Sarah's direction as the cause of my migraine. I heard my late father calling her a bitch and laying the blame squarely on her shoulders. I got my sorry ass out of the bed and told them all to fuck off and leave her alone. For some strange reason they fell about laughing and found the episode extremely amusing.

I wished to be out of there and back home in London. The desire to leave this hellhole was stronger than ever. Sarah was losing weight and had become withdrawn. I asked my cousin to have the tickets for the flight changed and soon we were on our way back to London. It felt a relief and colour soon returned to Sarah's cheeks. Upon our return I did not have a penny left to my name. My car was left for sale at the auction to cover the mortgage payments was left unsold. There were bills everywhere. It took me three weeks to sell my car, pay the mortgage and have some cash to spare.

It seemed like Sarah was beginning to grow up and take notice of the realities of life. She proposed signing on welfare. We could not survive like this for ever, she said. My pride had long gone out of the window. At least we would be fed and could try our hand at business. There seemed good money in it so why not. I can give you four reasons now, a father, a mother and two brothers in Pakistan.

We went to the bank and had a meeting with one of the corporate managers, Duncan. Now whenever I recall our meetings fond memories come to the fore. He really was a most intelligent, well meaning and knowledgeable person. Here I was naïve, very naïve indeed. Everything he said then was to come true later in life. We left the meeting with a five thousand pound overdraft facility and a family of Pakistani entrepreneurs to deal with, who did not know their arse from their elbow. I the wise one, in hindsight) was a true Neanderthal in every way possible.

I got busy organising and visiting prospective clients from London to Edinburgh, Wales and beyond until the sea stopped me from travelling any further. I travelled the country like a lunatic and these days they call it market research. A new enterprise centre had recently been built in Stonebridge Park Wembley with the patronage of the Prince's trust. I acquired a unit at minimum rent and began to work like a man possessed. We opened our first letter of credit and waited patiently for the stock to arrive.

Aisha was dropped at the in-house childcare centre and Sarah came to help. She agreed to manage the office and call prospective clients while I went on the road. It seems, I spent more time on the roads than tar macadam and the traffic cones put together. First consignment arrived and was promptly sold to courier bike riders. Ordered a second consignment and the Pakistani clan came up with another ingenious plan, sports goods and footballs and decided to send a consignment for which I had no money left to pay. They smelled money, lots of it while I was busy busting my ass selling goods at close to cost hoping to build a client base.

By now, my head was planted so far up my rear that I could not tell daylight from the stars. I rang to tell them that I had no money and stick to leatherwear while it was moving. You are worrying about nothing, said daddy from the Pakistani clan. I have money for you, no problem. Brothers of the Pakistani clan called me a coward and accused me of not wanting to see them prosper. Mammy joined in singing from the same hymn sheet, just different chapter and verse. It was my funeral while others dreamt of utopia and sang songs of joy.

Letters of credit are open for a maximum of ninety days. Now something wonderful happened. The leather motorbike jackets began to come apart from seams and salt began to appear. This happens when tanning process is not properly adhered to. This schmuck is fast learner if nothing else.

People wanted exchange of goods or their money back. Naseem came in handy, again. Now not only was I paying for repairs but also dead stock was beginning to pile up. Footballs stood there staring at me and then the demands came from Pakistan for money. All the previous rhetoric was forgotten and now everything was deemed my responsibility. I was screwed to the rafters. Then daddy dearest wrote a long vitriolic letter full of abuse narrating my incompetence and former shortcomings in life. Through all this, another consignment of leather jackets arrived to replace the first consignment. I was meant to pay for this as well.

I remortgaged the house to raise funds and promptly returned to Duncan to inform him of my current financial fiasco. I had always kept my promise of keeping him informed of all my comings and goings. He met me with moist eyes and a warm handshake. Why did you remortgage your house? He asked.

Because I owe you money and I don't like owing money, was my honest reply.

He acknowledged that in his twenty and more years of banking no one had ever done that. I told him of my intention of not letting him or his trust down. He became emotional, wished me good luck and we parted. I was never to see him again. The next time when I tried to meet with him, I met the devil, his replacement, a man of little scruples and no morality. Duncan had suffered a brain haemorrhage and was recuperating in a nursing home. I was not given his address as much as I had wished to visit him.

We sold the house in Southall and moved to Dunstable, approximately thirty miles from London. It was a semi with a large rear garden and double garage located on the main dual carriageway right next to the M1 motorway. Sarah liked the house and it was quicker to get to the office from there than it was from Southall. The hundred and sixty foot plus garden was big enough for Aisha to play in. By now I had had enough of my family and tried to get rid of the left over stock, over fifty thousand sterling worth and nowhere to go. I still owed £15,000 to my family.

It was announced that his royal highness the Prince of Wales, Prince Charles was due to officially open the centre. The big day arrived and I put on my only suit while Sarah took extra care and looked stunning. Aisha was as gorgeous and delectable as ever. We waited nervously until His Royal Highness the Prince of Wales arrived. It took him two minutes to notice our trio in the queue and walked straight over with the security people scrambling around him. He shook my hand and made polite conversation, admired Aisha and then turned to Sarah. It was a short humorous chat full of compliments. He appeared the most charming and down to earth individual one would have the pleasure of meeting before being whisked away. A most wonderful and memorable day was had by all.

Money was still tight but at least we had a roof over our heads, Aisha was happy and Sarah complaints had receded. I had decided to try to branch out into designing motorbike racing leathers and leather jeans. The demand was there but could not find a person competent enough in designing, pattern cutting and fitting. Upon professional advice, I enrolled in Barnfield College of fashion and managed to finish the three-year course in six months. Soon I had made friends with a wholesale distributor who ordered my first sample contract destined for Harrods.

At least now, there appeared a ray of light. I would leave home at six thirty in the morning and return home at around seven thirty in the evening. Sarah had made new friends and Aisha was full of chat and worldly wisdom. Mother and daughter spent their time shopping while I was away at work.

An amusing anecdote comes to mind. Aisha was close to two years of age, inquisitive and full of questions. One day she wanted her mother to buy her an item that she liked only to be told that Mummy had no money. Oh mum why don't you get money from the wall, everyone else does was Aisha's wonderful reply. She had been watching people make withdrawals from cash points in shopping centres. And her mother thought that money grew on trees!

It was announced that cousin Joe was getting married. His fiancée was a primary school teacher who was kept a secret from the extended family. It was later discovered that like Joe, she was a reformed alcoholic. Neither I nor Sarah or her family had ever met this woman but we were invited to the wedding. They lived in Uxbridge and wedding was organised in Ilford, Essex because this was where his fiancée's family once lived!

Then there were more revelations. Allegedly Joe had entered the vocation of priesthood but never finished his training. It was rumoured that he had interfered with children and was ordered to leave the seminary. The gossip train was on the move and gathering steam. Sarah's parents arrived for the wedding and I performed my usual chauffeuring duties. We all got spruced up as Sarah's mother fussed while her father was his usual calm and cool personified. Aisha was dressed for the event and I received orders to take the wedding pictures. After all I had a camera and what harm.

As soon as the church ceremony was over word had travelled that there was not enough food in the hall. Well you should have seen the gathering disappear in haste. It seemed as if Luftwaffe was in air and the siren for air raid had sounded. Women hitched their skirts and dresses as they ran across the churchyard towards the smell of food with men in tow. Sarah's mother ran the fastest hundred metres I have ever witnessed by a woman of fifty plus. It was hilarious. My darling daughter was hungry while Sarah looked bewildered. By the time we got to the hall there was not a morsel of food in sight. Sarah's mother offered us a share of the last remnants of a half eaten sandwich while trying to swallow the other half. I walked out with Aisha in my arms as Sarah followed quietly.

We saw a Donner kebab shop across the road and thanked god, profusely. I was famished, Aisha was hungry, Sarah looked empty headed and her father stood silently by my side. Sarah went to buy food while I coaxed, cajoled and amused my darling daughter. We had a donner kebab and a feast of chips among us three. Poor Aisha was hoovering chips, she was that hungry. I had lost my appetite while Sarah looked stunned and thoroughly bemused. Another wonderful new experience was had by us all.

Then I was introduced to another member of the clan, Sarah's uncle who lived in Kentish Town with his wife Margaret and daughter Mary. They were a close knit family and Mary doted on her dad. Johnny Kelly was a retired builder, a tough man in his time who gave room to many an impoverished newly arrived Irish immigrant. Sadly he had terminal cancer and was surviving on a diet of liquidised food. We got on very well and had many a hearty conversation. For some ungodly reason it was always Sarah's mother's side that took precedence in all matters of life and the living.

The father's family was barely spoken of even though they were described as decent people. In his teens her father had lost his parents and held memories of carrying his mother on his shoulder across fields looking for help. She soon passed away and the family had disintegrated. And yet this matriarch only had eyes for her own family.

One day Johnny Kelly broke down and told me what he had told no one. He did not wish to die and was not ready to go yet. I consoled him the best I could. Sadly, he was gone within months. I got a call at work that he was very sick, on his last legs and wanted to see me. I closed the factory and went to visit him. He seemed frail, scared and too weak to talk. All the time he kept a tight grip on my hand and did not wish for me to leave.

I promised to return the next morning but sadly never got the chance to see him alive again. The next day was his funeral. He had passed away soon after I left. It was a large funeral, the biggest in Kentish town for years, I was told. At Mary's request the priest made exemption allowing me to take pictures of the late John Kelly and I duly obliged. Taking pictures of the dead was not acceptable to the Irish. I could hear people tut tutting which was heard by the priest who in turn had a stern word or

84

two with the gathering. Still I could feel piercing looks at the back of my neck which I chose to ignore.

This was Mary's request and she was extremely grateful. She also told me that her dad had great admiration and respect for me considering the short period of time we had spent together. I felt honoured with her sentiments. At least Mary and Margaret were happy with the day's proceedings despite their sudden loss. Sarah's Mum and Dad left the next day.

We returned home and normality resumed. One day while visiting one of my customers, I saw a motorbike in his showroom, Honda CBR 600 FK, Rothmans colours. My mouth began to water and I wanted to take it home with me. I was sick and tired of sitting for hours in traffic. This bike would get me through the traffic I thought, wisely. It was bought and loaded into my van in the next twenty minutes. What was I going to tell Sarah soon hit me?

I drove home slowly, and took my time thinking while decent excuses eluded me. Eventually I arrived home. I have a surprise for you, I announced sheepishly. She looked perplexed and was definitely not amused to see the occupant of the van. I told her the excellent deal I got with discount and little to pay in cash, and how I would save on petrol and insurance. She looked like a three humped camel that had swallowed a barrel of sour apples. Now you have to get me a car, she demanded and I readily agreed. Phew! That was close is all I could think.

Life was beginning to settle into a routine. I still had to do the daily cooking and help clean the house at the weekends. My evenings with Aisha were something to come home to and forever she had new tricks for my amusement. Posing, singing and dancing were being added to her portfolio. The Irish clan was still coming and going and I had learned not to take notice of their eccentricities any more. Young Johnny was back on the scene the odd time. He found it difficult to comprehend that Sarah was married and had become a mom.

Now another character appeared on the scene, Benny Mace. His younger brother worked next door as a mechanic. He seemed a nice guy and an unmarried 23-year-old father of a two-year-old daughter. His girlfriend Jacinta seemed a little strange and I did not know how strange she was until a few years later.

One day they came to my office and Benny wanted to buy a jacket and a pair of leather jeans for her. As I appeared with a couple of pairs there she was starker's in only her knickers and a skimpy top. Benny looked amused, Sarah looked horrified and I did not know where to look. In later years, I was informed that they had broken up. Apparently, while Benny was working in London Jacinta agreed for a bet to tackle an entire rugby team in bed, in their home town of Cavan and won. Poor Benny was lost without her and missed his baby daughter. He looked a broken man. One day I walked in and Benny was telling Sarah his story. He appeared drunk as a skunk and I was told nothing except Benny was distressed.

Two comical events happened. First the anti terror squad turned up at my doorstep. I heard a thunderous knock on my front door followed by a yell ordering me to open the door or they would break it down. When I opened the door, a cop was ready to knock the front door down. They thought IRA sympathisers were living there. You should have seen the look of horror on his face. Safety jackets, helmets and armed to their teeth only to find a Paki, not a Paddy. They all looked confused, very confused indeed. Apologies were made as they left looking rather sheepish.

Then Sarah told me the story. Cops had stopped Benny during a routine traffic stop. One of the occupants was his cousin, whose mother was a petty criminal as were three of her male offspring. She was a known IRA sympathiser and had been monitored while providing B&B to convicted IRA personnel but nothing serious had ever occurred. She worked as a dispatcher in a taxi office but not for money. She made a lot more money by telling her sons the location of vacant houses as the owners called for taxis to the airport. Then they went and robbed the houses. They had several criminal convictions between them and when asked, Benny became nervous and promptly gave the cops my address. Hence, the appearance of the anti terrorist squad at my doorstep. Sarah promised to be more careful in her choice of friends from thereon. Future events were to prove otherwise.

Then Benny pulled another stunt. With the departure of his girlfriend and daughter he had decided to stay a while in London and bunked with a few Irish friends. One late afternoon I heard a knock on the door and there was Benny huffing and puffing, out of breath and once again running away from the cops. Obviously Sarah had not told him to stay away from us, hence he had returned to the public rest house.

Nothing serious happened this time. Often post gets delivered to wrong addresses and this morning Benny and his dimwit friends had found a blank credit card addressed to Mohammad Aslam. With a flourish Benny had signed on the back of the credit card. Paddy thought Christmas had come early and decided to go shopping, all four of them with ginger hair, freckles and an Irish accent while in possession of a credit card bearing a Pakistani name.

They went shopping in Tesco on Dunstable road, where over 80% of the clientele and staff are of Pakistani origin. There appeared four Paddies with two trolleys full of shopping, at a cash register manned by a Pakistani and produced a credit card bearing the name, Mohammad Aslam.

Instead of being angry I burst out laughing. I wished I were a fly on the wall when all this happened. The cashier had pressed the alarm and while waiting for security, Benny, his cousin and the others made a dash for freedom. They left the shopping trolleys blocking the aisle, hopped over the counters and ran in different directions like bats out of hell. Well fair play to Sarah; at least she was reliable and consistent in somehow always managing to bring shite to my door.

Now Sarah decided to get broody and wanted a companion for Aisha. She had made friends with an Afro Caribbean woman who lived a few doors away from us who just had a baby with her philandering husband. This man was so good and virile that he managed to impregnate his wife and the blonde mistress at the same time. Within a week he was daddy to two babies of different complexions.

Now men, here is a word of warning. When a woman becomes broody all logic flies out of the window. You can try rationalising and intellectualising with your wife but she only sees you as a humping camel. And if you try to duck and dive; she will make your life a living hell. It all began in earnest. I would arrive home with nothing but humping on offer. I was starving and all she wanted was a baby and it had to be quick. Just the involuntary donation and then I was allowed to go and cook my dinner.

For a year and a half old child, Aisha was becoming independent and had an opinion, about everything. She and her mother fought like cats over feeding time and would not sit down and eat the dinner when ordered. Yet she would sit in my lap and eat curry by the spoonful with her mouth on fire and gulping water by the gallon. Time and again she made my life worth living.

One day Sarah announced that she was pregnant and I thanked god mostly humbly. It was costing a small fortune in pregnancy tests. Every week there were more pregnancy kits in the shopping than groceries. Most of Sarah's time was spent in her friend's company. Every evening I arrived home to the sight of her afro Caribbean friend and her three kids and almost always this woman appeared in tears. By now Aisha was quite capable of keeping herself amused while Sarah fed herself on sandwiches and I was directed to the kitchen.

This became my darling daughter's fun time. She sat on the worktop while I cooked. Then it was one plate for me and another for her little majesty. She finished her food, nose running, watery eyes and a smile followed by her chubby cheeks muttering, look daddy, all gone. She looked so proud of herself. Then daddy and daughter would snuggle up and watch some TV, her favourites of course.

Soon it was time for daddy and daughter to go to bed. She always looked so much at peace as she lay next to me and would soon fall asleep. Then I would gently place her in her bed. Sometime late in the evening Sarah would appear to talk about her friend's tales of woe while I tried to sleep.

Her family had not visited us in our new home and soon her sisters, Mary and Kate, arrived followed by the elder brother Jimmy and his wife. These two were still trying to kill each other without ever succeeding. Then I got to meet Charlie, her other brother. His wife, Sheila had survived a kidney transplant and been to hell and back. She is a lovely person and I got to meet her in later years.

Almost seven months into pregnancy, Sarah decided that she wished for her mother's visit, as she needed company and help. By this time, her tummy looked huge in comparison to her earlier pregnancy and she could barely lift herself out of the chair. To this day, I do not know if it was a relief to see her mother or an act of resignation but at least for now, I was left alone. It was happy days for darling daughter and me. Sarah was getting good support from our GP and kept under constant care. In the meantime the house felt strange. Wherever I looked her mother was omnipresent, wherever I went she was there ahead of me. At times, it felt like I was living in a haunted house. Sarah was sure the baby would be a boy. She and her mother narrated all the old wives tales and managed to convince themselves of the impending arrival of a boy. She had already visited our doctor several times for information and organisation of circumcision for the baby and had everything organised. Then the day arrived when Sarah declared that the baby was on its way. If this was anything like the first pregnancy we would be waiting a long time, I thought.

Everything was packed and we arrived at Luton and Dunstable hospital, which was a hundred yards away from our home. Dr O' Sullivan was on call with Irish brogue and all. She was a lovely Irish lady doctor with a hint of a moustache which met with Sarah's amusement.

Chapter Five

Now as experienced parents we were, relaxed, calm and patient. At midnight, I was ordered to go home and rest. Baby was in no rush and they had a bed prepared for Sarah's overnight stay. I gave her a hug, kissed her goodnight and left for the night.

She was smiling as I waved goodbye to her. In retrospect I was about to lose my wife and had no inkling of the events to follow. I was feeling tired but excited as I arrived home. Sarah's mum was looking after Aisha. As I tiptoed to my bedroom, I could hear grandma snoring in the spare bedroom. The train was parked but the engine was still running.

Aisha was sleep until I heard a dopey little voice calling for Daddy. I walked in to my bedroom and there she was waiting for her hugs and kisses before falling asleep, again. Then I changed and went to sleep with Aisha's head neatly tucked under my chin. She was rolled into a cuddly little ball. I put my arm over her to snuggle her close and fell asleep.

I was jolted out of my sleep by the harsh sound of the phone ringing. I calmed Aisha and rushed downstairs to answer the phone. It was just gone past midnight. Mr Anjum can you please come down to the hospital straightaway, the voice sounded urgent. Your wife is about to go into labour, I was informed.

I'll be there in five minutes, I replied and asked Sarah's mum to take care of Aisha as I ran to the hospital. It took me less than ten minutes to get to the theatre and there was Sarah, looking flush and drained but smiling. Dr O' Sullivan was applying stitches and I had missed everything. It was over in two minutes, said a smiling Dr O' Sullivan. Congratulations, you have a baby daughter, she declared. Soon thereafter Sarah was taken to the maternity ward and my request to accompany her was met with, no you can see her in the morning. Everybody is asleep in the delivery ward and its best not to disturb the other patients. We will have your wife there soon. Sarah nodded her consent and I was sent home packing. I wanted to see my daughter, even if only for a second to give her a kiss and a hug and welcome her into this big bad world. No, I did not get to see my darling daughter and felt miffed like a dog without his bone.

Bloody women, I muttered quietly to Sarah. Even the little woman decides to announce her arrival at this time of the night. Sarah gave me a smile. She looked amused and nodded her head in agreement. After a kiss and a hug I asked if there was anything she needed for the morning. No thanks, just be here first thing in the morning she ordered.

I went home, happy. Aisha woke up and asked if mummy was ok. Yes darling and you have a brand new baby sister, I said in a hushed tone. I was bursting with joy and wanted to see Aisha's face when she met her baby sister for the first time, first thing in the morning. Grandma staggered in and asked if everything was all right. Yes, I have another darling daughter, I said with a big smile. Good is all she muttered and went back to bed.

It felt like a nightmare that made me jump. The bloody phone was ringing again at a few minutes past three in the morning. I had less than two hours of sleep and felt wrecked. In a rush to reach the phone I almost fell down the stairs. Aisha was awake and calling for me. I returned to pick her up and carried on my hip as I picked up the phone.

Hello Mr Anjum, said the voice. I am calling from Luton and Dunstable Hospital. Can you please come down, quickly? Your wife needs you and before I could ask any questions the voice was gone. I ran upstairs two steps at a time while poor Aisha looked sleepy eyed and confused.

What is going on, I heard Sarah's mother from the top of the stairs. There she was with her eyes half shut and talking. I don't know but I have to go to the hospital. Can you look after Aisha for me? I asked. She did not seem pleased but agreed.

I put on a shirt, pulled up my jeans, slid on the shoes without socks and ran out of the front door with the flies' wide open. It is not easy to close your pants while running as I found out that fateful morning. I was at the hospital in two minutes and less. Still out of breath with my right hand struggling with the zipper, Dr O' Sullivan met me in the hallway. She looked pale and worried. Sarah wants to see you, she said with her eyes still full of sleep. Her bleeper had awakened her.

We ran upstairs to the ward till one of my shoes came off and I tripped. She paused and then I followed her to the ward still trying hard to catch my breath. My chest felt ready to explode. There was Sarah, sitting upright in bed looking embarrassed and a little confused. Her face looked white as a sheet as two auxiliary nurses hurried around her. She told me sheepishly that she had wet her bed. I searched her overnight bag and found clean underwear and a nightie while Dr O'Sullivan was called over by one of the auxiliaries helping Sarah out of the bed.

As I helped Sarah with her change of clothes, she began to faint and her body fell limp in my arms. It was the most horrible feeling and a frightening sight as life seemed to slowly drain from her body. Her right hand reached for my face as she began to collapse in a heap. Before her hand could touch my face, Dr O'Sullivan was by my side. I am sorry you have to leave; she said in a state of panic and pushed past me. I gently lay Sarah down in the bed.

I was confused, Sarah had passed out and a stretcher was being pushed in her direction when some women woke up to moan about the racket. Sarah was moved from her bed to the stretcher and then slowly the horror became apparent. The bed was covered in blood from pillow down to the end of her feet. She was soaked in her own blood and I could not see the white of the bed sheets. Her blood was everywhere.

Staff started to run around as I was gently but firmly led out of the ward and brought downstairs. In a state of shock I slumped into a chair in the hallway and found myself barely able to think before the mind went completely numb. Trying to comprehend what had just expired felt daunting, to say the least.

Every minute seemed to take ages and I was becoming desperate as I went from door to door but found no one who could give me any information. Then I saw one of the auxiliary nurses walking down the hall towards me. I approached her and asked her about what had just happened. She looked emotional, exhausted and barely able to speak.

Sarah had complained to the nurses that she did not feel too well and felt that she had wet herself. Upon her request the auxiliary nurse had phoned me and bleeped Dr O'Sullivan. By the time she got back to the ward, I had arrived and she seemed to know as little as I did.

By now Sarah had been wheeled to the theatre. I was told to sit there and wait while a doctor was paged to come and speak with me. It seemed like eternity before I saw Dr O'Sullivan walking towards me. She was wiping away her tears and looked like death warmed up. I am so sorry, I am so sorry, was all she could mutter. She explained that Sarah seemed in great form when going to bed and that was the last time she had seen her.

It appeared that because of the size of the baby, it was probable that some capillaries had burst and caused internal haemorrhaging. Hence the blood on the sheets but she had neither seen nor experienced anything like this before. Rihana was almost twelve pounds at birth. She informed me that the consultant on call was Dr Seligman, a very competent surgeon who was on his way and Sarah would be in good hands. She sat with me quietly and not another word was exchanged. I think we were both in a state of shock. I remember consoling her rather than the other way around when a nurse approached us with the news that Dr Seligman had arrived and was in the theatre scrubbing.

A number of forms were handed to me for signatures to consent. Dr O'Sullivan told me that one was for consent to operate on Sarah and the other was for further invasive surgery, if needed. I could barely see the writing through tear infested eyes and duly signed whatever was placed in front of me. Dr O'Sullivan had to leave and I sat there all alone in the hallway as the hospital seemed deathly quiet.

Then I saw a distinguished but tired looking doctor approaching with his mask hanging loosely around his neck while gently opening the ties around his surgical gown. Mr Anjum, he asked and I duly acknowledged. He sounded tired as he introduced himself as Dr Seligman.

We have just finished operating on your wife, he said in a calm but disconcerting tone. He seemed ruffled and did not exude confidence. We have not been able to stop the bleeding but have managed to slow it down. The main source of bleeding appears to be the capillaries and blood vessels that burst due to trauma caused by childbirth. What trauma, I asked. She had a trouble free birth and I was told that everything went smoothly.

The size of the baby and the speed of the birth had left unnoticed the damage that childbirth had caused. To find and stem the source of bleeding they had to slow down the flow of blood. In the meantime, they had packaged her stomach with bandages and she was under constant observation. Sarah was to be kept heavily sedated. I was told to wait there and a member of staff would meet with me shortly. Then he slowly turned around and walked away. I had so many questions to ask but none came to mind. I felt cold, my bones felt frozen and then I began to shake as my legs gave way and I slumped to the floor. In an instant all the life seemed to have drained out of me and I could barely move.

A member of hospital staff dressed in a green gown approached me and offered a hand to help me get up from the floor. I could not muster enough energy to lift my hand and he decided to sit down on the floor next to me. Then he started to explain the events in the theatre. Sarah was being given blood transfusion but they were running out of plasma. They may have to operate again to replace the packing but Sarah's condition was worsening and she was getting weaker by the minute. They were also worried about the risk of key organs failure and may have to put her in induced coma. There were no assurances and all we could do was pray.

Sarah was placed in intensive care and if her situation did not improve then under police escort she was to be transferred to Addensbrooke Hospital, Cambridge that was better equipped for such cases. I was to return at around seven in the morning for an update. There were another two and a half hours to go.

The mind was blank and my world seemed grey. Soon everything had lost colour as I waited until advised to go home. There was nothing left here for me to do, I was told repeatedly. I did not want to go home leaving Sarah behind till for the umpteenth time I was told to go home and tend to my darling daughter. Slowly the brain began to function and it came to my awareness that now I had two not one daughter.

After a while, I went looking for a member of the medical staff. My legs still felt weak and I was struggling with my walk when I saw a nurse approaching and she looked cross. She must have thought that I was another one of those fathers who had come to visit his wife and child once the pubs were closed. Maybe I did look like a drunk. How was she to know that I was inebriated with pain? Can I help you? Public is not allowed in the hospital at this time of the hour, she said sternly.

I mumbled something about the mayhem of the earlier hours and asked her the whereabouts of my newborn daughter. Her expression changed and she became emotional. She was so sorry, everyone in the hospital was, she said. They had all heard about this poor woman. We are all praying for her, she said quietly as she gently escorted me to my newly born darling daughter and then left.

I entered this large room with white walls, white ceiling and looked completely bare. It contained nothing. Where was my daughter? Just when I was ready to go looking for the nurse again, something caught my eye on the left hand side of the room. There was a steel trolley tucked into a corner, like the ones in restaurants for serving food.

It all seemed so surreal as I slowly approached the trolley and found a bundle of off-white baby blankets. Two tiny little pudgy feet protruded from the other end of the blankets. Then the blankets stirred and I gently removed one after the other to find a baby in deep sleep. This was my newborn daughter and I did not recognise her. My eyes became moist and emotions took over.

Once again I looked at my new born daughter and immediately knew that she was mine. Sound asleep and almost motionless. Complete opposite of her older sister in looks yet absolutely gorgeous just like her with chubby cheeks and a mop of thick black hair. She appeared in deep thought as I felt pensive. Then the dam broke and I began to cry. There was no one but me and my beautiful baby daughter. She was a baby so beautiful, so innocent and had no inkling of the hell around her. What a welcome she had received. A scary thought hit me. She may never get the chance to see her mother, ever. Suddenly I felt a surge of rage inside of me. I felt burning anger, extremely intense and frightening.

My darling daughter was left in this empty room all alone where no one could see or hear her cry. I had enough problems searching for a member of the staff. How would anyone know if my daughter was dead or alive? How dare they? I was sobbing and getting angrier by the minute and finally I had made a decision. Darling I am taking you home, I whispered in my baby daughter's ear. I will look after you, always and ever, I promised.

I called her Rihana as I gently picked her up, held her close to my chest and walked home. No one saw me and no one challenged me as I walked out of the front door of the hospital. I felt a sea of emotions, turbulent and full of torrents which carried me home. I wanted to see Aisha and the thought kept me sane as I walked home in early morning darkness with Rihana glued to my chest and tears rolling down my face. I felt so helpless and alone. Then there was no pain, just a huge sense of loss and emptiness. Someone had managed to scrape the inside of me and left me with nothing.

Gently I opened the front door and went upstairs to the spare bedroom. Aisha was fast asleep. She looked so sweet and peaceful untouched by the unravelling events. I gently put Rihana down on my bed and went to fetch her new clothes. The sight of hospital clothes was literally making me sick. I needed to dress my daughter pretty and dressed my little princess while she slept blissfully. I prepared four bottles of feed for Rihana and lay down exhausted next to her. My head was out of control and buzzing. A million and one thoughts were going through my head while a steady stream of tears ran down my face winding their way to my chest.

I heard the tiptoe of little feet and there stood my darling Aisha, all sleepy eyed and looking confused. I picked her up and brought her into bed with me. You ok daddy, she asked so sweetly that it melted my heart. I kissed her soft cheeks, rubbed her forehead and lay her on my side as she drifted to sleep. My little angel, I thought as I stared at her contently. She was my whole world and now I had another little darling to nurture and protect who did not have a clue about the comings and goings of the night.

Rihana was a big baby and went through a bottle an hour. She would feed and fall asleep. No dirty nappies, just a few droplets. I was none the wiser until a year or so later her 'condition' was explained to me. That fateful night I just lay there thinking of what lay ahead of me. Two innocent little girls, their mother staring at death's door and I had to cope as my world collapsed around me.

Then the games in my head began and I began to pray. Yes this gobshite prayed like he had never prayed before. I swear I prayed to every god that exists. Muslim, Hindu, Christian, Catholic and the ones those are unknown. I made deals with each one of them. If they allowed Sarah to live, what I would and would not do for them.

Some of the deals were remarkable and I will not disclose but I can tell you this, when I ran out of gods, I even spoke with the devil. I think I sold him my soul, my life and my motorbike in exchange for my wife's life for I had nothing else left to give. These business meetings ended when I heard Sarah's mother and her footsteps outside my bedroom door. Her head popped in as she asked, are you awake? I slowly got up and walked out of the bedroom, leaving my two little angels fast asleep. We went downstairs and I explained briefly, what had happened. I asked her if she could mind my daughters because I had to go to the hospital in less than an hour. I had to start planning for what the future had in store for me. Hell, I was creating so many plans that even my back up plans had back up plans. My darling daughters were my priority and survival was foremost in my thoughts. Today I was not prepared to take shit from any one. She sat there stony faced and I heard no response. Maybe she was in a state of shock only God knows but I had no time to waste. I had better tell the rest of the family, she said as she left to make phone calls to Ireland and elsewhere. You should have seen the bill when it arrived and yes, I paid the damn thing. Thankfully, by then the clan had departed and I had no one left to kill.

I could hear Aisha awake and Rihana was crying. I took Aisha to the bathroom and carried Rihana in my lap till Aisha had finished. Then Rihana's bottle was nicely heated and I fed her as she lay in my lap. Aisha had her daily wash, changed her clothes and the prettiest picture in my life was ready. Then it was Rihana's turn, clean, wash, dry, baby soothing cream and baby oil were passed in order by Aisha, who sat there looking inquisitively while trying to comprehend this little bundle but was most helpful.

Slowly she began to understand that the baby was all hers to keep. Now she wanted to hold her sister. I cleaned Rihana's umbilical cord and dressed her. She looked so cosy and promptly fell asleep. Aisha sat against my pillows, resting her back as I gently placed Rihana in her lap. It was a remarkable sight. Rihana was far too big for poor Aisha. Her little arms were unable to wrap around as she tried to hold her baby sister. Every time she tried Rihana slid off her lap as poor Aisha looked at me helplessly. Eventually she allowed me to put Rihana to bed while she lay next to her newly acquired baby sister.

I went to see Sarah's mum who was walking around in a daze with little to say. The family will be here today, she announced as she narrated their itinerary. I heard nothing but did see her lips move. I have to change and get to the hospital, I informed her. Would you be ok with the girls or shall I take them with me, I asked. She said that she would look after them and asked me to keep her updated.

I got Rihana's bottles ready, four of them and the rest of her clothing and baby items were left next to her bed. Aisha's belongings and necessities were in a bag for whatever and whenever she needed. I asked her to feed Rihana very hour and a half and her face became contorted. That is too much, she is only a baby, she said. This woman will never learn is the thought that crossed my mind.

Even when facing an impending hell she had to try and fuck with my head. Before further protestations and dispensing of her wisdom began, I told her that I did not have time to argue with her as my wife, her daughter was on death's door. Either help or leave me alone to take care of my daughters. By now, I had frightening composure. I had decided that from now on it was to be just my daughters and me and garbage was out. I had no time to waste and really could not give a shit. For the first time since we first met she knew not to fuck with me. I felt cold, calm and completely in control.

I had a shave, showered, donned clean clothes, got ready, and walked down to the hospital. I had no idea of what to expect but felt ready for all eventualities. I was frighteningly calm and nothing could shake me now. All I could think was Aisha, Rihana and their mother. The rest of the world had simply vanished.

In the hospital, everyone was so kind. I informed them that I had taken my baby daughter home and all was well. I enquired about Sarah while the poor nurse looked stupefied. Soon there appeared another two, one from paediatrics and another from the ICU (intensive care unit). The thought of a baby disappearing in the morning must have sent shudders down their spine. You should have seen the look on their petrified faces. At least now, they were acquainted with the whole picture.

The ICU nurse started to give me an update on Sarah's progress. The bleeding had stabilised but she was still losing blood. They had her on alert for liver and kidney transplant if the trauma caused her vital organs to shut down. Kidney dialysis machine was on standby. They were running low on plasma but were trying to source more and she was still heavily sedated. The police escort was due to arrive in the next twenty minutes and a nurse and a doctor were ready and waiting to accompany Sarah to Addenbrooke's Hospital in Cambridge. This was seven thirty in the morning of 7 September 1989. The nurse was most kind and talked in hushed tones as we walked towards the ICU.

There were two other women in the same predicament as Sarah, but their condition was deemed less serious, she told me. Sarah was being kept separate from them. This all sounded as gobble de gooks to me as I was only interested in the news about the welfare of my wife. The rest did not seem important. I had already begun to insulate myself from the outside world. I needed to survive, I suppose!

We arrived at the ICU and I was asked to wait outside. There were two middle age couples huddled separately and a man in his early thirties was sitting with one of the couples. We exchanged good mornings, how's your uncle and I sat down. The nurse went to speak with the team dealing with Sarah as I waited patiently. There seemed nothing else to do? It also gave me time to start thinking about plans for the future, which became a good distraction and temporarily deflected my attention from my current state of distress.

She returned with a mask and a gown, which I promptly donned and followed her. To my right I saw two young women in their mid twenties fast asleep in their beds with drips attached to the back of their hands. Each had a nurse monitoring their progress. The only sound was the beeping of the heart monitors, three of them gentle but frequent.

Then we walked through some plastic curtains and there lay Sarah in isolation with a doctor holding a clipboard standing on one side of her bed and a nurse stood on the other. They were monitoring her progress and were to accompany Sarah on her ambulance journey to Cambridge. In addition, we were informed that police escort had arrived and were awaiting further instructions.

They had to wait for the trauma specialist who was still busy in the operating theatre. Sarah was in too precarious a state to be moved and needed to be stabilised. I had all this information to absorb while I stared blankly at this lifeless body just lying there. She looked pure white as if all the blood had been sucked out of her. I had never seen anything so white.

I saw drips surrounding her, including one containing morphine, which was keeping her sedated. I stood there willing her to fight and stay alive. She looked deathly white and barely breathing as the sound of the heart monitor created an eerie atmosphere. This definitely did not feel like the land of the living. I went over to touch her but was advised not to go near her for fear of infection and contamination. I was allowed to plant a gentle kiss on Sarah's forehead and then asked to wait outside. Please don't give up I said to her in a hushed tone as I was gently led out.

All I had ever wished for was a simple life and now only wanted to take my wife home to my beautiful daughters. She had two absolutely gorgeous daughters waiting for her at home, to kill and die for. I sat outside staring at the floor. This place felt so detached from the real world outside its four walls. It's simply impossible to describe what I was feeling. Then my thoughts were disturbed with the sound of rushing footsteps inside the ICU. One beep had stopped its rhythmic sound and became constant. The two couples sitting next to me both began to cry and their eyes filled with fear.

There was a flurry of movement and a nurse approached one of the couples. I am so sorry; your daughter has passed away she said in a whisper. The couple trying desperately to maintain their dignity and composure walked in behind her tightly clasping each other's hand. I could see the white of their knuckles and my heart went out to them. But at least unlike me, they had someone to hold on to.

Ten minutes later, they emerged talking about making arrangements for collection of their daughter's body and her belongings. I stood up to pass my condolences, which were graciously accepted. The man looked shaken and in tears while his wife maintained decorum. They wished my wife and me the best of luck and left, their departing steps short and deliberate.

I have no recollection of what was going through my head, except that there was a hell of a lot going on. I sensed that people were watching me and became aware that I had been talking to myself. The woman came over and sat beside me as she held my hand and uttered words of encouragement while the two men watched. The younger of the two appeared inconsolable. Humanity has a strange way of turning up when least expected.

I heard another monitor go monotone. Shit! Who next is the thought that raced through my head? Please god, not Sarah, I begged. My hands began to shake as my entire body convulsed with fear. The door opened yet again and a different nurse appeared. All four of us stood upright waiting for the bad news. The nurse gently asked me to sit down and approached the couple. She whispered something to them and the young man began to bawl and seemed inconsolable. The woman gave me a hug before entering the ICU.

Once again I was all alone and talking to myself. Hey I had been alone all my life, and survived thus far. I'll manage, I told myself. I think I was giving myself a pep talk. I could hear people crying and the voices were getting closer. The couple and the young man emerged, holding onto each other for dear life. The young man was in hysterics. He looked lost and in pieces. Individually they gave me a hug and wished the very best to my wife and me as they left. Now it was just the silence to accompany me only to be disturbed by the beeps of the solitary monitor at work. I realised that I was counting the beeps and willing the monitor to keep beeping. I knew that if that damn machine stopped making that friggin noise that would be it. End of story, chapter and verse and there was no way I wanted that annoying sound to stop.

Still there was no update from the team. My bum was sore, my head felt light and full of thoughts about Aisha and Rihana which brought me back to reality. I told the nurse that I was going home to check on my daughters and will be back shortly. If needed, I would be there sooner. I was assured that this was the best thing to do as Sarah was in no condition to be moved and when it happened, would be in the afternoon at the earliest. I arrived home and it felt deathly quiet. No one gave out to me. No one quizzed me. This was not normal and felt very strange.

Later in the day a lady health visitor came to check on Rihana's well being. I seemed to have all bases covered until it came to Rihana's feeding routine. Rihana was hungry every hour and a half and I was trying to stretch it to two hours. The Lady Health Visitor was not happy. I was feeding her too much she insisted. Well pray tell me how often and when I should feed her and she gave no answer. Then Rihana started to cry. I warmed the bottle, which the Lady Health Visitor insisted on checking, temperature and all, before giving the all clear.

I picked Rihana up and sat on the settee with Aisha tucked neatly on my right observing everything from under my right armpit as Rihana's head rested on my left arm. Lady Health Visitor was monitoring me like a hawk as she observed Rihana hoover the full bottle in a single breath, or so it seemed. If only you could see the look on her face. It was priceless.

She looked stupefied. I raised Rihana, made her sit up with my right hand firmly but softly tucked under her chin while gently rubbing her back with my left. To Aisha's amusement a burp came up in no time followed by another. Her eyes were closed and she seemed asleep. Gently I lay her head on my shoulder as I rubbed her back, Aisha followed suit with her little hand comforting her baby sister while Rihana raised her head, burped audibly and fell asleep, again.

The Lady Health Visitor changed her tune. It seems you are coping well and I will call again in a week's time. Call me if you need me before that, she said and departed. What about Rihana's feed, I asked. Oh, we will discuss it at my next visit, was her reply.

Sarah's mother was walking around in a world of her own and appeared occupied in her thoughts. I suppose life is not made easy with a single barely functioning brain cell. The family will be around soon, she informed me; some were coming by air and others by coach as if I gave a shit. She busied herself with preparations for their dinner. I have little recollection of who arrived when and in which order except that Sarah's father was the first to arrive that afternoon. Then I think the two brothers Jimmy and Charlie along with Jimmy's wife, Louise followed by the two sisters, Mary and Kate. All I can remember is that the full cast of the pantomime had gathered within forty-eight hours.

I was at home getting everything ready for my darling daughters and our journey to Cambridge, 72 miles away when Sarah's mother came over and asked me to wait a while. Sarah's Dad was on his way and should be here this afternoon. It would be nice if he could accompany me to Cambridge. I agreed to wait but could not sit still. There was only so much feeding with Rihana and poor Aisha looked lost. Her dad was crushing her with hugs and kisses and she looked confused. God knows what she may have thought of me but I do know that I became extremely protective of them both.

I decided to pay another visit to the hospital and needed to know how Sarah was doing. Soon I arrived at the hospital except this time I did not have to run. Everything was much the same and her state was precarious with no sign of improvement. Now they had decided that they had no choice left but move Sarah to Cambridge.

I was not allowed to accompany her in the ambulance as there was no room and I was considered more a hindrance than help. The police escort was still waiting patiently with blue lights going around in circles but no sirens yet. The medical staff asked me politely to go home and advised me to travel to Cambridge in my own time when traffic had eased and Sarah would not have missed me anyway. The rush hour was fast approaching and 5 pm was always a nightmare for driving.

I went home and as always found Aisha a pleasant distraction. Rihana was in a world of her own. With her it was feed, sleep and not a bother. She was the most placid and content baby I had ever seen. All things considered this baby had the patience of ten saints and a loopy dad thrown in for good measure.

Sarah's dad arrived. He looked concerned, tired and drained with little to say. I had to wait till the matriarch had fed her husband while my itchy bum was raring to go. For some reason I felt angry as I watched them both busy eating, looking so calm and mechanical while Rihana lay in my lap and Aisha huddled next to me. We somehow did not seem important to them. They appeared distant from our presence as they spoke in hushed tones with each other.

Thankfully, the feast was soon over and I gathered Aisha and Rihana with bottles prepared, baby feed, nappy bags, clothes and everything else that I could think of. I had recently leased a brand new Mercedes van for business with a double seat on the passenger side and plenty of space in the back. That day the space came handy. Rihana's carry cot was fastened with the seat belt, Aisha was tied with the second seat belt and the Royals sat in the back. The journey was calm; my daughters were with me and the rest of the world could go to hell. I only had time to think about my wife and our daughters.

An hour and a half later, we arrived. The ambulance had arrived only a few minutes before us. It is a huge hospital, I observed as we were directed to ICU where Sarah was being kept. Her condition was described as critical but stable. After a short while, a nurse arrived to speak with me and yes, she would only speak to me. For the first time since I had known the matriarch, she did not make an ass of herself and remained quiet.

The nurse explained that Mr Robinson will be operating on Sarah. There was something in the way she pronounced his name, which oozed respect, the kind reserved for deities. It seemed her head bowed a little every time she mentioned his name. The rest of the staff offered me their best wishes and also assured me that Sarah was in the best hands possible. They all sounded so sincere and kind. Somehow, I knew I could trust them. It took me less then twenty-four hours to figure out why.

I was escorted to meet with Mr Robinson as he strode towards the operating theatre. An aura surrounded this man and his entire demeanour demanded and commanded respect. He was polite yet firm, assuring but truthful and kindness seemed to surround him but he looked a little tired. Having finished one procedure, he was on his way to perform a miracle. He assured me that he would do his best and gave Sarah an evens chance of survival. Then I left him in peace and returned to my darling daughters who were in the waiting room. For once I did not feel the need to ask questions.

This man was special, the thought had repeatedly crossed my mind and he did not let me down. Somehow, I did not feel afraid anymore. Against all odds, he managed to save my wife. To this day, even though Sarah and I are now divorced, I feel I owe this man an awful lot of gratitude because the mother of my daughters is alive today because of him.

As soon as the procedure was over, I was called to see Mr Robinson. We met in the corridor where we talked as he walked towards the surgical ward. He had managed to stop the haemorrhaging but the next twenty-four hours were critical for Sarah and he still gave her an evens chance of survival. He stated that this was one of the worst cases he had ever come across and then he looked exhausted.

We were scheduled to meet at half past eight in the morning for a meeting as we said goodnight and parted. I thanked him profusely and went back to the waiting room to relay the news to mam and dad. It was close to two in the morning and all of a sudden pangs of hunger hit me. Dad are you hungry? I asked. He nodded.

I checked on Aisha and Rihana before heading to town. The nurse on duty gave me precise directions to the only safe to eat takeaway at that hour of the morning. We gorged on Donner kebabs and greasy chips and they tasted like a feast fit for a king. We returned with some take away and chips for the matriarch. I asked Sarah's dad if he would like to accompany me to the meeting in the morning. I had noticed that he had been suffering quietly and saw the intensity of pain in his eyes. We sat around and dad dozed off till the daylight broke. I sat through the night staring like an owl while Aisha and Rihana slept peacefully. Even the matriarch had a good snore or two.

The news in the morning was encouraging and a source of relief. A nurse led us to Mr Robinson's office for our meeting. Once again I sensed and experienced a feeling of awe in his presence. He was in his civvies this time and pointed towards the two empty chairs for us to be seated. How is Sarah? I asked nervously. He wished to speak with me alone. I requested that Sarah's dad be allowed to stay. He politely but firmly stated that it was a matter of importance which he could only discuss with me.

I pleaded yet again that her father had travelled from Ireland to be with his daughter, and I wished for him to hear firsthand what Mr Robinson had to say. He gently nodded his consent. She is stable but critical. The next few days would be crucial; she would be kept on a morphine drip and an induced state of coma, he stated. But! I did not like the sound of but!

She may have to spend the rest of her life in an institution, he added in a very solemn tone of voice. It felt like a thunderbolt from blue and beyond comprehension. It did not sound real that my wife could be confined to a psychiatric institution for the rest of her natural life. What would I tell my daughters? That I committed their mother to a mental institution. I simply refused to accept this fact. There had to be another way as there always is.

There was no other way, I was assured. Sarah was given a hysterectomy to help find the source of her haemorrhaging. One of her ovaries had been removed, her body had endured a severe trauma and while in an induced state of coma, there was a risk that lack of oxygen supply to the brain may have occurred. At the age of twenty four, my wife was about to enter menopause and nature had given her the gift of psychosis for the rest of her natural life. I could stick it in my pipe and smoke it, but had no other options.

I chose to ignore the wisdom. Instead I told him that I wished to take my wife home. I wanted my wife at home with our daughters and that was it. If she ever needed a reason to live, now she had two of them. Her dad sat there stupefied. I don't think he understood the gravity of what had just been said. Dad, Sarah will be fine, I tried to reassure him. You could see relief travel all the way through his body. He got up and shook the doctor's hand. I sensed that handshake had more gratitude than words could ever say.

Mr Robinson's only other advice was to seek mental health supports for Sarah and then I shook his hand while sincerely expressing my gratitude and left his office. It did not sink in then but took the best part of fifteen years to experience what he had politely tried to warn me of. What he told me was that my wife was gone and I would be taking home a person suffering from psychosis. She could have killed us all and shown no remorse. Destruction was promised for the rest of our future and I was reluctant to accept it because I loved my wife dearly.

Mr Robinson had given me a curious look as I thanked him with all my heart and took our leave. I had told him that there was no way I could have had my wife sectioned and hoped against all odds that she would be fine. She needed her daughters as much as they would need her. As you wish Mr Anjum, he seemed to have said ruefully.

Dad seemed relieved, happier, and alive. Throughout the evening I felt that he was slowly dying with his daughter. We returned to the waiting room and gave Sarah's mother the news. There were no tears, just relief. I was told that I might be allowed to see her later, if only for a short while. She would not be able to recognise anyone for at least a few days. This piece of news was good enough for me.

We drove home and Dad was beginning to talk. I felt wrecked but relieved, Aisha looked drained while Rihana slept and soon we were approaching Luton when the matriarch decided to come to life. I want to go to a church to say thanks to god, light a candle and say a prayer, she said. Dad looked a little surprised and said that Sam and the girls were tired and he would go to the church with her later.

You should have seen her snout fill with air while my heart filled with dread. She was indignant and announced that she was going to church before going home. If we did not wish to bring her to the church then we could drop her in town and she would make her own way home.

I told you this bloated biddy would drive anyone bonkers. If there was a river nearby I would gladly have dropped her in among the piranhas or so I felt. I saw a church spire in the distance and promptly pulled up outside the door. This is not my church, she exclaimed indignantly as Dad let out another sigh. Well how the feck was I to know how many churches this woman owned and their locations. What kind of church do you want to go to? I asked. I was too tired to argue with the numbskull. Our lady's, a Catholic church of course, she sneered.

112

Now someone pray tell me, the situation that I was in, where do I find the yellow pages, there was no satnav and I had loony tunes singing in my ears. If I wasn't so tired, would gladly have pushed her out of the moving van and her husband would have lent me a hand with gratitude, probably. I stopped several times to ask for directions and got a few queer looks in return. Then a passerby gave me directions to a Catholic church. We arrived and she took the best part of three minutes in her church to do what she wanted and thankfully, without another utterance we arrived home.

Charlie arrived soon thereafter. He is a decent person and has a heart of gold taking into consideration the opportunities in life he was given. If given a chance he would have done even better in life. Despite a lack of education he had worked hard to become a success story. He had little time for his mother but took his obligations seriously. He had a loving wife and doted on his son. He had taken the first available flight out of Galway.

Older brother Jimmy and his wife were on their way. Now this couple is a very different kettle of fish. If you look in the Pictionary under dysfunctional, their pictures would stare back at you. Jimmy was a child in an adult body but apple of his mother's eye and could do no wrong. His wife is of good heart but possesses a brain which slipped gears at random.

They had two lovely daughters and two sons. The couple had made sure that their children saw all the colours of the rainbow in their short lives. Suffice to say domestic bliss and violence ran on the same track, colliding frequently.

I had my daughters to look after and matriarch did what she does best, tend to her brood. Soon after their arrival the sons went for a pint across the road with their dad while she fussed around getting their dinner ready. I was in a world of my own and the kitchen was taken over by her highness. I will be out of your way soon, she said repeatedly. I urgently needed divine intervention. Who else could get this woman out of my way? God was not being helpful at all. The day he created her, he probably knew the fuck up he had made and went into hiding.

Every time I went to the kitchen she was there with pots, pans, plates, peeled vegetables and god knows what else with little or no space to spare. Then shit happened again and there she was with slices of ham. Alcohol and pork, not in my house she had been told, repeatedly.

All four returned from the pub and matriarch asked them to sit around the dining table. Sarah and I had bought a round glass table for four which suited the clan perfectly. Plates piled with food arrived. Jimmy's pile was the highest, as always. I did not know whether he was meant to eat or climb the mountain. I was sitting with Aisha and Rihana on the other side of the room watching TV and trying my best to ignore the proceedings. We will soon be out of your way, the matriarch announced with a regal flair and a wave of her hand as she walked back to the kitchen to carry more plates laden with food.

I could not give a rat's ass to whatever she was saying. Aisha was neatly tucked into my side as only she can. Rihana made very little in demands and was fast asleep most of the time. Charlie seemed pensive as others dug into food with dedication, passion and commitment. Little was being said as I walked to the kitchen to see what I could cook. I still had not tackled the issue of pork with this woman. Being a Muslim has its own peculiarities and rewards.

I did not feel hungry anymore, the girls were fed and I had to make travel plans for our visit to the hospital. I had Aisha and Rihana ready. There was a quarter of a tank of diesel in the van and a princely sum of five pounds in my pocket. No loose change, not a penny more and I was prepared to set out for a

114

round trip of 144 miles. Jimmy finished first and came over to sit next to me. After a decent burp and settling the folds of his bum he described with a nonchalant air the way his mother had phoned him. They had all thought that Sarah was gone and they were coming to make her funeral arrangements. This panto seemed to have more asses than the donkey sanctuary.

Now their demeanour was the least of my concerns. Charlie noticed that something was bothering me and I narrated to him the episode of ham I had found in the fridge. He was furious and told me to throw the shit out. You do not have to put up with this kind of crap, he added. I don't know whether he meant the ham or the mother. To date I am none the wiser but pretty sure he meant the mother.

I got my darling daughters in the front seat and the clan got in the back. Where are we going to sit? Someone had asked. On your backside you dumbass, I muttered even though I had felt a compulsion to yell. Good people treat all people with respect; I heard one of my mother's teachings whisper in my ear and I told her to feck off.

Charlie got an ingenious idea to get a plank of wood, shove it under the driving seat while the other end rested on the hump of rear wheel and for the next hour and a half and I heard nothing but moaning and cursing. It seemed like one of their perfect family outings. When fed, they farted and were always feckin ready to moan. My monologues were keeping me occupied till I heard my darling daughter Aisha's inquisitive voice.

Where are we going daddy? She asked. For a drive darling, I replied. But where? She asked again. To see mummy, I replied. Where Daddy? Questions only a child can ask without causing offence. She looked so sweet with her eyes slightly closed and a little frown on her pudgy little forehead. Now aged twenty four she is still the same and now questions me instead of asking questions.

We arrived at the hospital and went straight to the ICU. Louise very kindly offered to look after my darlings while I went to speak with the nurse for the daily update. Sarah was stable, heavily sedated, her bleeding had become negligible and she was holding steady. I was allowed to see her lying in a surgical bed, surrounded by breathing apparatus, two drips, one in each hand and her hands lay neatly by her side. There was the sound of the ventilator at work with its hose disappearing down Sarah's throat, heart monitor and its steady beep and I there stood a dialysis machine nearby.

For the first time her cheeks showed some colour as she appeared alive and peacefully asleep. A mountain of worry suddenly rolled off my back. I gently kissed her forehead and said a quiet hello in her left ear but got no reply. I pulled a stool and sat down. Then I began my non-sensical talk as I told her about our daughters, especially our newborn. I told her how wonderful Aisha was and how she was helping me with her baby sister. For the first time in her life, she was listening without answering or snapping. She stayed quiet and not a word was uttered.

The nurse walked away quietly, gently wiping an errant tear from her eye. She knew we had a lot of catching up to do, especially Sarah. I talked while Sarah listened and the odd time I saw a hint of a smile.

Then it dawned upon me that the clan was here. I asked the nurse if they could see Sarah. One at a time, only for a minute and no more were the instructions. We do not want to distress her, she said politely but firmly. For once the whole clan behaved.

Except for Jimmy who upon his return to the waiting room found that, Louise had changed the TV channel and a tussle began for the remote control. Voices were raised, a nurse appeared and decorum was restored. One thing for sure the clan never let the side down. There was always a feck up waiting to happen and it usually did.

Aisha wanted to see her mummy and I took her and Rihana to see Sarah. The nurse had done her best to cover Sarah and the protruding tubes were covered to save Aisha distress. I told Aisha Mummy was resting and would be coming home soon. She gave her mum a kiss on her right cheek and sat down quietly in my lap. I gently lay Rihana beside Sarah and sat there trying to stop tears from leaving my eyes. I did not wish for Aisha to see me cry. Rihana was no trouble at all. As placid, a child as one would ever see. I was hoping the feel of Rihana's touch; her closeness would help bring Sarah back and give her the will to fight probably the biggest battle of her life. Rihana lay there quietly, opened her eyes for a moment or two and then fell asleep again.

It was a sobering sight to watch the mother asleep as her new born baby lay next to her. Aisha looked a little lost and whispered occasionally while I sat there pensively. This was my world and I was trying my best to hold it together. Sometimes I wished to do more but did not know what or how. I was trying and had the two biggest reasons to help me survive who were completely reliant on me. Sarah was facing her own demons.

I sat there all day every day with Aisha in my lap as Rihana lay next to her mom. At other times Rihana was in my lap while Aisha sat staring at her mother. This was our world and I believe all of us never felt alone. We were all there fighting for our survival and the rest of the world barely existed. Then there was the clan outside, full of its peculiarities and uncertainties. Another day had passed and Charlie had to return to work, as did Sarah's dad. Louise went to see a father she had not seen for years and then Mary and Kate arrived. Now there were three of them, cacklin, arguing and talking in their alien tongue while my daughters and I found solace with Sarah or in our corner at home. We three were doing fine as Sarah slept.

I was scrimping and scrounging for money as the business was closed. The odd cheque came alongside threats from a customer who threatened to bring his gang around to beat me up as I had not replied to his phone calls, all two of them. He needed his jacket repaired or replaced. I returned his call to say that I had just received his message. As for the rest, he was welcome to take whatever action he deemed fit and I would contact him in a week's time to have the matter sorted. He uttered some apologetic nonsense which meant nothing to me. I was becoming more self aware of people and had little time left for their crap.

I had been on the go nonstop for seventy-two hours and needed to calm down. Louise told me to take a little break from the girls and we decided to get some Chinese. It was also a good distraction from the constant humming and hawing of the matriarch. Louise took care of the girls while Kate came with me on the motorbike to collect the food from Luton. Food was not great but it was nice to taste a little normality.

As time went on I was becoming more possessive and protective of my daughters and at times found it impossible to leave them in anyone's care. As days went by everyone had left except Mary, Kate and the matriarch. My daily routine became getting the girls ready and leaving for our daily stay in the hospital in Cambridge. We were there by 9.30 the latest. I waited, sat by Sarah's side, talked a little, and walked a little, sat and played with the girls before returning home by 9pm every evening and we did this, seven days a week.

Sarah was holding her own. They had reduced the morphine drip due to fear of addiction and she was beginning to show signs of movement. At times she grimaced with pain as she tried to squeeze my fingers. Then there was a gentle caress of the hand. She was coming back to life and it felt wonderful. A miracle had happened and our daughters still had their mother.

One evening I asked Sarah's mother if she would take care of Rihana for the night to allow me to catch up on some long lost sleep. She was still waking up every two hours for a feed. To make matters worse, Mary and Kate's boyfriends rang every night at 11.30pm sharp. The two of them were neither light in weight nor on their feet. It sounded like a herd of Rhinos racing to the phone and one spent the next half hour talking while the other sulked. Then the phone would ring again and only one Rhino would run or so it seemed. In between, I was trying to catch up on sleep, hence the request to the matriarch.

She looked neither sure nor reassuring. Prior to this I had done deals with the devil so why not with the devil's disciple. There seemed little cohesion between my mind and body and I felt close to mental and physical collapse. Give her to me after the last feed and I will mind her, she replied.

It was 1.30 in the morning by the time I put Rihana to sleep, handed her to her grandmother and literally collapsed into my bed where Aisha was fast asleep. I thought I was dreaming when I heard noises. As I slowly managed to open my eyes the hovering shadow of the matriarch was leaning forward to put Rihana next to me. I looked at the clock. It was 3.20 in the morning.

I am not able to do this anymore, she said flatly. I made room for Rihana and soon Daddy and daughters were back in the land of nod. We did not need help from anyone, I had finally decided there and then.

119

This woman had often told me that she had helped raise kids and plenty of them and small wonder when they turned out to be such fuck ups, I often felt compelled to blurt but sadly never did say. Trust, faith and respect had long departed. Now only the words shameless and brazen were left etched in my mind.

No one from the clan had ever offered help financially or otherwise. Once Charlie had offered to contribute towards the cost of diesel, the rest god love them felt entitled to take what they could, especially the matriarch. Now it was mostly Aisha and Rihana travelling with me to the hospital. The matriarch and her daughters did not see any point in visiting as Sarah was never awake and I thanked god for small mercies.

On the sixth day of our daily visits, I exchanged greetings with the duty nurse who knew our daily routine. She told me that Sarah had begun to move her limbs and moaned with pain quite often. This was a good sign as her senses were returning and the dosage of morphine was being gently lowered. She sat in her office peering through the glass window as I lowered Aisha to give her mum a kiss and gently lay Rihana beside Sarah. The bed was raised about four feet off the ground and the floor was tiled. The nurse smiled and waved at us. Aisha waved back and began to amuse herself as I sat down on a stool two feet away, next to Sarah's bed.

I felt Sarah stir and saw her grimace with pain. She was trying to move her left arm which lifted slightly before dropping by her side and the drip lines were pulled a little as she slowly tried to move her body. The nurse looked through the window and gently began to rise and then it happened. The event that is firmly etched in my memory and probably would haunt me forever.

Sarah gently opened her eyes and turned her head towards me. She saw Rihana lying next to her fast asleep. Suddenly her eyes opened and burned with fire. They appeared full of hatred and venom and the memory still sends a shudder down my spine.

I had never seen such a look that could kill. In a split second I saw the nurse jump and reach for the door of her office as one of the drip stands found its way to the floor. Sarah with all her might had pushed Rihana away and instinctively my arms reached out to catch my baby in mid air.

Sarah was staring at me, while her eyes seemed unnaturally wide and ablaze. It was a look beyond description and scared the living daylights out of me. Then Sarah gently turned away, lowered her head onto the pillow and looked away to her right as her eyes began to well up. I knew she was awake because she did acknowledge when I called her name.

What had just transpired seemed beyond belief and my hands were shaking as I held Rihana tightly in my arms. I had never seen such putrefied hatred, ever. What the fuck had just happened. The nurse was there by her side, picking up the drip stand and checking the drip lines while fixing the tape holding them to the back of Sarah's hand. She had tears in her eyes and was trying hard to contain her emotions. Then she gave me a wistful little smile with a little nod of her head.

I turned my attention to Aisha. The poor thing was stunned, surprised and stood there looking mesmerised. I called her over and she stood nestling close to me with my arms filled with Rihana. My heart was racing and I could hear the thud of my heartbeat. My chest felt ready to explode and the blood went rushing to my head as I felt faint.

I did not wish to black out. My arms were feeling weak and hastily I held Rihana even closer as I bent over her. Darling Aisha was standing next to me with her right hand rubbing my back and the left hand resting on Rihana's forehead.

This child was incredible. She had always been my beacon of hope and she was not going to let her silly dad down. She looked so mature and grown up at the ripe old age of two years and seven months. I was crying tears of blood inside of me. Rihana was stuck between my arms and my chin as life returned slowly returned to my arms and the feeling of dizziness began to dissipate. I sat there motionless, too scared to move.

Sarah had gone back to sleep as I rose gingerly and slowly walked to the waiting room where I held and rocked Rihana for what seemed like eternity. I wanted her to feel safe. I wanted to reassure her; I wanted to tell her that this would never happen again.

I always had Aisha and all through this she remained glued to my side till she asked, 'daddy, are you ok'. I said yes and gave her a kiss on those delectable chubby cheeks. She smiled and soon was herself again, a picture of joy to cherish and behold.

I informed the nurse that I was taking my daughters home and to call me if my presence was needed. Upon arrival I informed the matriarch and her daughters that Sarah was awake, back amongst the living and all the visible signs were promising. Nothing else was said or repeated.

Chapter Six

Nothing much had changed in our daily routine. We got fed, washed, dressed and then went off to the hospital. Many a time on a wing and a prayer as cash was sporadic and the needle on the fuel gauge always seemed to hover near empty with never more than ten pounds in my pocket but thankfully, I never ran out of gas or food. The terror trio were travelling with me, but managing to keep their distance. The phone calls in the middle of the night were still coming but I had stopped caring by now.

I had started to mix baby rusks in Rihana's feed as milk by itself was not doing much for her appetite. Then it was time for Lady Health Visitor to re appear. She was horrified to hear that I was mixing rusks in baby feed. It seems that since her first visit, she had learned nothing.

She had no new information except insisting that baby food was too soon. She provided me with no new pearls of wisdom and left in a pensive mood promising to return with a solution. If she ever found a solution I would become a fairy, is the thought that crossed my mind.

I felt angry and it got worse with what was to follow. Sarah had been moved to a private room to recuperate and still could not bear to look at Rihana. I would arrive at the hospital, let the girls settle and then carry Sarah to the bathroom followed by a shower. I washed her, shampooed and dried her hair, helped dress and settle her in bed before the regal trio was allowed in.

Sometimes I plaited her hair and at other times she wanted a ponytail. In between, I would cut and file her nails, trim her fringe and then got out of the way for the rest of the day. I gently encouraged her to try and hold our baby daughter. She would always push poor Rihana away without a sideways glance.

123

Over a period of time she began to soften up but to this day, she has shown Rihana neither affection, nor love or care. At least then I managed to persuade her to hold Rihana for half a minute at a time. The way she looked at her seemed scary at times and I have no idea what was going through her head. However, gradually she was beginning to hold and feed her.

One day after my daily chores were done and with Sarah propped up in her bed, I left her with the matriarch, Mary and Kate and went for a stroll down the hospital corridor with Rihana in my arms and Aisha by my side. I still could not trust Sarah with Rihana and even the thought of them two together petrified me.

As I returned, something had changed. Sarah started shouting at me for not making her family feel welcome in our house. They always had to tip toe around me and were scared of me. I had no respect or regard for her family, especially her mother, she screamed.

Mary the moron became sheepish, her mother flushed and Kate looked embarrassed as I got up and walked out of the room and straight into the lift. I wanted to go for a walk and get as far away as possible from these three. Before the lift doors closed, Kate had entered the lift. She was extremely apologetic. Well you know Sarah, she said. She should know better about Mary and mum. It's about time that she stopped listening to those two. Poor Kate was always trying to pacify and be the voice of reason.

I still felt a desperate desire to get away as I lit a cigarette and Kate stood there talking to me, trying to be supportive. Look, your daughters need you and you have to come up, she said. The thought of my daughters calmed me down and after a few minutes we returned to Sarah's room.

It was as if nothing untoward had occurred and they all tried to be nice to me. Oh, you always take too much notice, said Sarah. Why won't you let mum stay? You could do with some help and she wants to help. I would rather have had a hole drilled in either side of my head, without anaesthetic, I thought to myself.

Slowly Sarah was returning to her normal self but there were subtle changes that I did notice. The blank stares and emptiness in her eyes were a constant source of discomfort and confusion. Sarah was off morphine and it was over a fortnight since all hell had broken loose.

Mary and Kate were making preparations to leave when I asked Kate to stay a while; I could have done with some help but she was dying to see her boyfriend back home and had to go. Mary was of no consequence and unfortunately for me the matriarch was staying. Both sisters left the next day and slowly peace and quiet returned as I began collecting the marbles in my head. They still seemed out of place but I at least I could find most of them. Matriarch was making every effort to stay out of my way and thankfully, we barely spoke.

Then out of the blue Bridget of all people rang looking for her dear sister. Where is Sarah's mother? She wanted to know. I told her that the matriarch had gone pottering around town to buy presents for the folks back home. Ok I will call her again and tell her that for the last two days Willie is off his rocker again. I cannot cope with him and she had better come down and sort him out, Bridget sounded very angry.

Master Willie often fell off the wagon and this time he was off his train. He held a bottle of Vodka in one hand and had been reciting Shakespeare for the past forty-eight hours. It must have been some sight. I was so preoccupied that I forgot to savour the thought. Upon her return, I informed her of the call I had received and that Bridget would ring again. All of a sudden, she was like a hyena on heat having swallowed a packet of speed for good measure. One minute she was on the phone, next she was in the bathroom and soon she was all dressed with her handbag on her arm ready to go.

Will you give me a lift? Willie needs me, she asked curtly. Lift to where? I asked. Willie lived in Harrow and Bridget was in Hayes. I had no idea where this woman was heading. Just drop me at the bus stop and I will make my own way, she said. I told her to give me a few minutes to get the girls ready before I could drop her at the bus station. She could not wait and the next minute she was gone.

Now I had the house all to myself and the company of my darling daughters. There was the daily trip to the hospital, washing and ironing, hoovering and some shopping to do before Aisha, Rihana and I could sit down in front of the TV. Rihana remained asleep most of the time but Aisha and I loved trying to keep her awake, mostly unsuccessfully. Then Aisha wanted to hold Rihana in her lap while watching TV but seldom succeeded.

Rihana looked like a great big pink bundle and poor Aisha in her little nightie with hair scattered over her forehead looked a picture of confusion trying to hold on this bundle that kept slipping out of her arms and off her lap. I would breathe a sigh of relief and allow myself a smile because somehow I knew that from then on everything would be fine, I reassured myself. What a fool I was, the thought often crosses my mind.

Before we went to bed, the house was spick and span, everything was clean and organised for the following day. Rihana was still sleeping in my bed and Aisha crept in every night abandoning her cot and her room. She was spoilt rotten and loved snuggling up to daddy. Daddy hug, she would request with outstretched arms as she would stand by my bed knowing that a hug would entitle her to sleeping on the other side of me, in my bed.

Rihana lay on one side and Aisha on the other. Five bottles of feed on the bedside table, a kettle full of water and we were off to snooze. They were happy days. Next morning, seven sharp, as per my routine I woke up to get myself ready for the day. Aisha and Rihana had their routine, even where sleep was concerned and I could set the clock by them. Aisha woke up at seven thirty, Rihana at eight and both were ready to be fed.

I had bottles to wash and feeds to prepare when I heard a knock on the front door and the doorbell rang simultaneously. Then there was the knock again and I cursed under my breath. I was worried that they were going to wake my darlings up. Who the hell was it and what was their rush? I thought as I walked to the front door.

I opened the front door and there stood a woman, mid to late thirties, arms neatly folded against her chest, holding some files and a stack of papers. I am here to take two children into foster care, she announced. You what? Who sent you? You must have the wrong address; I blurted it all out at the same time.

She dropped a file as she pushed her right hand against the door. Mrs Anjum gave birth to a baby girl on 6 September in Luton and Dunstable Hospital, she asked. Yes, I replied. Oh, you must be her husband, she cooed. Well how perceptive of her. Yes, I replied, again. And, you have a daughter, Aisha? She asked and got another yes for the umpteenth time.

The hospital had informed the social services that the mother is in intensive care and we have to put the children in foster care until she recuperates and returns, she stated matter of factly. Now this woman was beginning to annoy me and I had loads to do. Look I am their father and quite capable of looking after them. I do not need foster care, nor do they and then heard my darling daughter calling me. Daddy, daddy what's wrong'? Aisha was standing at the top of the stairs, bleary eyed with her arms stretched. She wanted me to pick her up.

I turned to the woman and told her that I have my children to look after and now, please go away and leave us alone. She had an ID card in her hand which she put in my face as if I gave a shit.

I have the power to remove them so please step out of my way, she ordered. I slammed the door in her face and went to pick up Aisha. She needed to go to the bathroom. When finished I cleaned her, put toothpaste on her toothbrush and leaving her occupied had a quick peek at Rihana. God bless her. She was fast asleep

There was a huge thud on the front door and that literally made me I jump out of my skin. Then again, bang, bang and it was repeated. It sounded like someone was trying to knock the bloody door down.

I asked Aisha to keep brushing; re assured her that everything is ok and ran down the stairs two steps at a time. As soon as I opened the door a size thirteen foot appeared and wedged between the door and the doorstep. A police officer stood there, six foot two and a bit more. Please step aside and let this woman in, he said in a booming voice. From behind him appeared the woman, the social worker. I had told you that I have the authority to remove the children and would call for help, she announced triumphantly.

Behind her stood two more police officers on my driveway, one asking the other if the rear of the house was secured. He had his baton drawn. There was another cop walking from the police car, which was parked blocking my gate.

Someone called out a few names, probably cops at the rear of the house, I assumed. I asked him to remove his foot from the door he did not budge and proceeded to pull the flick stick from his side. Its impressive to see a six inch stick become a foot long. One of his colleagues was pulling out the handcuffs from his belt. Sir I will advise you not to approach or touch the door, said size thirteen. He looked serious and the tone was threatening. In fact, he looked very fucking serious and meant business.

Then I heard Aisha calling for me and Rihana began to cry. Fuck this I said and left the front door open as I walked upstairs. The social worker, like a ferret ducked under size thirteen's outstretched right arm and shot straight past me as she scooted upstairs. Aisha was upset and crying while Rihana was bawling. As I reached Aisha she slid into my arms and put her little head down on my shoulder. Then I walked towards the bedroom to comfort Rihana.

The woman was emerging from the other bedroom. She had gone from one room to the other and found Rihana. She was holding my baby in her arms but then a strange thing happened. She calmly walked down the stairs as I followed her to the front door. She stood at the doorway and asked the cops to go away. Everything is fine, she told them but another drama was in the offing. I am sorry ma'am but we can only take orders from our super, he stated matter of factly and you do not have the authority, said the size thirteen as he slowly retracted his foot from my front door.

The other two cops including Mr Handcuffs looked very confused and the two gently began to retreat towards their car. One went on the walkie-talkie but I could not hear ensuing conversation. The woman proceeded to pass Rihana back to me but I had my arms full with Aisha. I gently put her down, gave her a hug and a kiss and asked her to go in the front room and

129

put the telly on. God bless her, she did as I asked. Now I had Rihana in my arms and she had calmed down. She was staring at me, my poor baby. I gave her a gentle squeeze and kissed her chubby cheeks repeatedly.

Then an argument began between size thirteen and the social worker. He was talking to base, she was talking to her superiors, the front door was still wide open but I really could not give a shit. I went to the kitchen with Rihana in my arms and put the kettle on, a couple of slices of bread in the toaster and an egg to boil. Aisha loved to have a boiled egg in her cup and then I lay Rihana on the carpet to change her nappy. Yes, I had the baby blanket and a sheet under her!

The woman returned and her eyes appeared moist. I shall remember the words that escaped her mouth until the day I die. 'If one per cent of women were as capable a parent as you are, then they ought to be very proud of themselves'. She handed me her card and asked, 'how are you coping financially, moneywise'? I have none was my honest answer. I will cope as I always do, I replied. I am sure you will, she said as she jotted something in haste on a piece of paper and handed it over to me.

I will not bother you again. Tomorrow morning, please go to the social services office and ask for this woman, she pointed to the piece of paper. There will be a cheque waiting for you as an interim payment and you will receive weekly payments as a carer. In addition, you are entitled to; something she said which I do not recall.

The morning's events were simply too much to comprehend. One minute she was creating hell in my already turbulent life and next she was soothing my sores. I wish you the best of luck with your family. You have two beautiful daughters and they are lucky to have you. I hope your wife gets better soon and please do not hesitate to contact me if you need anything, she added as she wiped away an errant tear, turned around and walked out of the open door. I never saw her or heard from her again.

The next morning before heading to the hospital, I went to visit the social services. They were based in Luton city centre. I parked the van outside the social services office. Usually the place is packed and it's impossible to find a parking space. This morning I found a parking space without much effort. Aisha jumped in my arms as was her usually game. Catch me Daddy, she would say then arms extended she would jump and dare me to catch her. I had not let her down thus far.

She helped me with the buggy as I picked up Rihana and then she helped me tie her baby sister while Rihana sat there placid as ever. There was not a bother on either one of them. Rihana was in the buggy and Aisha on my shoulders as we approached the front door. As I pushed the front door three men rushed to hold the door open. Somehow everything seemed wonderful this morning.

I thanked them for their kindness, Aisha gave her priceless smile of gratitude and I walked towards the counter and joined the queue. Aisha wanted to get down from my shoulders and Rihana was awake and getting a little restless. A young woman came rushing out from one of the offices and asked me to follow her. I had no idea who she was and I was reluctant to leave the queue which was getting longer by the minute. Don't worry, said one of the young men, I'll hold your spot. I followed the young lady into the office as she closed the door behind her.

She was busy fiddling and fondling her paperwork till she found what she was looking for. She handed me a cheque for over three hundred sterling and pushed a piece of paper towards me for my signature. This is to confirm that you have received this payment and will be getting the same every fortnight till your wife gets better, she informed me. I know that you have enough on your plate and I will have everything sorted for next week, she added.

Then she shook Aisha's hand, smiled at Rihana and held the door open with the warmest smile I had seen in a long time. She told me how beautiful my daughters were and I thanked her for her kindness as Daddy and daughters departed. We had a long but this time a happy journey ahead. I fed Rihana in the van while Aisha listened to music. We had the most enjoyable drive to the hospital. Aisha always made sure that my life was anything but boring.

Sarah was beginning to walk unaided and I was still doing her hair, manicure and pedicure while bringing daily delivery of clean nighties and undergarments. Buying new ones and washing the old was a piece of cake. I think I bought more tights, bras and underwear for her than she ever did. Gradually I had become a master in Denier description and bra cup sizes.

Aisha was happy, Sarah began to look good, Rihana looked content and I began to breathe normal for a change. My gentle pleadings had persuaded Sarah to hold Rihana and feed her. Then the good news came that Sarah would be allowed to return home in the next day or two. I had everything ready from the bathroom to the kitchen, bedrooms were done and everything was in surplus. I was ready to bring my family home at last. It had been some journey. Sixth of September was destined to be etched in my memory forever, remembered daily and never forgotten.

Sarah still felt very sore and was not aware that part of her stomach had been removed and menopause was about to hit her like a runaway train. Even I did not know what the future held in store and for then I was thankful to have my family and had a life to live, one day at a time.

132

We arrived home and were a family once again. Sarah's first priority was to get back into her size ten jeans. After giving birth to Aisha, it took her three weeks to get her figure back but this time it took a little longer. Seven weeks I think or thereabouts which included much starvation and a handful of fancy diets.

But I was beginning to notice something different about her. Her mannerism, her habits, her way of doing things had changed. At times she seemed distant, almost detached as if daydreaming.

She was becoming more stubborn than ever before. Often she would not hear what we said, as if she were in a world of her own. One thing no one could miss was her temper. She was having bouts of rage which were frightening and often occurred without warning.

She was very angry indeed!

Chapter Seven

It was good to have Sarah at home but often she appeared distant and pre occupied. Usually she had great fun with Aisha but it was not the same anymore. Her affection and loving seemed timid. It felt as she was playing a role by doing all the right things but the spirit was missing.

She had also become very needy and reliant on me. If I were not available, she would become nervous, angry and agitated without any apparent reason. She always seemed preoccupied and had started to go to meetings, when, where and with whom, she would not divulge. It all appeared very secretive to say the least. Then one day she told me that she had been meeting with health officials and had visited several offices including citizen's advice centre. She was angry at the hospital and the surgeon and the way she thought they had treated her.

They had almost killed her, she had said with a voice full of venom. Even for Sarah this sounded a little extreme. She was going to make them pay and it was going to cost them dearly, she had stated. I had no say in the proceedings and was given the choice of either being with her or she would do it all single handed. She was going to make them pay, she had insisted.

A meeting between the surgeon Mr Seligman and hospital officials was organised and a man from some government agency was to accompany us. Sarah had several meetings with him and I was due to meet with him for the first time prior to our meeting in the hospital. We met and Sarah was present even though only he and I were scheduled to meet prior to the official meeting. He seemed a very amicable chap and came across as polite and accommodating. It was not a meeting as Sarah had explained but to examine the facts of events that had occurred since Rihana's birth.

This was organised for Sarah's benefit to help her get the answers she needed, he told me quietly. Sarah had been pestering him and this was the least he could do. In the end, it turned out to be a formal meeting without any new disclosures.

I already knew and had experienced more than what was disclosed at the meeting. No apologies were made, meeting was professionally conducted and events were narrated while Sarah sat there looking angry but remained quiet. I knew she was raging beneath the surface. At the end of the meeting the gentleman shook our hands and left. Best of luck with the future he had said.

I could feel the fury rising within Sarah. She was seething. Someone had to pay but she did not know what to do next. I was at the receiving end as she went about grinding her teeth. Every day and every minute she needed to know that either I was with her or against her. I assured her that I would do whatever she wished and would fight whosoever but did not know who we were meant to fight. This decision was left to Sarah.

It was back to work and I began travelling to Wembley, opened the office, tried to renew the contacts, made apologies, rectified orders and tried my best to normalise our lives. Now I would travel back and forth sometimes twice a day to see how Sarah was coping with the children.

Sometimes she seemed happy while at other times looked distant as she sat staring into space and the odd time her past friend from few doors down would drop in. Even their relationship was not the same anymore. Her husband had fathered a child with one of his flames and had left the marital home leaving her to raise three children single handed. Forever she appeared in tears. I still had to go to work, cook the dinner, help with household chores and amuse my darling daughters.

There was little time to spare but life seemed fine. Aisha was well able to keep herself amused while Rihana was placid as ever. I decided that instead of paying machinists for repairs, I would try and open my own little manufacturing unit in East London, the home of leather garments manufacture and wholesale.

I consulted with Naseem and opened a factory in Romford Road, East London. It was a small unit employing five people on piecework and doing most of the pattern and garment cutting myself. Alongside I did the finishing, visited clients and searched for new clients. It was a cutthroat industry which I found out in no time. The odd time Naseem turned up to lend a hand and sometimes when bored Sarah brought our daughters to the factory and life was beginning to settle into some form of normality.

Then she began to complain about feeling bored. She had nothing to do and her constant complaining began to wear me down. She seldom smiled or showed joy, no matter what. Only when talking to Aisha was her tone kind and even that was becoming rare. She always appeared fed up or angry with everything around her. I was under a lot of pressure with worries about Sarah, my darling daughters, suppliers, the bank and the new corporate manager was an absolute treat.

I owed the bank approximately 2,000 Sterling in overdraft but had an agreed facility for £5,000. At all times I had kept them informed of my current situation. It became fashionable with Mr John Bowler, my new corporate manager to write to me, the same letter over and again and carry a charge of £75.00. Then he would unilaterally decide to pay me a flying visit and the charge for this unexpected pleasure was £80.00. He was keeping an eye on things as he regularly stated and well within his remit, he would add.

This was wholly uncalled for but he did not seem to care. According to him my agreement was with Duncan Murray, the previous manager and now he was re evaluating and re assessing the bank's relationship with me and my business. One day I told him that I felt that he was being unfair to me and I did not feel happy dealing with him. He gave me the option to clear my overdraft and save charges or it was going to be his way. Before long, the £2,000 had become £4,000, without me drawing an extra penny.

Eventually I decided that I had had enough and sat down with Sarah to discuss our future. How about starting a new life in Ireland, I suggested. I needed help and Sarah had me drained, psychologically, emotionally and physically. She was a little apprehensive but after a while became excited at the prospect of being near her family. They could help me take care of her, get her off my back and hopefully, I would have some form of normality restored to my life, or so I thought.

I remember my late father telling me more than once that a wise man learns from other people's mistakes, an intelligent man learns from his own mistakes and a fool never learns. What would I like to be? I think I was about to answer a question he had asked of me two and more decades ago.

An entirely new can of worms was waiting to be opened but I did not know it then. It was decided that we would return the house to the building society, clear business matters and she would ask Charlie, her brother to help move our belongings to Ireland. It was done and dusted which made her happy and I felt relieved.

It was the October of 1989 when Sarah spoke with Charlie and our schedule for move to Ireland was finalised. Sarah packed a couple of suitcases full of clothes and necessities before flying to Ireland. All the household furniture and belongings were put in storage while she planned to stay with her parents and find a place for us to live. I was going into the unknown having placed all my faith in her capabilities.

It was a lot to ask, I must admit but life had reached a stage where something urgently needed to happen for the good of our family and my sanity. She flew to Ireland with Aisha and Rihana and we spoke every evening. I had never been away from my daughters and it was killing me but the girls seemed happy as did Sarah. Her old self was beginning to return.

I handed the keys for our house to the building society, lost equity and began sleeping on the factory floor. I had found an inch thick sheet of foam to serve as my bed for the next four months. It was freezing in London and often the water mains froze. Snow and black ice covered the roads. If it got too cold, I moved my sheet of foam and slept on the cutting table. The only drawback was, inhaling leather dust, which is lethal, literally.

In the morning, I filled a bucket from the hot water tap in the sink and washed myself while sitting on the toilet seat. I needed a daily shower. What in god's name I was thinking or doing, I have no idea. This was to remain my daily ritual for the next four months. Most nights the water in the pipes froze and I used the blow drier to heat the pipes before gaining access to water. It was that cold.

If cash was scarce, I had to starve. At other times I got a take away but it had to cost less than five pounds and had to last the day. Payment of my invoices always appeared to be on a very long finger. Its common practice in trade that the distributors like holding on to payments for as long as they possibly can. This allows them to keep the supplier under control and tied to their business.

Breakfast was a nonentity and my washing was done in Naseem's house. Life was hard, appetite was gone and there was the imminent move and urgent need to save some money which I possessed none. Whatever money I had was gone and what I earned was going to Sarah. The only other monies I possessed were in the hands of the distributors and they were reluctant to part with it.

One day I decided that I had had enough and called in the receivers to value the stock. In the meantime I started to sell anything and everything for cash at knockdown prices. Then I called all the suppliers and began to clear their accounts. It was a slow and painful process. People who had supplied me with leather got their hides back plus more and they were most appreciative.

I had one machinist retained to finish the orders that I needed to fulfil. Personally I was doing an 18 to 20 hour day to try to save some money in wages while I regularly sent money to Sarah, which kept her complaining to a minimum. In fact, this is the best I had seen in her demeanour for a long time. Well at last, something was agreeing with her and I thanked god for small mercies.

In October she returned with Charlie to collect our household belongings but nature had another surprise in stock for us. As soon they drove past Liverpool, snowstorms hit Britain and they were trapped in miles of traffic which was going nowhere. Blizzards had brought everything to a standstill. M6 was blocked, M5 was blocked, M1 had problems and the whole country was suffering. It took them over 24 hours to get to London.

Charlie looked shattered; Sarah looked tired but strangely appeared affectionate and loving. I got more hugs in five minutes than I had in the previous twelve months. Maybe life was turning for the better. I was hopeful and felt elated to put it mildly. We ate kebabs and chips and went to sleep on the floor with only an inch of foam between a freezing floor and us. Charlie was exhausted and soon lost to the world while Sarah held on to me while we slept. It was a wonderful feeling and the best I had felt for a long time.

Two days later, they were gone. Charlie was most considerate and caring. He warned me again that if mam had anything to do with it, my marriage would soon be over. You do not know her as we do. Keep Sarah away from her, was his parting advice. These words were destined to haunt me forever because I failed to fathom the gravity of what he had stated.

Christmas week came and I decided to surprise my darling daughters. On the 23rd of December, I flew Ryanair after paying five times the normal fare for the flight but it was worth it. Only Charlie knew of my planned surprise and came to collect me from the airport. I did not know where their parents had built the new bungalow. It was somewhere out in the countryside, I had been told. Pitch-black roads with poor surface were the norm and I had never seen so much darkness in my life but thankfully, eventually we arrived.

Charlie went in first and announced that he had a Christmas present for delivery. After a pause, I emerged from behind him to see Aisha's face light up and almost explode with excitement, hugs, kisses, and then more hugs. Sarah stood beside her and her face broke into a huge smile. I had not seen her this much happy for a very long time. Rihana was there looking shy and I could no longer contain my joy at seeing her as I picked her up and launched her high in the air. I hugged and kissed her and almost swallowed her in between kisses. Oh god I had missed my daughters so much.

Aisha was busy telling everyone her Daddy was here. She was on fire and no one was safe. Come and see my daddy, she was shouting with her face lit like a Christmas tree. Rihana got squashed between me and Sarah as I received one of the loveliest hugs ever. Maybe she was getting better and it felt like bliss indeed.

Everyone seemed happy and even the matriarch welcomed me. Dad was his usual self, warm, quiet and courteous as always. The rest of the clan was amiable. Matriarch even opened the front room, her good room but only for the opening of the presents. Other members of the extended family came to visit and were most pleasant. All the right things were said and done.

I slept like I had not slept in years. All two nights and could have slept more. Then it was time to return as there were matters of urgency that needed my undivided attention. With a heavy heart, I kissed them goodbye. As per usual Aisha got more than her fair share, Rihana was still shy but I had to have my quota of hugs and kisses. Sarah appeared emotional like I had never seen before. She was loving, caring, hugging and all I could wish for.

I assured them that I would have everything done and dusted in no time and would return in no time. It did not feel good but I knew I will see them soon and would never let them go, again. I had never been away from them for a day never mind weeks and it was eating away at me. By now Sarah had rented a house in Riverside, Galway and signed on social welfare which was helping her existence plus whatever I sent her on a weekly basis, which was almost every penny I earned.

Upon my return Naseem insisted that I come and stay with him. He was sick and tired of looking at me living like a dog. There were only two matters left for closure, the bank and the auditors. I informed the auditors of my intention to close the business and put it into voluntary liquidation. They were reluctant because I had invested so much time and effort into my business and it was beginning to pay off. I am sorry I have decided and I have a young family to look after was my final answer. The matter was not open for discussion thereon. They asked for forty-eight hours to prepare statement of assets, means, income, savings etc. and two days later I put the company in voluntary liquidation. Total cost came to approximately £428,000. It was my personal loss, house and all but, I did not care. All I could think of was my daughters. Now I did not owe anyone a penny, except to Mr John Bowler, my friendly corporate manager. I had a special treat waiting for him and this was personal.

In early January 1990 I invited him for a meeting. At the time there were interested buyers evaluating the stock and were forever coming and going. The auditors had sent them invitations to peruse the stock and thus far the best deal on offer was 4% of the total value of the stock. The auditors tried to advise me to hold on a little longer and get a much better price but I refused to listen. I was ready to go and my darling daughters were waiting. Eventually they gave up trying.

Now I only had eyes for my darling Mr Bowler. I was at peace and looking forward to enjoying this moment, no I was going to savour it. I had not forgotten the stunts he had pulled while my wife lay at the death's door and my darling daughters almost lost their mother. I remembered every gory detail vividly. I distinctly remembered every word and every iota of pain he had caused me. He arrived, regal and full of grandeur wearing a silk tie to match the silk shirt. I had the cups ready for coffee, biscuits neatly lay on a paper plate and the kettle had come to boil. I was ready. He seemed excited with the comings and goings of people chatting and talking business. Business looks good. I hope I have been of some help, he chirped.

Oh yes, thank you John, you have been great help, I quipped. Coffee, two sugars, I enquired. Yes please, he replied with the smile of a choirboy. He held the mug of coffee in one hand and a biscuit in the other, Bourbons, his favourites. How is life? I asked, making polite conversation.

He had managed to get his son in to Malvern Boys School with a lot of effort and pull of course and his daughter was in Cheltenham Ladies College. They were to cost him close to £30,000 in fees but he would manage somehow, he said in mock horror. I consoled him. Oh, I am sure you will manage somehow, I said. Life is tough right now, he sighed, but what is the good news, he asked cheerily. I am closing the company, I replied.

I saw coffee spurt out of his nose as he began to cough and splutter. The bourbon cream had dribbled from the side of his mouth and did not look pretty. He looked a sight as he tried to wipe his chin and then managed to smear his shirt. Coffee marks stained his silk shirt and I knew that it was screwed. Absent-mindedly he was wiping all over and appeared deranged. But you can't do that, he exclaimed. Let me introduce you to my auditors and liquidators, I said calmly while pointing in the direction of the two men holding clipboards.

But what about your suppliers and your clients, he asked. They have all been paid and taken care of, I told him. But you will lose a lot of money, he exclaimed. I do not care, I said calmly with an air of satisfaction and a mission accomplished. It is all done and dusted and today I am closing the factory and the auditors will have the keys. He started to get up on his feet and looked visibly shaken. He knew that he could squeeze me no more. The sonofabitch, I thought and extended my hand to wish him goodbye. His hands were shaking as he asked meekly, what will I tell my superiors? You will manage, you always do, was my reply.

He seemed pensive now. God help anyone who underestimates you were his last words as he turned around and departed. In later years I heard from Duncan who informed me that soon after the episode with me, Bowler was fired from his job. He had been pulling similar stunts with other small businesses.

I went to stay with Naseem for next eight days before my impending departure. It felt so good to feel the bed sheets under my aching body as I literally sank into the bed. Even his cooking seemed delicious though he could barely manage to cook his speciality, an omelette!

Then another incident happened. That day, I had four hundred sterling cash in the upper pocket of the shirt I was wearing and this was my worldly cash, which would help me get to Ireland. But fate had another scenario planned for me probably as a going away present. Naseem arrived home and he was livid. He had just given out to a twelve year old across the street for hurling snowballs at him. One had hit him in the face missing his glasses by a fraction of an inch. He was cursing as he wiped his glasses and walked to the bathroom. His left cheek looked bruised and swollen.

Then the doorbell rang. As I opened the front door, a punch hit me right under the chin. There stood a man six feet and more ready to swing at me again. He did not get a chance and landed on the icy concrete surface outside the door. My right fist had reciprocated his good intent and he looked stunned. There appeared a nasty gash on his elbow and now he looked scared. Who the fucks are you and what's wrong with you? I asked. No answer came but he wrestled me to the ground. This man is an asshole I thought. He was cut and bruised but did not give up until I had his arms restrained.

Are you going to stay calm or what? I enquired politely with my right hand firmly entrenched against his windpipe. He nodded his acknowledgment. I got up and pulled him off the ground. His elbow was bleeding badly. I asked him again his reason for punching me.

He lived across the road with his girlfriend who had a tearaway as a ten-year-old son from a previous relationship. As he arrived home from a hard day at work, she tore into him about some paki from across the road giving out to her son. He had been ordered to go and sort the Paki out. He was told that he wears glasses and the front door was pointed out to him. Hence moi got the fist because I wear glasses and this dumbass with brain the size of a pea had crossed the road to appease his betrothed.

I invited him in to help clean his wound as Naseem appeared from the bathroom. 'That is the man who gave out to your precious girlfriend's son', I pointed towards Naseem. Poor Naseem is a foot shorter than me and this fact seemed to amuse the moron. Then he genuinely looked embarrassed. Naseem is about five foot two in high heels and glasses, the least threatening individual you will ever meet. The moron was struggling for words. All he could remember was glasses, hence when I opened the door, he saw a pair of glasses that he had been instructed to sort out.

The shithead could not even apologise properly as he waffled profusely. Soon he left expressing gratitude for the bandage and the courtesy that was afforded. I was getting ready for bed when something hit me. My money in my pocket had vanished. All the cash I possessed in this world had gone. I went out and Naseem followed. We searched in the snow; we looked under the electricity mains box, the guttering and every nook and cranny we could think of. The money had simply disappeared and my heart sank. I was sitting in the snow, on a winter's morning and broke down.

Over the next two days I managed to sell some stock and a £4,800 worth of industrial sewing machine for £1,500 to some Pakistanis who had a leather manufacturing business and were always on the lookout for a deal. Then I went to British car auctions in Brentford and bought myself a Renault long wheel base van to carry all my machines and the leftovers to Ireland. Naseem came to help me with the journey. He was always there whenever I needed him.

I had exactly £300 Sterling left in my pocket when I reached my new home in Galway, Ireland and still had my motorbike, a Honda CBR 600FK which was to become a novelty in Ireland.

Chapter Eight

It was the January of 1990 and it was raining which did not stop until the month of May. Ireland was about to have the wettest year in its history. The first couple of days were spent unloading and packing the stock in the garage. It was neatly packed to the rafters. The van was allowed to be parked in the matriarchal house for the next year or two before being returned to the UK for sale at a princely sum of £250. A car was purchased with the proceeds and brought back to Ireland. Naseem collected the van from Ireland, drove back to England, and returned with a Toyota Corolla, which served us well for the next three years until stolen by joy riders and destroyed.

The girls appeared to have grown in the past four weeks and Sarah seemed more in control and independent yet something still appeared amiss. I just could not put my finger on it. However, our daughters were still as loving as ever and Sarah appeared caring and affectionate most of the time. Aisha still wanted rides on my back and Rihana spent most of her time wrapped around my right leg. If Aisha wanted to play leap jump, Rihana rushed to wrap herself around my legs. That's how she got her nickname of Koala bear.

Naseem returned to the UK and I began to take stock of my surroundings. I had to visit the local police station for registration. It was called, alien registration. At last, I knew who I was; a bloody alien and now had a card to prove it. Compared to London, this was heaven; I could sleep in peace until some students rented the house next door and my utopia was rattled. They introduced me to Saw Doctors and 'I used to love her once', which was played over and again till early morning hours.

We had a semi detached house with garage, a lovely large front garden and a garden to the rear. The kitchen was large and rooms were spacious but the house was very cold in its nature.

We literally had to sit on top of the fire to stay warm. Sheets were covering the windows to keep the draft out and going to bed seemed a scary proposition. The bed felt like icicles until the body heat managed to warm the sheets. Oil-fired gas heating was expensive to say the least and the words Polish coal became the synonymous with money. Coal burnt night and day to keep the front room warm and this is where we spent most of our leisure time.

At least for the first time in a long time I could park my car in front of my house and sleep in peace. Petrol stations closed at six and seldom opened at the weekend. Shops had very basic merchandise at exorbitant prices and almost everything had to be ordered from Dublin but at least the basic necessities were there.

Rules of the road were ignored, cars had rust holes and bald tyres, MOT was unheard of and drivers drove at will without a licence or care in the world. People felt free to do whatever they liked as long as it suited them. This was the land of the free. Sometimes it felt like an intellectual nightmare but the people were good in demeanour and meant well. I had to adjust quickly if I was to survive but sadly, there was little in jobs and the clic (nepotism) was in vogue. There were eccentricities and peculiarities that were confusing.

It rained nonstop until May and it was the wettest year ever and brought me back to my childhood and memories of my favourite teacher, Sister James at the Presentation, Convent High School in Risalpur, Pakistan. I was nine years of age and she was a wonderful human being and an exceptional teacher. She came from county Longford in Ireland and had many an amusing anecdote. One came to the fore; 'children it rains when god washes our sins'. What a statement and the prophecy was about to unfold thirty-two years later. Was this truly a land of the sinners, for it rained so much?

I soon realised that besides the nightlife in the local hostelries, there was not much else on offer.

There were two major employers in town and then it was survival of the fittest. Finding a job was a nightmare and money was always in short supply. Almost every second family seemed to be on social welfare. Most of their conversations involved financial entitlements and planning claims from the state. In between cash in hand was in vogue.

Sarah's routine involved daily interaction with her mother and sisters at her mother's house, which was located twelve miles away. Brothers mostly kept to themselves. I had the choice of being alone or accompany them to Clarinbridge where the same conversations repeated, religiously. The family home could easily be called 'The Ground Hog Palace'. It was gossip detached from reality and always went around in circles. It was frustrating and depressing and felt the need to find a job and earn a living.

Sarah's mother, Mary and Kate worked as part time childminders, Charlie had a cleaning business and Jimmy worked with him full time. Sometimes Dad's services were required if an extra pair of hands was required. At other times the whole family was brought in on an hourly rate if Charlie got a contract that required extra manpower. From there on Sarah's money was hers to keep and spend as she wished while mine was deemed communal property.

She was the highest qualified among this family with a high school certificate yet mother and daughters claimed worldly wisdom. They had to have a say in everything, especially my life, but it was mostly communicated through Sarah. Cracks in our relationship were beginning to appear and getting wider by the day. Now there were regular occurrences of one of the sisters turning up at two or three in the morning, with Jimmy and

Louise's children. Whenever Jimmy and Louise sat down for a drink arguments ensued often leading to bouts of physical violence.

Sarah's family were called for help and while Louise headed for the women's refuge with the youngest, Jimmy remained home drinking and the aunts turned up at my doorstep with the other two children Julianne and Gemma. The poor things in their nighties always looked sleepy and scared. It became my job to trawl the streets looking for Louise, just in case harm came to her. My portfolio of responsibilities was ever expanding.

Then came the day when Louise arrived at our door with her children and settled in the front room. I was busy reading while Aisha and Rihana snuggled either side of me. Greetings were exchanged and children sat down to watch TV. Suddenly Louise exploded for no apparent reason and a flood of vitriolics began to pour in my direction.

I was accused of being too smug, self-important and did not give a fuck about anyone else. She did not feel welcome in my house and the tirade went on until she got up and left with her poor kids in tow. They looked gobsmacked. I had said nothing and done nothing. Ah sure she is like that sometimes, was Sarah's reply.

We had no money but Sarah never missed a birthday, anniversary, Christmas or any special event where her family was concerned. My family or I were seldom if ever mentioned. It was amazing how this clan operated. Mary was diagnosed with diabetes and she could not have children. Now there were more histrionics and every new panto seemed to pay a visit to my house.

She was advised to give up drinking and smoking. She did neither even when she drifted into a coma. Chocolate bars

150

brought the sugar level up or else she would have been in serious trouble. A few drinks were always on hand; especially pints and her skin began to deteriorate. Instead of losing, she gained weight and was forever covered in sores that refused to heal.

'Ah sure what harm', was the common consensus. Now the wisdom was focused on me, again. What more could I sell to raise cash? I could sell the motorbike, the sewing machines and some of the stock I had brought home but how, were the questions that needed an answer. Everyone admired the quality of garments I had on offer and matriarch often asked for freebies for her poor Jimmy but never offered a dime in return.

Then I heard of a motorbike show being organised in Kilmeaden and I was advised to go and sell some leather jackets there. We decided to attend the show and Sarah accompanied me. We slept overnight in the van and nearly froze to death. People were extremely nice and we managed to raise over £600 which Sarah kept. We will sort it out when we get home, she said. Upon return to Galway she informed me that she owed her mother £150 which was duly deducted from the takings and by the time all the sums were done, I was left with nothing. A full year had gone by before I was given £2.50 to go to Supermac's for a treat, a snack box. I held on to that money for a rainy day. There were many of them to come.

Telephone was a novelty with an eleven-month waiting period for a connection. It was longer if you lived in the suburbs. Public transport system seemed primitive, as did everything else. Subconsciously I was comparing everything to London and becoming fed up and depressed. Every day after the girls were washed, dressed and fed, I plaited their hair and sometimes they wanted ponytails. Then we sat around the fire where Aisha did her reading and writing as Rihana played with crayons.

Sometimes Sarah joined in but mostly she remained aloof and distant. At times, she would gather the girls and announce her departure to her mother's house. It was probably one of the loneliest times of my life.

I was advised to make contact with IDA (industrial Development Agency) Ireland and had many a meeting and prepared multiple business proposals for them. It later transpired that they were interested only in major proposals and as a small business; I was not worth the effort. The banks were not interested in giving loans unless collateral was on offer.

In Bank of Ireland, Eyre Square I met with a corporate manager who advised me that based on my business proposal they were prepared to lend me money but could not offer less than £80,000. I was only looking for £5,000 and sadly had to say no. I met the very same manager some fifteen years later who kindly informed me that they were making available my business proposal documents to their new clients as a template for preparation of business and cash forecast plans.

I returned to the IDA and eventually they agreed to give me a £5,000, once off grant. I intended to restart by business in leatherwear and promptly rented an industrial unit in Ballybane, which opened for business in June of 1990 and lasted a mere ten months. Those days the Irish were extremely suspicious and untrusting of foreigners.

I found the only tannery in Ireland in Carrick on Suir and paid two visits to see if they could supply me with leather. Now I had to raise more money and sold the motorbike for £2,600. In the first year more than £10,000 was raised and spent. All Sarah's family had to offer was their worldly wisdom and nothing else.

Soon a cruel aspect of Irish life began to raise its ugly head, racism. It was silent, discreet but extremely nasty. My first experience was on a visit to the local pharmacy in Mervue for Sarah's prescription. Sarah had a medical card, which allowed her free prescription. Firstly the Pharmacist stared at me as if I had just landed from the moon and then he told me to wait while he served a paying customer. And I waited. In the meantime another paying customer came and got served, then another. I was getting annoyed but said nothing and still I had not learned my lesson. About twenty minutes or so later, the pharmacist turned to me and said that if I did not like waiting, I was free to go somewhere else. I waited until I got the damn prescription.

When asked what took me so long, I narrated the whole episode without receiving a word of comfort or understanding in return. I was never to return to this pharmacy. Twenty-one years gone and I still have not frequented these premises.

The next incident occurred when I visited the Bank of Ireland in Eyre square. I was waiting patiently in the queue until it was my turn to approach the window when a woman standing behind me approached the window and wanted to be served. The cashier looked surprised and told her not to jump the queue. This is my country and he can fuck off back to where he came from. This woman was no down and out. She was well dressed, well heeled and well spoken. It is only the vocabulary that let her down. When she parked outside, I had noticed her car. A two-year-old Mercedes, which was a novelty in Galway and only the very rich, could afford.

The third incident occurred when I accompanied Mary's boyfriend Noel for his stag night, which started in Paddy's Bar in Prospect Hill. It was just him and me. I did not drink alcohol and he seldom took a drink. A pair of muppets we must have looked like. He had no known family and as an orphan was brought up by the brothers of charity in an industrial school. He had endured the most inhuman form of torture a state could impose on its children. I learned a lot more about Irish history in later years.

He had survived that experience and now he was to take on an even bigger challenge of surviving Mary. I wished him good luck and was sure that he was going to need it in abundance. After frequenting Paddy's we had plans to meet Charlie and Jimmy in Crowe's Bar before proceeding to meet with the girls at Bentley's night club, Eyre Square.

I followed Noel into the bar. Dear god it was something from the Stone Age. Uneven brick floor which made me wobble and the dimly lit bar showed a barman and a customer holding a pint in his left hand staring at the floor. He looked in deep thought. Noel knew him and went to say hello and they shook hands. Noel proceeded to introduce me; I extended my hand and got a dirty look in return before the word British bastard was uttered. Then the man turned to his right and spat on the floor. Well I should be thankful for small mercies. He could easily have spat at my outstretched hand or me. Noel looked embarrassed but continued the conversation with this man. The bar man gave me a blank stare while I looked at the paintings on the wall. Thankfully, my complexion hid my embarrassment.

Soon we proceeded to Crowe's bar. It was a small family run bar with a couple of armchairs, three stools and the rest of the clientele had to stand. A few minutes later Charlie and Jimmy arrived, separately. I had my small glass of coke, Noel caressed his pint, and Charlie had one while Jimmy was soon on his third and getting merry. Soon they were getting bored and we decided to go to the Bentley and meet the girls. There was no sign of them and Charlie decided that we should go in and I followed suit. We paid for the entry and got ourselves some drinks. This time I settled on an orange.

The place was depressing to say the least. I saw some girls dancing around handbags, young men inebriated, others legless and leaning against the wall while others swayed like headless chickens. A strange smell hung in the air and music was blaring. Charlie looked bemused, Jimmy got another pint, Noel looked clueless and I wished to be somewhere else.

Eventually the girls arrived and we all heard a commotion at the door. Sarah looked animated as she came looking for Charlie. Their conversation made Jimmy laugh, Noel looked sheepish and I was none the wiser. Charlie told me that the doormen would not let Mary in and he was angry. We all filtered out slowly and were met with the sounds of Mary's wailing. She sounded like a harpooned sperm whale in agony. Her tonsils were at full throttle as tears rolled down her ample cheeks. 'I want my ma, I want to go home'. I want to see ma was heard over and again, in stereo. Everyone in the square heard it. You could not help but hear it.

A couple of passersby called her a stupid fat cow and I gently drifted away as it seemed the safest option. Kate was trying to console Mary while Sarah was running from one to the other trying to mediate but the doormen did not budge and would not let Mary in. On a previous occasion, she had been barred from returning to the nightclub. Only god knew what she had done but the door staff were adamant that she would not be allowed in despite Sarah's diplomacy and Charlie's protestations. Let's get the fuck out of here, Charlie announced. It's only a shit hole.

I was becoming aware that no matter what, family came first and common sense and common decency often took leave. We were all ordered by Charlie to go home. All Jimmy could mutter was, feckin sisters and their feckin shenanigans. A year or two later Kate managed to get married. She was firm with her mother, completely ignored her wisdom and never allowed her a say in her wedding. Mary's was the complete opposite. One would think it was the matriarch who was getting married. I was asked to take her wedding pictures. Sarah told me that everybody loved my pictures and I could do a better job than the professional photographer on Kate's wedding. I suppose it was a compliment but a dangerous one. I knew that if I fucked up would never hear the end of it. In this family nothing was either forgiven or ever forgotten. Sarah pleaded many a time and eventually I agreed. While they got ready with Mary's wedding plans I was dreading my impending funeral.

I got on with life and kept myself busy with darling daughters. Rihana refused to sleep anywhere but her own bed but recently she was getting used to sleeping in my lap and it felt wonderful. When it was very cold, she slept in our bed between Sarah and me. Aisha had her own room. Madam was becoming independent but still needed attention before going to sleep. Daddy tell me a story, daddy rub my head, daddy, daddy, daddy! And I loved every minute of it. Many a time this irked Sarah but she loved her mum the same.

Rihana was often restless in her sleep and the night before Mary's wedding she decided to play football with my face. The next morning both my eyes were bloodshot and I could barely see a thing. Somehow I muddled through the day, took the pictures as and when ordered and thankfully the day passed without too many mishaps. Sarah's mother had her moments but I think by now most people chose to ignore her antics.

Now everyone was married and living their own life. The clan religiously gathered for Sunday dinner at their mother's house. Charlie was very protective of his family and the matriarch was never allowed a say in his family affairs. His wife Sheila is an absolute lady and their son did not have much time for his father's family. Norman is a few months older than Aisha.

To everyone's amusement Jimmy was always served first and then it was the turn of us peasants. Sometimes Louise and the children came along. She did not like Sarah's mother and blamed her for all of her husband's shortcomings. Sarah advised me that it would be wise to attend these Sunday gatherings. It was a family occasion and we all had to be there. She was beginning to sound more and more like Mary.

One weekend I committed a cardinal sin. I heard a gentle knock and answered the door to find four sheepish looking Asian looking men standing on my doorstep. They were visiting the local mosque which was located in one of the houses on our road. Someone in the mosque had informed them that one of their kind had recently moved to the neighbourhood.

The one nearest to me was making polite conversation while the others remained quiet. They were well dressed and looked respectable. I have always been weary of preachers and pastors but they looked like professionals in their demeanour and appearance. They introduced themselves as doctors working in the regional (UCHG) hospital in town. They wished to invite me to join 'them' in social gatherings and Friday prayers.

I cordially invited them in. It was a novelty and a pleasant change to see people of my own ethnicity. They were aware of the isolation and prejudice people of colour were facing in the West of Ireland and had decided to organise functions for social and moral support. They brought sweets and chocolates as gifts for the girls and sought my approval. One, after receiving a nod of acknowledgment handed my daughters their presents.

Aisha and Rihana were politeness personified but looked a little bewildered. They had never seen anyone come to see me except Naseem and then to see four non white strangers in a room was a novelty. In walked Sarah dressed in summer shorts and a tee shirt and sat on the right arm of my chair. She wanted

157

to know who they were and why they were here. I could sense trouble ahead. Her tone was always a warning sign. Their eyes hit the floor faster than a hooker's knickers. If it weren't so serious I probably would have split my sides laughing. But this was serious and I could smell trouble brewing. She stared at them but said nothing. Her answer to their greetings was short and sharp, devoid of any respect.

They looked visibly uncomfortable. I asked her to accompany me to the kitchen but the request was ignored. As I asked Sarah to put the kettle on, she told me to do it myself. They were making an effort with small talk but Sarah was direct and wanted to know the purpose of their visit. What did they want from her husband?

I went to the kitchen and she followed. What do they want? Why are they here? Questions came in succession. They are being polite and making contact with people from their own country, I told her. Sarah declared that she did not want them in her house. I made tea and Sarah helped me carry and they left a few minutes later never to be seen again. I often wondered, why?

My life was destined for isolation but did not know it then even though all the warning signs were there with neon lights flashing. This was just another incident in many that were to follow in later years. Anyone within a mile of me was dispatched with undue haste. My alienation process had begun and was slowly being applied to the children. One minute we were sitting there playing with our daughters and then without warning Sarah would get up, gather the girls and announce that she was going to her mothers. She always kept Aisha close while Rihana got functional attention.

I was the only person with whom Rihana felt comfortable. One evening I was pleasantly surprised when Sarah offered to put

Rihana to bed. Aisha and I were busy painting when it dawned upon me that mother and daughter had been gone for over an hour, which felt rather strange. Aisha did not like me leaving her company and I made the excuse for the need to go to the toilet. I gently walked up the stairs, just in case mum and daughter had fallen asleep. It was 7.30 in the evening. I had a peek though the banisters and found the door slightly open. Sarah was sitting upright in the bed staring blankly at the facing wall. Rihana must be asleep, I thought. Still something made me feel uncomfortable and the look on Sarah's face was disturbing. I quietly walked to the bedroom and opened the door. Are you ok? I asked but got no reply. Where is Rihana? I asked stupidly and still got no answer.

And then it hit me. She had a pillow on Rihana's face and her left hand was pressing it down. What the hell are you doing? I screamed as I ran towards her, grabbed the pillow and flung it across the floor. She looked at me without a hint of expression or uttering a word. I was frantically searching for Rihana's heartbeat with my right ear stuck firmly to her chest. I lifted her up and put her head against my shoulder while gently rubbing her back. Her chest started to move gently at first and then she let out a little cry.

I was in tears as Aisha came upstairs and asked, what's wrong Daddy? Nothing darling, everything is ok. Everything will be ok, I replied. What else could I say? She climbed onto the bed and started chattering. I looked at Sarah and her eyes told me that she wasn't there. My head flooded with thoughts, mostly of fear. I had no idea what was going through her head. I got Aisha ready for bed, tucked her in and still holding Rihana against my shoulder went back to see Sarah. She was awake, lying on her right hand side and gazing towards the window. I took Rihana with me to the other bedroom and lay her down by my side and soon she was asleep.

159

Right then I could not bear the sight of Sarah but didn't know what to do. Sleep was the furthest thing from my mind. I felt so scared. What lay ahead and fear of the unknown frightened me even more. Where to go, what to do, who to talk to and I felt that I had no one. Sometime during the night, I drifted to sleep. The next morning everything was back to normal as if, nothing untoward had happened. Sarah seemed a little distant, pensive and quieter than usual. I was afraid to broach the events of the previous night. I decided that from now on I would never leave Rihana alone in Sarah's company. All this sounds so pitiful now. She was at liberty to leave for her mother's house as and when she pleased and I could do nothing and told no one.

Now she wanted Aisha to go to a playschool which had opened less than a hundred yard from our house. She wanted Aisha to mix with other children but we could not afford the cost and settled for part time care. Time was moving along and soon it was time to start thinking about Aisha going to school. I had little or no say in it. There seemed something wrong with every primary school in Galway. Too far, too near, too many traveller children and the saga carried on. Thankfully, we settled on the Mercy Primary School in town.

Initially Sarah wanted to drop Aisha at school and I was allocated the job of collecting her. Soon she got tired and the novelty wore off as it always did. I would prepare the breakfast and get Aisha and Rihana ready for the day. First Aisha then Rihana would sit in front of me to have plaits in their hair, one sometimes two and then I would take Aisha to school. Her fringe had to be perfect, just above the eyes, not too short and definitely not touching her eye lashes. She was just four and a bit and looked absolutely beautiful; a cherub's face with flowing long black hair and the navy uniform with white blouse. Out came the camera and I took some pictures, a good few actually.

I took pictures of her packing her bag, eating her breakfast, in her uniform and as she walked out the door with school bag on her back. I felt more nervous than she did. She was enjoying the attention, delighted with her new clothes and excited about this place called school. There was my bundle of joy walking along the path, heading for school, care free, excited, confident and full of energy. Her school bag was hanging below her knees. Everything seemed prim and proper.

She had to be like her old man, a chip off the old block. Her long black hair hanging down her back gently flowed with the breeze. I watched her and walked with her. She looked incredibly cute and confident as hand in hand we strode to the car. She looked confident and self assured. It felt as a part of me went missing. The girl knew what she wanted. She was becoming very particular in all aspects of her life. If something displeased her, the dreaded frown appeared. She was ahead of her class as she had learned all the basics at home. Reading, writing and simple sums were not a problem. Soon she was reciting tables. She is so intelligent and gifted.

First thing, she made me do. Quit smoking. Daddy I don't want you to die, the chubby cheeks requested. Who was I to argue? And smoking was gone. I wish I could have done more for her. Now she was getting the odd racist remark and beginning to notice that she was different from the rest. A priest came to visit her school on a weekly basis and talked about religion and hell and heaven, while condemning all things non Catholic.

Sarah had a word with the Principal of the school who described the priest as a bit of an ass and could do nothing but ignore him. The Catholic Church was the benefactors of the school. I was upset but Sarah would not allow me a meeting with the principal. Thankfully it was not long before the fecker disappeared and Aisha settled down. She was organised, methodical and soon became the teacher's pet.

I found a job at the local golf range, nothing much, £2.50 an hour and all the golf balls I could hit. Joe Greene was the owner and I soon found out that he had hay for brains but liked spending money, which did not belong to him. His favourite past time was emptying the till. He soon tried to talk me down to £1.50 an hour but did not succeed. He was a strange man. Forever the suppliers chased him for overdue accounts and it became my job to serve golfers and fend off the creditors. He spent money from sales, did not pay the suppliers or replace stock but constantly moaned about the drop in takings. I should do something, anything to improve the income, he ordered regularly. In the meantime, he was always playing golf, had membership of four golf clubs but in reality could not afford one.

Every time it rained, the sewage overflowed and faeces were seen floating around the car park. Do something, he would declare. There is shit floating around and customers can't get in. The only shit I could see stood in front of me and the place had serious problems all around him. He hated spending money on the upkeep of the shop or the golf range, which interestingly was built below sea level. Now I felt perfectly balanced and had a chip on either shoulder. Shit at work literally and shit at home, metaphorically. Sarah and Joe would have made an ideal couple. This thought had often crossed my mind.

It appeared that I was quite natural at golf. The resident professional would give me the odd tip on a golf swing technique and within twelve months, I was playing off a handicap of six. He advised me to bring the handicap down to four, enrol with the PGA (Professional Golfers Association) as a trainee professional and qualify as a professional in three years time.

I was beginning to meet some of the nicest people in my life. I strongly believe they kept me sane over the past fifteen years.

Doctors, nurses, solicitors, teachers, unemployed, juniors, housewives and they were very kind to me. However, no one ever knew the hell I was enduring. By now, it was becoming customary for Sarah to tell me what I could and could not wear and where I could or could not go. Else, there was hell to pay. Once or twice even a tee shirt or two were burnt because they looked good on me and would attract the wrong kind of women. Aisha and Rihana were very close to me and it used to make Sarah extremely jealous. She still displayed fits of rage but seldom in public.

Repeatedly I caught her slapping Rihana for no apparent reason. She pretended as if nothing had happened. She was living in a constant state of denial and there seemed little that I could do. The more protective I became of the girls, the slyer, more manipulating and controlling Sarah became. Moreover, she was firmly in the clasp of the clan.

One day I received the news that my youngest aunt's husband had been diagnosed with bowel cancer. He had complained of severe stomach pains for months, until my other aunt's husband had him admitted to his hospital. When operating they found that the cancer had spread and they could not stitch the surgical incision. He died a couple of days later. I am sorry to hear is all Sarah could muster before getting on with her normal day while I bottled my emotions, just like a man. Aisha comforted me and poor Rihana had no idea what was going on around her.

A few months later, the other uncle in law died of a heart attack. I broke the news to Sarah. So sorry to hear, she said but you should not be upsetting the children. She picked the children up and left for her mother's house to allow me to grieve in peace. They had all treated Sarah like royalty when she visited Pakistan and now she did not show an iota of respect or remorse. At least they were dead and could not see or feel anything but sadly, I was not.

If the children protested against visits to the matriarchal house, they were forcibly taken. Soon they learned to conform to their mother's wishes. That night, after putting children to bed, I knew I would not be able to sleep. It was approaching midnight, my head was hopping and it would not rest. Sarah and the girls were fast asleep as I decided to go for a walk.

There was a new dual carriageway built around our housing estate. Approximately six may be seven miles in circumference with an accompanying footpath. I put on my tee shirt, slid on a jacket, pulled up a pair of jeans and went for a walk. I was in pain and could not shake off this feeling. Then it began to rain and I started to cry. I felt utterly helpless and did not wish to return home. My past was swimming in front of my eyes, the tears were flowing and I did not care. Memories, painful memories came in droves to haunt me.

It rained all night and I know, because I was walking in the rain, all night. I had walked around in circles for more than seven hours, nonstop. It was 7.30 in the morning as I put the key in the front door and saw Sarah walking down the stairs. Did you get the milk, she asked. Shit I had forgotten. She had told me last night that we were out of milk. I promptly turned around and went to the local shop to get a litre and returned. She had not noticed my absence from our marital bed.

Every day after school, Aisha and I sat down for homework after lunch. She used to love her maths and practised hand writing for ages. Colouring pictures with crayons was my darling daughter's favourite pastime. Every time someone suggested presents it had to be colouring pencils, crayons and colouring books. Rihana had her familiar smelly pillow for company and did not ask for much but often joined us in colouring.

164

Sometimes Sarah joined in or took the initiative, yet she had something to say about everything I did with our daughters and yes, I was always wrong. It was during these times that I first began to notice Sarah hiding outside the door, eavesdropping while Aisha, Rihana and I did homework or had playful fun. I first realised when one day Aisha felt frustrated with her homework and started to cry. Sarah barged in and started yelling at me. It was my fault that Aisha had got upset.

Yet it was always Sarah who punished them and hit with a wooden spoon, slapped or hit them with whatever was in her hand. It was seldom Aisha but she was extremely antagonistic towards Rihana. She always blamed Rihana for the loss of her figure and the cause for her hospitalisation. Subsequently she also blamed Rihana for corrective surgery she had to have for the removal of dead skin around her waist. Then she upped the ante and started to accuse Rihana of trying to kill her. To date she has not allowed Rihana to live it down.

Now she had a new mantra. Love me the way I am and if you do not like it then leave. At least she had stopped making comparisons between loving her or my mother, who was seldom if ever mentioned. A new script was added to her repertoire. Often she would say that she could not have more children but I could and this became an obsession with her.

If ever I held a door open for a woman, I was accused of giving them the wrong ideas. If an acquaintance from golf said hello, how I knew her and what she wanted from me, were the repetitive questions.

Public embarrassment and humiliation were becoming the daily norm.

Chapter Nine

Alienation and isolation had become the norms of my life as Sarah told me repeatedly that as a married man I did not need anybody else. I had a family and responsibilities. Her life revolved around her family and often dictated by them. She dictated mine and in between our daughters were being conditioned to this dysfunctional norm. I worked in the golf range from six in the evening till closing at ten but seldom managed to close before eleven. As people got acquainted with me they spent more time in conversation than hitting golf balls. They seldom seemed in a rush to get home.

Then came the news of us being on the social housing list and were informed that an apartment had become available with no option but to accept. Rahoon flats, the very name seemed to send a shudder down the spine of local people. It was lovingly referred to as Galway's Beirut. If we refused to take the apartment, we stood to lose our rent allowance plus our place on the housing list.

We hired a removals company to help with the move and Sarah's brothers in law were most helpful. Leftover business stock was neatly packed in the van and parked in Sarah's mother's driveway, children's toys, unbeknown to me, were packed off to Mary's house in Tuam. The apartment was on the top floor of a four-storey block and centrally heated. The tenants had no control over the heating. It was on twenty-four hours a day, seven days a week, which meant having the windows and doors open in summer while never having to experience the cold of winter.

As Kate matured, Mary became stupider and the matriarch more destructive while dad pottered around his garden. Charlie and Jimmy were busy with the cleaning business and I was busy with my normal routine of cooking, dropping off and collecting

Aisha from school. Rihana came with us while Sarah slept. Aisha and Rihana were becoming very close while Aisha acted like a little mummy to Rihana which was heartening and amusing. Aisha hugged and kissed Rihana while telling her to be good and encouraged her in little tasks. She became very protective of her baby sister.

When Sarah wished to visit her mother, she collected Aisha from school and spent the afternoon and sometimes the evening in Clarinbridge. I had to walk to the Golf range, which was a mile and a half away, and then back after work as Sarah had the family car. Sometimes it was midnight by the time I arrived home. On the way home repeatedly I would meet characters who hated, black bastards and foreigners and often threatened to kill me or fuck me off onto a banana boat for return to my homeland.

It is difficult to describe how our family was progressing. At least, the bills were paid on time. Sarah regularly visited her mother and sisters three or four times a week and other days they appeared at our apartment. They did not seem to have a life outside their coven. Sarah often asked if I would prefer for her to stay at home and expect their visit or was it more amenable to visit them. Both the choices were equally painful and appeared the same to me.

Charlie disclosed that while the parent's house was being built, they had asked to stay with him. A firm no was his answer and he refused to let them inside his house. Eventually he relented and allowed them to park their caravan in his driveway for the best part of ten months. They were only allowed inside the house for the use of toilet facilities. How the mother, father and a teenage daughter had survived, I have no idea. Charlie had no wish to have his family disturbed or his home destroyed. He was a very wise man indeed and I duly noticed. His focus of life and his priorities were his son, his wife, his business and him.

Jimmy's priorities were him, drink and him. Oh yes! and his boys, as girls were deemed as not being important. By now he had two sons. For the sisters the only thing important was them inclusive of their mother.

Upon marriage, Mary and her husband Noel bought a Mobile home and parked it on the matriarchal land for the best part of two years. Soon Noel's life was to become hell. Mary's inability to conceive was creating dramas and Noel bore the brunt of her tantrums. After a couple of drinks Mary would let loose with an aria of childlessness and fuck god to heaven and above in the process. Her wailing could scare the living daylights out of the dead and this panto was developing sequels. Even the sequels appeared to have sequels with frequent repeats. It was a bit like a cheap version of Sky One.

In later years, Kate and her husband occupied the mobile home until they got their own house. Slowly but gradually even her husband was driven around the bend, several times and seemed lost. The daughters brought three scared crows home and nailed them firmly to the cross. This family seemed like destruction in perpetual motion. The lack of common decency, values and home economics was becoming more apparent and transparent.

One day Mary's husband was attending a social occasion and she had no iron. It became an excuse for the females of the clan to gather in our apartment. That was the first time I observed Mary attempt to iron a pair of trousers. Putting up the ironing board was not a problem; it took less than ten minutes. Switching on the iron was ok. Where to put water was a conundrum as she could not locate the hole and then the real drama began.

She did not know how to iron. Well she did not know much but this was hilarious even by her standards. She did not know how or where to begin and my help was enlisted. There were more creases ironed into this pair of trousers than the face of a sixty-year-old red fem. They were diagonal, they were parallel and then they were everywhere. In fact there were more creases on display than the fabric itself. I did help avert a major catastrophe. In contrast, Kate, the youngest sister was most capable. Eventually, she and her married bliss were destroyed by the joint efforts of the matriarch and Mary.

Dad never interfered. Most of the time he was so quiet that he may as well not have existed. At least his clothes were ironed daily and neatly placed on his bed alongside his socks and underwear. His food was cooked and placed in front of him like clockwork. And what the three scared crows got does not deserve a mention.

Now Mary was learning to drive. She had no licence but she was would often venture testing the patience of other road users. I witnessed her driving skills and the display of her abilities first hand when she came to visit us. She spent more time hitting kerbs than on the road. How she had not managed to cause an accident was beyond comprehension.

One weekend an event was organised in Clarinbridge and we had to attend by matriarchal command. We came out of the complex and headed for Clarinbridge. Sarah and the girls were with me while Mary and her husband drove behind us. We arrived and the mother enquired about Mary's whereabouts. I don't know was our honest reply. We had not seen them since getting on to the main road. Matriarch started to pace up and down, looked out of the window, looked out of the door and we all instinctly knew that she was ready to explode.

And then shit hit the fan. Where the hell are they? She roared at Sarah who did not answer and then she looked at Kate who did not have a clue either. And now the canon turned towards me. I told her that once we got on the main road, I had not seen them. Why did you not wait for her? She yelled at me. Then she looked at Sarah and exploded, why did you not make him wait for your sister? She is only a learner, I hope to god nothing has happened to her. Her darling, the lunatic and the incompetent was now a menace on the roads, but it was everyone's fault if she got hurt, especially mine. Sarah looked nervously at me and murmured please do not say anything.

Then there were instances of family discussion where brothers and sisters would end up in heated discussions about the inheritance of the family home. The boys narrated the culture of it being the inheritance of a son, before turning on each other while the sisters berated about who would wipe their mother and father's backsides in old age and were thus entitled to the family home. Eventually they would all agree that Mary should get the house and invite everyone to visit. This was intellectual torture of the highest calibre.

Aisha was maturing fast and Rihana's years of freedom were coming to an end. She had to prepare for her entrance to school. Now at least the sisters would have company and space away from their mother, may be even me. Rihana was developing her own personality, a mixture of innocence, naivety and wisdom imitating her older sister, which was extremely amusing.

On her fifth birthday she got extremely upset when it came to cutting her cake. It would be spoilt, she said adamantly and no amount of coaxing would do. Daddy it is so pretty, I don't wanna, she said. She looked heartbroken and so damn cute that I could have eaten her never mind the cake. Her hair was so silky and beautiful which fell below her lower back and seemed to go on forever. She looked like a doll, the most beautiful ever. I offer my sincere apologies, as beautiful as her older and wiser sister. Phew! That was close and too close for comfort.

170

Sarah and her sisters after consultation with the matriarch and Sarah's approval decided to crowd around the table and Mary the wise one put a knife into the cake and cut a slice that she brought over to Rihana. Rihana became inconsolable. She wailed, Daddy my cake, daddy my cake. Big tears ran down her big brown eyes and Aisha rushed over to console her. She was livid and shouted at her mother demanding an explanation. Why was Mary allowed to cut the cake? She wanted an answer but none was forthcoming.

I took Rihana out of the room and we did a little wheeling dealing where it was decided that I would buy her a brand new cake if she calmed down and gave me a hug. I love you daddy but I hate Mary, she said between her salty tears. Then another deal was struck. She would have the cake and the slice could be shared between the other fifteen or so guests. I agreed. Then music began and soon the episode was forgotten.

I noticed that Rihana was becoming introverted. She was becoming withdrawn with little show of emotion but remained loving, just like her sister. Hugs and kisses were still in unlimited supply. All this time I was dealing with Sarah's multiple personalities and did not know which would appear at a given time. My migraines were killing me. Paracetamol, Ponsin, Migralieve, Solpadeine, I tried them all and the doctors were worried. They had no clue of what I was enduring at home.

One night I found myself banging my forehead on the concrete floor. While asleep, a sharp pain had hit me which felt like a cold poker piercing through my head. It began at the right temple and shot through to the left and felt unbearable. Aisha woke up and offered to gently rub my forehead. She looked worried. I managed to get her back to bed until she fell asleep. She had to go to school the next morning. All night I sat next to the toilet, just in case I got sick. Sarah looked worried. There were times

171

when she was caring and loving, but sadly, they did not last long.

These headaches were to become more frequent and severe, as did the back pain. I was diagnosed with suffering from sciatica. It was so painful that at times I could not draw breath, sit or lie down. Often I had to crawl on all fours if nature called. In the meantime Sarah's family was continuously raising the bar in dysfunctionality. One weekend at one of the family gatherings Mary got drunk and began shouting obscenities at her husband for no apparent reason. Noel is a quiet and decent hardworking man with no family or extended attachments. Charlie and Jimmy had seen enough and ventured outside for a cigarette. Jesus if she was my wife I would have killed her long time ago, one said to the other. I don't know how he puts up with her.

I was offered a 'hot whishkey' for the umpteenth time, which I politely refused. Mum, you know he does not drink, Sarah piped and the rest laughed.

Her mother noticed Mary's behaviour and for once looked worried. Noel had had enough as he got up and walked out. Mary followed him to the back door still yelling without making an iota of sense. I hope he doesn't hit her or Daddy will go mad, the matriarch shouted. After a few moments she changed tack and shouted into the back garden. Someone go after him and do something, don't let him hit her, I think he is going to hit her, she yelled. I have no idea who she was calling or talking to.

Poor Noel could not harm a fly. I walked over to him and he was close to tears. I think he was beginning to realise what I had been experiencing for years. How did you put up with that shit all these years? He asked. My wisdom had long left my head and I had no answer for the poor soul. This was meant to be a special day. The priest was coming to bless the house. According to Sarah's mother a catholic priest is the son of god and they and the house needed his blessing. She had his presents ready and the 'besht' bottle of whiskey took centre stage on the table. The house was full of guests and the shenanigans had raised many an eyebrow. Visitors had gone quiet while the family dispersed. It was a quiet mayhem except for Mary's rantings and ravings.

For once Sarah had detached herself from the circus. She made herself a sandwich and sat calmly in the kitchen. Aisha came inside looking visibly upset. Her cousins were grabbing Rihana's toys and she was in tears. They were much older than Aisha and Rihana. Rihana had a couple of well worn toys that no one was allowed to touch and they had taken them. I asked Sarah to sort it out as I had learned not to interfere with her family affairs by now. They will be alright, is all she said and did not flinch. Aisha and Rihana appeared in a state of distress. I asked her again politely if she could sort the kids out. Go do it yourself, she barked. I took the girls outside and retrieved Rihana's toys from her cousins.

I came across a heated discussion between the two brothers and they seemed close to fisticuffs. It was their inheritance once again. Jimmy wanted the family home for his family inheritance; he is the eldest he was insisting. Over my dead body was Charlie's repeated retort. Drink always brought out the best in them. It was later revealed that the brothers had many a fisticuff on their nights out and everyone in the family was well used to it.

I found Noel sitting in his car, looking desolate and lost. I sat down with him. He looked bewildered. You'll get used to it is all the wisdom I could muster.

Beer was flowing freely and another disclosure was about to be made. Sarah whispered, dear god mum is going to lose her rag. Apparently Kate disclosed that elder brother Jimmy had tried to kiss her and grabbed her boobs on several occasions. If her husband was to hear there would have been murder. Michael was a decent guy but very protective and possessive of his wife. By now the matriarch had heard the whisper and confronted Kate. Stop telling lies about your brother, she scolded.

This evoked memories of an incident at one of these family gatherings when I caught Kate's husband in the kitchen lavishing praise on Sarah's boobies. It appeared that it was a joke for him to grab her bum or her boobs in jest. I never saw this occur but Noel and others vouched to have seen it happen in the matriarchal house. The same had occurred in Noel and Mary's house.

I was always the last to know and by now I had given up. On rare occasions if invited the mother always turned up at our home with a bottle in tow and insisted that Sarah take a little drink. It's only a little drink what harm. If he does not want to drink that's his problem. We are celebrating, aren't we? She would ask. Often she asked Sarah why did she did not marry a nice catholic boy. This question was asked loud and always in company. By now the gods must have tired of her and decided to teach her a lesson.

The story broke about Bishop Eamon Casey fathering a child and hiding the fact for seventeen years followed by the story of Father Cleary having a son. Her heaven went on fire. Her Utopia was collapsing all around her and she was spitting venom. Her offspring were quietly enjoying her antics from a distance. She stomped and slammed as if the gorse in her fanny was on fire. Humpty dumpty had fallen off the wall to the amusement of her kin and no one wanted to help her pick up the pieces. The women were whores who had taken advantage of the poor men. Now she saw these women as Pariahs.

Throughout this I worried that my two darlings were becoming accustomed to these scenarios and their mother saw nothing wrong with such happenings. By now the scenes were plentiful and the matriarch often sought help from her husband who often walked away blaming her for all the destruction within the family. He refused to get involved. She caused the harm and she could sort it out, was always his retort. Even the brothers and sisters were singing from the same hymn sheet. If he had stood up to mum our future could have turned out better, was their common consensus. Then Mary would pipe up. Better not let mum hear this or it will kill her. They would all agree but their resentment towards their parents was barely concealed yet never revealed.

I think there is a god after all. Once when the house was blessed and holy water sprinkled Charlie brought his new dog into the house which promptly proceeded to urinate in the middle of the floor. The matriarch's face looked like a baboon's backside, red as a cherry and ready to explode. Charlie could not give a shit. She knew not to mess with Charlie. He is the only person who gave her little in importance and she knew not to mess with him.

Since my first job, a joint account had been opened. Sarah never put a cent in it but had complete access to the account. She was working quite regularly with Charlie and often they finished late in the night. Cleaning after special events like the race week or pub cleaning after closing hours was the norm and brought cash in hand. They would finish late as I and the girls slept. I had all the housework under control. I never saw a penny from her earnings. In all our years together she had bought me two presents. A cigarette lighter with my name engraved while we were courting and a fifteen euro watch for my fortieth birthday.

I never missed her birthday, wedding anniversary, Christmas, our Eids, we Muslims have two Christmases and I was giving her cash and presents on every celebratory occasion. In return I got sweet fuck all. She often stated that she had never claimed to have done anything for me.

Aisha and Rihana were nicely settled in their routine when we got the news that an offer of a newly built house was on the cards. Sarah was excited and we were all jubilant. No more living in Alcatraz. She regularly drove to the estate and watched the finishing touches being applied. Sometimes she took the girls with her and started to choose the house she would like to be allocated, as if we had a choice. There were 33 houses mostly semi detached. It was a quiet estate just on the edge of the city, looked nice and my heart lifted. Go and talk to someone and make sure we get the house outside the circle; preferably the last one was her recurring demand. The requests were piling up and I had a hesitant word or two with a former mayor, the current mayor and a few councillors and whoever I could grab at the golf range. It wasn't difficult because most of them were frequent visitors to the golf range.

Sarah was busy doing the rounds of the city hall. Eventually we got the house of our choice. The girls seemed happy and excited which made me happy. They were the only two things of importance in my life who gave me a reason to live. Hope and happiness accompanied them. There were fleeting moments when I had thought of taking my life for which I feel thoroughly ashamed.

Most important were their hugs and kisses from the time they woke up till they went to bed. When being dropped at school and collected from school. This continued through university years till all hell broke loose in 2004.

At the golf range, ownership changed and my services were no longer required. I was not surprised to say the least. At last Mr Greene had succeeded in draining the well dry. I had become acquainted with a taxi driver who played golf. He was forever looking for a driver for night work and always promised that the money was good. One third of whatever I made was on offer and all expenses for the maintenance of the taxi were his responsibility. Clean money, he had insisted. I decided to take him up on his offer as I had no other choice. Life was bad enough with money. It wasn't worth thinking what it would be like without money. Sarah's money was hers to keep. She was worried about my loss of income, whereas I had found another source of experience which was to become more painful than the previous one. A whole new way of life was about to begin. To know the true personalities of the inhabitants of a town one needs to drive a taxi at night when inhibitions alongside airs and graces are gone and alcohol has taken control. Then appears no sense of decency and definitely there are no boundaries.

Mr Tommy Murphy, my boss, was a most amenable guy, fond of the Amber nectar to excess and seldom had his car serviced. There was always tomorrow and now I knew why no one would work for him. His car was a death trap on four wheels but I managed to keep everyone who sailed in it, alive. Very quickly I became popular as everyone in town seemed to know Tommy and his car and I became their new target of jest.

A blow in, the first brown foreigner to drive a taxi in Galway and to make matters worse, I drove at night. Bile and venom came from all sides, taxi drivers and punters alike. I was hit by a tsunami filled with shite. The people in the taxi office were kind to me. Roisin had been the controller for the past eighteen years and more and she made time for me. She soon realised that I was there to work and made no excuses. I was getting more work than others to the ire of my fellow drivers. Other taxi owners began approaching me to come and work for them with offers of more money. But first I had to organise the house. Sarah did not like the paintwork in the new house. I painted it. She wanted new furniture and I bought it. She wanted new

177

curtains; I had to pay for them. What she wanted she got and I paid for it. Her money was for her to keep. If I asked a question, I got an earful.

The work suited me as did the hours. I was still weary of leaving Rihana in Sarah's care. Now the routine began which was to follow till our marriage breakdown and separation. I would finish work, go home and be in bed by three am. The girls would wake up at seven thirty and use the bathroom. Then I would follow suit. While they were getting ready for school, I would have the table laid, bread, butter, eggs, milk, cups for tea with teabags and sugar ready. They would come downstairs and prepare their school lunches while I cooked their breakfast. All done and we were off to school while mummy slept.

I would return home, lie down for a while, do some house work till it was time to collect darling daughters from school. When girls sat down with their homework, I prepared lunch. Now Sarah would join us and we would eat then it was back to homework. While I prepared dinner, girls would watch telly or help me with the dinner preparation. We all ate dinner together.

Aisha would return to homework while Rihana kept herself occupied in her room with her dolls or watched TV in the front room. Sarah watched Coronation Street, Eastenders and other favourites with passion mostly in the confines of our bedroom. We also had TV's in Aisha's room, Rihana's room and there was one in the kitchen.

Aisha finished homework and watched her favourites, Buffy the vampire slayer, Angel and others. God help anyone who disturbed her including and especially Rihana. Aisha was becoming independent, demanding and liked her own space. By nine I was ready to go to work with a goodnight kiss and it was time to face the music.

178

Soon I knew every nook and cranny of Galway. You can't find an address, ask Sam, you can't find the front door ask Sam, if you want to find out where your one (Irish way of referring to someone whose name you have forgotten) lives, ask Sam. As the customers got to know me there were regular requests for my services as a taxi driver. At other times the requests were not so appropriate but I respectfully turned them down. I was learning more about shades and colours in life here than all my years at college studying Physics, Chemistry, Biology and Psychology. The degree in Psychology was to come in handy later.

Racism was rife, ugly, vulgar and at times threatening. One episode comes to mind when a child holding his mother's hand turned around and said, mum look man with a dirty face, he did not wash his face properly. I was at the taxi rank and he was no more than three feet away at the bus stop. Four may be five years of age. The mother got red in the face and hastily walked away.

Four examples of vulgarity and racism follow which occurred in the presence of a patrol car which was parked nightly across the road with two policemen inside. It always carried the same clowns, Joe Lally and Paddy Shield. Taxi rank was the hub of trouble, arguments and fisticuffs, male and female. Every night threats and racist abuse came my way but somehow I managed to keep my peace. I had repeatedly been told at the police station that they could not provide me with a guardian angel. I was also receiving abuse at home, verbal and at times physical.

The first incident occurred when I was sitting in the taxi rank waiting patiently. Normally it was quiet till midnight when the revellers came out of the pubs which signalled a journey home or towards the night clubs. It was Wednesday evening and a coach pulled up on the other side of the taxi rank. In between is a footpath. The coach was full and people started to get off the

179

bus and waited patiently for their luggage. Next minute a man in his late twenties walked gingerly down the steps and fell between the pavement and my parked car and created a commotion. I saw a woman jump off the bus and run towards him.

He ran over me, said the man as he pointed towards my parked car. All the passengers looked bemused as this woman in her early thirties walked around my car and yelled, you fucking black bastard why did you drive over my brother? Before I could answer her fist had smashed into my face and broke my glasses. She was wearing a ring with a large stone embedded in it. There appeared a cut under my eye which started to drip blood. I got out of my car and as she was about to punch me again, I grabbed her wrist. What are go going to do? Hit a woman, she sneered. Today I wish to god without answering I had. Then I had little idea how far the female vulgarity had progressed.

I looked across the road and saw the police car disappearing in the distance. This is not the first time they had responded in such manner. Two of my colleagues, Michael and Gerry Kelly were on the scene within seconds. Someone rang the Mill Street police station. Now the drunken brother was standing tall and looking the worse for wear as he swayed from one side to the other.

One of their fellow passengers walked over to me and disclosed that brother and sister had travelled on the coach from Holyhead and had been drinking nonstop. They were abusive towards their fellow passengers throughout the journey till falling asleep. They had made life hell for all around them and now it was my turn. They were Galway natives working in England and were returning for their mother's monthly mass.

Michael rang the police again and twenty minutes later, my favourite keystone cops turned up. We had to answer an emergency they said. They were lying. I checked later and there were no calls logged for another emergency except mine. They were not aware that I had some friends at the police station that did care about their uniform and wore it with pride. This was not the first incident involving me and the cops. I was considered a nuisance for making reports of abusive behaviour and racist slurs which often involved threats. In later years one of these clowns was promoted to the rank of inspector.

They took statements from witnesses and one them told me that he had recovered £175 in cash from the woman which would help pay for my glasses. This money was confiscated and a year and a half later the case went to court. It made the local papers, woman admitted assault and criminal damage, brother admitted to lying and I got a call from one of the keystone cops informing me that she was fined £350 while the brother had received a £110 fine plus costs. When the fines were paid I would be reimbursed. What about the £175 which was confiscated, I asked. He stated that no such monies were ever taken from the woman. Did he tell a lie before or was he lying now?

Four years after this incident occurred I received a call from Mill Street police station informing me that the cops were closing the file as the couple had disappeared from their radar. This anal lot could not find their anus even if all the arrows were pointed towards their hole. No monies were ever recovered. If I ever saw either of them, I should inform them immediately were the instructions given and the case was closed. It never happened, I never saw them and not a penny was recovered.

The second incident involved receiving a call from the office to pick up a couple at the Spar supermarket outside the bus station in Foster Street. I found an elderly couple standing outside the entrance of the supermarket. It was around three on a Sunday afternoon. I opened the rear door of my car and assisted the lady to sit down. Then I turned around and opened the boot of the car for their luggage.

As I approached their luggage, a man in his twenties who was passing by began hurling abuse at me. It was the usual, black bastard, why don't you fuck off back to where you came from. I ignored him and picked up one of the suit cases and walked towards the rear of my car. The elderly gentleman stood beside his cases. I returned to pick the last of the suit cases and as we both turned his wife had started screaming.

There was another fecker in my driving seat trying to take the keys out of the ignition while the first was trying to block my way to the driver's side and shadow boxed. There is a release button under the steering to press for the release of ignition key. I could hear on my taxi radio the office calling for help. Sam is in trouble again. A lady passenger in a passing bus had noticed the trouble and called the taxi office. The number is on top of every taxi and she had also called the cops, but there was no sign of the cops.

I got past the first idiot and grabbed hold of the other through the driver's window. Now he was hanging out of the window, half in half out. The lady passenger had got out of the car and started screaming. She looked shaken and her husband was consoling her. As the boxer came towards me, he was met with a sharp fist which helped land him on his backside in the middle of the road. He got up and ran like a headless chicken almost run over by an oncoming car. The second was trying to wriggle free. I grabbed him by the collar, pulled him out of the window and threw him on the ground. I think he literally wet himself before getting off the ground and running in the opposite direction of his friend.

I got the passengers back in the car. The woman was finding it hard to speak. The gentleman said quietly that he felt ashamed

182

to see the Irish with this kind of behaviour. He never knew that racism existed in Ireland. I told him not to worry, told the office I was on my way to Ballybrit and will meet with the cops upon my return. Half an hour later I returned to the scene of the incident and still no cops. Forty five minutes later I saw a lonely uniform walking toward me and I knew him.

Hi Michael how is it going, I asked. Ah sure I think there is some trouble out here. What are you up to? He asked. I told him about my experience and he started to laugh. Well I was told no rush, just a couple of lads acting the maggot. Well fair play, he added. You are well able for these little feckers, was his final answer and we went about our business.

The third incident involved a local thug who for his merriment often picked on me for no apparent reason. His name was Cutter Dodd and belonged to one of the nastiest families in Galway. He was reputedly dangerous, always carried a knife and had been in and out of the prison throughout his life.

On several occasions he had kicked my car and pulled the knife on me as he happened to walk by. I had reported the matter to the cops and had been advised to stay away from him. He is nasty and a dangerous bastard, they informed me. I don't go near him, he is the one who approaches me, I had told them repeatedly. Well keep your distance and drive off if you have to, was their advice and that was it.

This Saturday night he decided not only to kick my car but pull the knife out while standing next to my driver side door. I locked the doors and called the office. Across the road I saw the keystone cops amusing themselves by one pointing to the other as the comedy commenced. It was just after two in the morning and people were beginning to filter towards Supermac's in Eyre Square. He was sniggering as he became boisterous and hit the car window with the back of the knife handle. Next I heard the chant only an Irish crowd is capable of. Kill the black bastard, kill the black bastard and they sang the damn thing over and again in complete harmony.

I felt I had had enough, released the door locks, put my right foot against the door and pushed it with all my might. All the taxis ahead and behind of me had long vanished like rats abandoning a sinking ship. He was grinning from ear to ear tossing the knife from one hand to the other as the chanting from the crowd got louder. Driver needs help, driver needs help, Eyre Square and hurry, was the continuous message on the taxi radio. It was being repeated over and again. Next thing I remember Cutter Dodd flew over the bonnet of my car and into the newly erected bus stop before collapsing into a heap. The right hand was once again my saviour. The crowd went silent and began to disperse. The keystone cops were on the move again, slowly disappearing in the distance. They had not stepped outside their patrol car. Two weeks later a nineteen year old student from Tipperary was beaten to death in Eyre square just where the patrol car was regularly parked and it made national headlines. For me it was all in a day's work and worse still, I was alive. Cutter Dodd never came near me again.

The fourth incident occurred at around ten on a Thursday evening and I was the first taxi on the rank. This guy six foot three but looking taller asked if I was free for hire and would take him out of town. Sure, I replied. He looked ok and at least he was observant. What could go wrong? I asked of myself. By now I had acquired a sense of Irish humour.

He got in the car and closed the door very gently. Where would you like to go, I asked. He turned slowly towards me, a bit lop sided and asked, where you from. After all these years I was still being asked where I was from. It's a very Irish habit but becomes annoying after a year or two. From London, I had replied. No fuckin really, he persisted. From Pakistan originally,

184

was my answer. He continued, what brings you here? This was another common denominator. Oh shit, went through my head. This was going to be one of those nights. My wife is from Galway and now where would you like to go? I asked. Just drive, he barked. Where to? I repeated. By now knots were beginning to appear in my stomach. Turloughmore, but don't go yet, he ordered. The taxis behind me were already leaving the rank while I was being interviewed by this gobshite. Only two weeks ago a colleague of mine, Eileen O'Shaughnessy was brutally murdered by her passengers in the same vicinity and the culprits have yet to be found. More than twenty years have passed and they are still at large.

By now this was getting too much and I asked him to leave and return when he was ready to go. Fuck off you cunt, was his polite reply. Get back in your banana boat and fuck off back to where you came from. Another Irish favourite was hurled. Land of the poets and writers and this was the best on offer.

There were plenty of people milling around and the keystone cops were there except officer Shiels had a different partner in the passenger seat of his patrol car. I decided that I had had enough. I got out of the car and walked to the passenger side and opened the door. Can you please get out of my car? I asked. He slowly got out of the car and slammed the door behind him. I walked away as people were watching and this was most embarrassing. The Irish are wonderful spectators. I had found this out by now.

Next thing I felt a thump on my right shoulder. The bastard had hit me from behind and was shadow boxing. I had a quick glance at the keystone cops and saw no movement. They were still there but showed no notion of moving but seemed very interested and observant. Another punch came my way as I swayed, and he missed. This guy meant business and business is what he got. One right hook to the lower jaw lifted him in the air before he landed on his backside. I heard a loud crack but I had no idea where the sound had come from. He appeared dazed and stupefied as he lay on the ground. A look of genuine surprise was etched all over on his face as he caressed his jaw.

Now the keystone cop made a move and came over to us. Now, now lads, what's all this commotion? We can't have this now, they said in their best professional demeanour. You go about your business and we'll deal with him, they told me. I got back in the car and shook with rage while emotions came over me. Now the damn car wouldn't start. I tried again and got nothing. I paused, sat there for a minute or two and looked at the ignition. The keys were there and I tried turning the keys but they would not turn.

Then it hit me. I was not able to grab the keys, my fingers would not respond and my wrist was limp. It dawned upon me that I had broken my wrist. I started the car with my left hand, rested my right hand on the steering and put the car in gear as I drove to the other side of the square and parked the car. I needed someone to drive me home. I called the office but everyone was busy. I thought about leaving the car there and walking home.

Before I could decide I heard a knock on my window and I opened the window absent mindedly. As I turned my head to the right a punch landed straight on my mouth. It was the moron again, pressed firmly against my door and I could not get out. Somehow I hopped into the passenger seat and got out. He was standing there, very still. Before I could say or do anything there was a cop standing between us. It was the pride of Eyre square, officer Shiels.

Sorry about that, he said. We had warned the fecker to go away. This time he handcuffed the fecker and took him away. I got in the car and somehow managed to drive home. Sarah came down to enquire what had happened. I briefly told her the story. Oh, well may be you should give up driving the taxi, she said and went straight back to bed.

I went to the kitchen, boiled the kettle, soaked the wrist in salted hot water and wrapped it with crepe bandage. I was well used to bandages and injuries with all my years playing sport. Thirty minutes or so later I heard a knock on the front door. As I walked from the kitchen, I saw blue lights flashing through the curtains. Dear God, what now? I sighed. Its cops outside, two cop cars, I heard Sarah whisper from top of the stairs.

I opened the door and there stood two policemen. Sorry to disturb you sir, does Sam the taxi driver live here, the young cop asked politely. Yes, I said hesitantly, I am Sam. Well we have a few visitors from Turloughmore who have come down to say thank you. There were two cars alright, with blue lights which were promptly switched off. One young cop, seven foot tall, well that's what I saw and another not much shorter, plus another two slowly began to emerge from the other car. They almost looked embarrassed. The first in the queue put his right hand forward. Wow I had seen shovels smaller than this hand. His girlfriend must be a very happy woman I thought as instinctly I checked his size fourteen shoes.

I apologised that my hand was broken and they took my left hand, one at a time. There was warmth in their demeanour which was heartening. They had come down to shake my hand and that was it. The local cop explained that the moron belonged to a family of local thugs, four brothers in all who had terrorised the town since their school days.

The news had travelled how one of the biggest feckers had been put on his backside by a blow in (Irish term for a foreigner) and out of embarrassment they would not be showing their faces again. Hence, they wished to express their gratitude. Sarah heard everything, said nothing and went straight back to bed.

187

By the time my head hit the pillow she was already snoring. I did not sleep that night. My head was throbbing and the wrist felt on fire but somehow I made it through the night.

Another two other little snippets come to mind. Every weekend night between grabbing and groping in public and sexual encounters in doorways, there were occasions of fisticuffs between couples and usually men came out the worse for wear with scratched faces and blows from sharp heels. They never got any sympathy. Ah the fecker must have done something wrong was the usual response. He probably deserved it. Even the cops turned a blind eye while taxi drivers were advised not to get involved. There was a case of aggravated assault in Ballinasloe and it made all the national papers. A Good Samaritan came to the help of a woman who was being assaulted by her partner. Apparently he caused injury to the thug but now the couple were suing the Good Samaritan for causing harm. She was appearing as a witness for the thug.

This Schmuck, that is I, is a slow learner, very slow indeed. One evening when approaching the taxi rank, I heard a commotion. A woman was screaming and everyone on the taxi rank heard it; people around the Square heard it but all went their merry way. I saw a woman lying on the ground screaming and there appeared a man on top of her. She was lashing out and he was trying to grab her wrists. They were in the middle of the road and I had no option but to stop.

I walked over to the warring couple and helped remove the male from the melee. Next thing, I felt a sharp pain from the back of my head. The woman had jumped on my back and was pulling the hair out of my head. Leave him alone you fucking black bastard she was screaming as she tried to take a bite out of my ear. Somehow I managed to get her off my back while the male stood on the edge of the kerb managing to look dumb as dumb can be.

188

She walked over, grabbed his hand and walked away laughing as if sharing a joke. We told you so, was all I heard from fellow taxi drivers. The cops once again advised me to stay away from the feckers. They are no good, I was told repeatedly.

Wednesday night was student's night and on many an occasion a female passenger, upon arrival at her destination would refuse to pay the fare and simply walk away. Did I say occasionally? It happened once maybe twice a night on the student's night. It was the same statement every time. I'll call the cops and tell them you tried to rape me and then she would laugh and simply walk away. I'd call the cops to be told don't waste your time or ours. This happens all the time and not worth the hassle. It was 2010 before this finally came to an end. A newly appointed female district court judge became the first judge to fine, caution and chastise one of these emancipated but intellectually emaciated female role models of the future.

Then there was the incident with four young lesbians. It was their favourite pastime to abuse taxi drivers especially once they found a foreigner. I became their favourite pastime. I was a dirty old man and I could keep my dirty dick to myself. They claimed they were clean because they licked themselves clean like cats. I was a man, a dog and a dirty black dog at that. Then they would proceed to throw loose change at me and walk out to the hoots of their laughter. By now there was no point calling the cops. I was wasting their time and mine.

Then there were three other comical events. One involved two young sisters in their twenties. On the night in question it transpired that both were single mothers and could not hook a man and were heading home empty handed. According to them the men had wised up and knew all their tricks, whatever that meant. One had two children and the other one with the eldest being five years of age and left in charge of the others to save on child minding fees. Now they were asking me if I would like to be entertained for free. I politely declined their kind invitation to be met with a response which stated that my kind was only interested in money and what would I know about real women.

On another night a nineteen year old trainee nurse asked me to come in for a cup of coffee at two thirty in the morning. To her distaste I told her that she was young enough to be my daughter. Well I don't offer this to everyone and I am not a whore as you may think before slamming the car door and walking away in a huff.

But the funniest of them all were four students from the local university, two girls and two boys who had hired my taxi to Corrib village, the student residences. The gist of the conversation throughout the journey was who had slept with whom the night before and none could recall. It transpired that one of them had used a plastic bag tied to his willy instead of a condom and would not be getting sex this night with either girl unless he could produce a real condom. Screwing around was and still is an optional module in all undergraduate studies.

Now there was a regular customer with the company where I worked. She was a German national married to an Irish Guy and lectured at the local university in social science. She lectured in Women's Institute studies was a feminist, she had informed me, though why, I have no idea. She had heard my episode from another taxi driver and wanted to know what had happened. I told her briefly and she wanted to know more about the way town behaved and how the taxi drivers coped. I gave her a synopsis of the passengers and their behaviours at night and she felt insulted.

Women could never do what I had just told her. They don't do such things, she said indignantly. Secondly Irish were the warmest, most charming and hospitable people and they were

190

not the least bit racist, she had further insisted. I met her three years later. She recognised me and came to apologise for her previous comments. It appeared that her son was being bullied at school and was called Adolf and Nazi on a daily basis. Apparently the girls were the worst as she told her story while holding back the tears. How life had turned full circle in three years. I accepted her apology but it did not mean much. I knew the truth and I was living it every day of my life.

Sarah was as inquisitive as ever. She wanted to know details of my days at work. When the events were recited, she wanted to know what I had done wrong. I must have done something to annoy them was always her esteemed prognosis. Soon I was driving a taxi in the day time, which was not easy to get because most owners worked in the daytime. It was night work they did not like.

Now at least I could get a decent night's sleep and have some normality in my life. The girls seemed happier as I was able to drop and collect them from school. They were happy times till Aisha went to secondary school and I was screwed once again. Rihana finished school at ten to one, Aisha finished at twenty to three and other times the school would close early without warning for teachers meetings. I was doing more taxi work for my daughters than for the office which did not sit well either with the office or the owner. Poor Rihana ended up taking the bus home, till she joined Aisha in the secondary school. Sarah's behaviour was becoming more erratic by the day.

Sometimes she spoke about my family with kindness but other times it was mostly venom. A few times she suggested my mother could come and stay with us and even thought of building a granny flat to accommodate her. This plan like many others never came to fruition. My mum was living with my sister in San Francisco, California. She was travelling between Pakistan and the U.S. till her age and failing health compelled her to settle in Pakistan.

Thankfully there became fewer visits from the clan and to their houses. They all had their own homes now and unlike Sarah always put themselves first. While they visited sporadically, Sarah seldom missed a week without visiting her mother or her sisters.

Then she proposed having single beds. Why, I have no idea but she seemed hell bent on destroying what little I had left in sanity.

Aisha and Rihana often talked about their mum and her lying. Whether she was getting her facts mixed up or blatantly lying, I can prove neither but her behaviour was definitely getting more erratic by the day. It's as if she was always on the look out to cause grief. If I went to the bathroom she checked the toilet seat, if I used the sink she looked for eye lashes, if I had a shower she looked for my hairs in the bath. At the same time she had no qualms leaving the bath dirty or leaving hair dye scattered around the bath and tiles. If I pointed these facts to her, either she became abusive or laughed the matter off.

If Aisha, Rihana and I were in the front room, Aisha noticed that Sarah stood outside the door listening with her ear planted firmly on the door. Whenever she suspected and opened the door, there she found her mother standing. Many a times I heard Aisha telling Sarah, mum we have enough friends, what we need is a mother while she was always trying to be their best friend or so I thought till one day I opened the front door and heard screams coming from the kitchen. Then Rihana was about six years of age.

I ran to the kitchen and there was Rihana running around the kitchen being chased by her mother with a wooden spoon in her hand swinging wildly. Rihana's little hands were covering her bum. She had tears streaming down those beautiful cheeks while she screamed and cried. Sarah looked like a raving lunatic. God forbid if it had been someone else, I would have killed them. I grabbed the spoon from Sarah as Rihana curled in my lap. Sarah walked out without uttering a word. My bum bum is sore Daddy, whimpered Rihana. She was in agony.

Then she told me that Sarah had attacked her on numerous occasions but she was afraid of telling me. She did not want Mum and dad to fight. She was craving for a mother that did not exist. I was dying a slow death and could nothing. Once again I swore to myself never to leave Rihana alone in her company but what could I do when on whim she was capable of taking the girls away from me. Sarah always attacked Rihana when I was not around. Her favourite accusation while beating the living daylights out of my darling daughter was that she had tried to kill her. She was referring to the events of 6 September 1989.

She always picked her moments and Rihana was too scared to tell me because it would make me angry and mummy had told her repeatedly not to make me angry. Whatever this woman was planning and how her mind worked, I have no idea. What was I to do? After all I had been foretold and it was entirely my fault. Would their mother have been better in an institution? What would I have told my daughters?

This continued till the day when Rihana was fifteen. Sarah went to hit her and Rihana kicked her on the shin. I swear I will kill you if you ever hit me again, Rihana had threatened her mother. Aisha was screaming down the phone and she was hysterical. This was post 2005 when Sarah and I had separated and the girls were in their mother's house.

Yet for my birthday, well one of them, she took the girls to make pottery for my birthday present. Little plates with Happy

Birthday Daddy printed on them. They are precious momentos which I still cherish and always will. They have the pride of place on the front room walls and in my heart. Pretty little hands making pottery, what a sight it must have been. I love presents that are personal and encouraged my daughters to make them. There is only so much after shave, socks and underwear a man can use. My aftershave lasts me more than six months. Whatever the girls drew for me, I have kept scribbles and all.

Aisha is so talented. In secondary school she made a bedside locker, better than a professional. In a play at primary school, she was a seasoned professional at the age of nine and played multiple roles in a play. I was amazed and felt so proud. I still have it on video, of course.

Rihana is more introverted. She made cushions, really pretty ones. I found some of her writings from her early secondary school years. There was so much emotion that it's over powering. She was not even fifteen then. On the day of her graduation she wrote a poem and was asked to make a presentation. There was not a dry eye left in the hall. Yet no one knew the life she was enduring at home. I always thought I did but was wrong. My darling has carried so much pain which is apparent in her eyes but she does not reveal. I don't dare question even though it breaks my heart.

Now back to Sarah and me. She would repeatedly describe our marriage as a sham but did not want separation. Sex in the marriage was nonexistent and only if she wanted. She decided and organised catholic marriage counselling and like a lemming I followed because I still wanted to save this marriage. It was the weirdest counselling ever. A nun in a habit grilling us both about our personal and private life including sexual practices while tut tutting. Even Sarah looked confused. How we had sex, where we had sex, what holes were being drilled. This felt more perversion than counselling.

My sincere apologies as I forgot to mention that I am in possession of several degrees in counselling. A BA in psychology, a BA in counselling and psychometric testing, a Masters in Cognitive Behaviour Therapy and a level seven Diploma in Community Education alongside being a certified mediator in conflict resolution which seems ironic. I am also in the middle of preparing and in the process of conducting research for my PhD. Hence I believe I know a little about counselling and this was counselling for the planet ape shit. Congruence, non judgmental, empathy and unconditional positive regard had never set foot within a mile of this woman. Even Sarah looked visibly shocked and vowed never to return.

Then another advised us that we should have had more partners and tried several relationships before settling down and getting married. Currently he acts as a consultant for the family courts. May god help us all!

Then the loony prince that is I took the family on holidays. Sarah wanted Aisha to see her place of birth, our first house, the second house and the rest. Even there conflict was plenty and created out of nothing. Only god knows about my demeanour because Aisha does not look happy in those pictures and seems distant and lost. I paid for everything and was still trying to play happy families.

I had noticed that Aisha was becoming moody. Either puberty was on the horizon or her parent's arguments were beginning to take their toll. But she was still the most loving daughter any father could wish for. Aisha takes her education very seriously. Every teacher, every principal showed adulation and showered her with compliments.

Many a time the principal would walk me across the road for a coffee instead of giving me reports about my darling daughter. We don't want to see you. The parents we need to see never turn up. What do you want to hear? How wonderful your daughter is? How wonderful your daughters are? He would say with a genuine heart warming smile, before paying for the coffee.

Rihana was never an academic but very sensitive and highly intelligent. She got praise as well. At times Aisha was jealous of her because she worked hard for her grades whereas Rihana did as little as possible but always finished her homework and received good grades. It drove Aisha bananas.

In all their years at school I believe there would be less than ten missed days, through illness if at all. Aisha wanted perfect records and Rihana was not far behind. They were always impeccable in their attire and demeanour. Words cannot describe how wonderful they really were and are.

Despite the shambles of a family they turned out as wonderful young adults while Sarah continuously played her mind games. Her attention was almost always focused on Aisha as she worked hard to get her sympathy and attention.

Chapter Ten

I have a baby sister who I had not seen in years. In fact it was 1976 when I had left Pakistan for the U.K. Now she was married, had a son and living in Castro Valley, San Francisco. We had opened communication and mum was living with her. Let's go visit her, one day Sarah suggested. It sounded like a great idea. I was excited and it made the girls happy.

I was €4,500 lighter before we set foot in the U.S and there was more to be spent during our stay by muggins that is I. My brother in law was there to pick us up and he seemed livid. We were over eighteen hours late and they were worried. My sister had waited and waited till she became tired and went home with my mum. They were wrecked and could wait no more. Well, a funny incident had occurred. We got on the plane as most people do, at Shannon Airport in Ireland and within an hour of the flight the captain decided to return as there appeared pungent fumes in the back of the plane and passengers began to collapse.

Rihana's eyes were watering and she began to cough. Aisha did not feel too well and I could feel fumes in the back of my throat. Apparently a problem had been reported prior to take off, nothing was found and the plane had been given a clean bill of health. Twenty minutes into the air and good ole paddy started chanting like father Jack drink, drink, drink, a favourite phrase from Father Ted. There were about fifteen of them idiots and only shut up once miniature bottles of alcohol were served to keep the peace. Thankfully it was one of them feckers who collapsed first. That shut him up.

The captain announced, ladies and gentlemen, we are experiencing a small problem and I have decided not to take a chance while flying over the Atlantic and will be returning to Shannon. Next minute after a u turn we were heading back to

Shannon. Lunch was due to be served but could not be served as this was an emergency and Rihana was hungry, gods bless her.

Well we had to wait till a plane stupid enough to fly us over the Atlantic could be found and the crew to go with it. For four hours we were allowed free of charge as many peanuts and crisps that we could eat. We were offered tea and coffee to go but no food from the restaurant. If we did we'll have to pay for it and couldn't anyway because we were not allowed outside of the holding area.

A charter plane was found and fuelled with no in flight entertainment and the seats felt like park benches. We were already late as we approached JFK when another funny thing happened. A jumbo before us had crash landed on its nose without the undercarriage and we were to be kept in the air, going round and round in circles burning fuel, just in case. Just in case what? Well just in case, we were informed. I could see the fire crews, the white foam, the jumbo, lying on its nose like a drunken elephant, pun intended! And every time we circled, I saw this view. By now my backside was painfully sore but we were to remain attached to our seats, with the seatbelts.

Then the honourable captain announced that we were running low on fuel and if not allowed to land in the next ten minutes would be heading for Newark. What did he expect us to do, piss in the tanks? I was beginning to feel a little cranky and my little darlings looked wrecked. Thankfully we landed within the next fifteen minutes but had managed to miss the connecting flight and there was no Aer Lingus staff to be seen at JFK.

It was close to midnight and I had no way of contacting my darling sister. We all sat down on the floor and it was freezing. New York was covered in snow and there were no seats in the arrivals lounge at the JFK. One young smart couple had found a wheel chair and he being the chivalrous character let the girlfriend sit, for no more than thirty seconds before being pushed out by the airport staff. This is for disabled use, are you disabled, one asked sarcastically.

It seemed like ages before a half awake, half asleep young woman turned up in her green Aer Lingus attire, trying to fix her hair while tugging at her underwear and she looked neither comfortable nor awake. Then another one turned up and between two half brains they managed to find a quarter. They had no answers to any questions and we were none the wiser about our overnight stay or connecting flights. This was one thirty in the morning in New York, Christmas week and 21st of December to be precise.

At ten past two in the morning they announced in unison, ladies and gentlemen we have arranged for transport. You will be taken to a hotel for overnight stay and in the morning please make your own arrangements to your destinations. Aer Lingus will reimburse and then the dimwits began to depart. For fuck sake this was the 21st of December and the whole of America was on the move. Arrangements, what arrangements, where, how were the questions but dimwits were reluctant to answer. Sorry you have to do it yourself; the small blonde one piped up looking completely disinterested.

The crowd had raced to the front and were busy pushing and shoving into the minibuses on their way to oblivion. They could not give a shit about anyone but themselves. This was Christmas goodwill, my ass. I asked Sarah and the girls to be patient as they appeared close to a state of collapse. All done, all gone and the schmuck family was still there. I did not know whether to wait at the airport or venture to a hotel. Sarah spoke words of wisdom, I acknowledge. Let's go to the hotel, she said. At least the girls can lie down for a while and we can shower and clean up. We returned to the nonplussed looking bimbos who were in a rush to vacate the Aer Lingus kiosk. Sorry is all they said as I stared at their departing backsides.

I was pondering the conundrum of transport when a kind looking Hispanic guy approached us. I can drop you at the hotel he offered. I asked him how much and no charge was his reply. He worked at the airport and was heading home for Christmas holidays. I would one day like to thank him again. He had brought my faith back to human kindness when I had felt hopelessness for the umpteenth time. He knew all the short cuts and we arrived at the hotel to watch the fellow sheep getting off their mini buses.

He appeared to know the hotel staff and got us a room and a key. We were the first to our room while the demented feckers were still wandering around the lobby. He wanted nothing in return and my constant show of gratitude made him feel embarrassed. He gave me instructions for which terminal to go to and what airline to approach in the morning. He advised me to be there before three thirty. Then with a wry smile he wished us a Happy Christmas and disappeared into the falling snow of New York leaving behind a wonderful memory of human compassion.

I stayed awake and soon it was time to wake Sarah and the girls. They had an hour of sleep. We got ready and went downstairs to the lobby. The mini buses were there and waiting. I put the luggage in the back when suddenly the herd appeared. Sarah, Aisha and Rihana were waiting for me on the kerb. By the time they came over, all three mini buses were full. Our luggage was on the minibus and we were left standing in foot deep snow. I got hold of the driver as he was about to drive away. We were here first and you have our luggage, I protested. Not my problem, he muttered as he offloaded our luggage drove away in a hurry. Lighting may not strike twice but shit sure did, repeatedly.

I went back inside and spoke to the receptionist, who spoke to the duty manager who spoke to the chauffeur and soon the hotel VIP transport was at our disposal. The driver appeared to be an absolute gentleman. He assured me that he will sort everything out as he took us to the right terminal, pointed to the growing queue and told us to hurry. We joined the rapidly growing queue when the minibuses full of sheep shaggers arrived.

Sarah got into a conversation with a member of the airline staff who promptly pulled us out of the queue and took us to a check in where she organised eight seats for the four of us, got our luggage sorted, pointed to the departure gate, wished us Merry Christmas and was gone. What a welcome after all that we had endured. Sarah and the girls slept all the way before we landed in sunny San Francisco. And all this time my poor brother in law had waited, departed, returned and waited for hours not knowing where the hell we were. Well at last we had arrived.

We got home to a tearful reunion and reception. I had not seen my mother for ten and sister for sixteen years and this was the first time that I had met my brother in law. Leyla was all over my darling daughters. The way she kissed and hugged, I thought she was going to eat them away. Her son Faran was standing behind her observing quietly but looking shy and amused. Four weeks flew and I found cousins I had never seen or met before.

They took us everywhere, museums, zoo, planetarium, Fisherman's Wharf, Chinatown, tram rides, any and every place of interest that existed within fifty miles of San Francisco. They took care of everything. The only time we were allowed to spend money was on presents for folks back home, well Sarah's folks back home actually for I had none.

One day when buying presents, I suggested that Sarah buy something for Faran. We were in a discount warehouse where brand names are sold at a fraction of their original price. She was busy buying presents for everyone, sisters, mother, father, nieces, nephews and whoever she could think of, with her money of course. Her retort, why don't you buy him something and matter was deemed closed.

I bought him one or two presents with pleasure. The smile on his face was worth the effort and I wished to do more. A gesture from Sarah would not have gone amiss. In later years I often wondered what memories the child held of the incident. He had heard her reply loud and clear and looked dejected. His parents had opened their home to us, his family was taking us everywhere and yet she was loathing in spending five dollars on him.

Somehow we managed to have a great time, the children seemed relaxed and Sarah behaved, which was delightful yet unexpected.

At San Francisco Airport Rihana started to cry. She wanted to stay with auntie Leyla and did not want to go back to Ireland. Aisha looked sad and Sarah seemed emotional and lost. She seemed calm and polite and almost loving at times. She had not wished to return to Ireland either. We returned to Shannon and arrived home without incident.

Chapter Eleven

Things were about to get worse. I had given up the job of driving a taxi and got work as trainee golf professional at the local Golf Club. One of my clients while driving the taxi was Alan Wannabe. His father Sean is a famous golf professional based in Lakeside Golf club. He had succeeded his uncle Rob, a renowned personality in his heyday. He was well liked and highly respected in golfing circles. Alan had asked me several times to work with him in his father's golf shop. I asked Sean if he would take me on as an assistant and after a little humming and hawing he had agreed. For me it was an honour to work with and learn from the master. He was one of the best in his craft. It also allowed me flexibility of hours which I badly needed.

Aisha and Rihana had settled in the secondary school and were doing exceptionally well. Aisha was under pressure, mostly self imposed. She always finished her homework which was plentiful and tiresome. I was becoming familiar with the Irish phenomena of putting students under pressure to perform in their junior cert and leaving cert exams. Without achieving high points entry to good graduate courses limited their choice of subjects and future prospects. Aisha had to excel at everything she undertook.

Every evening at 11.30 I would ask Aisha to go to bed. She was very sensitive and hard working and usually suffered headaches before the day was over. I rubbed her forehead till she fell asleep. At times she pretended to be asleep and as soon my snoring was heard she was back studying with the duvet over her head and she bedside lamp inside it. She thought I did not know her tricks but I did.

Monday, Wednesday and Friday I worked from nine till noon and on Tuesday and Thursday it was twelve till six. Also I had to settle for working every Saturday from ten till six. This allowed me to drop my daughters at school every morning and collect them in the afternoon. The other two afternoons they were collected by Seamus a taxi driver friend of mine. We became best friends when I drove a taxi and he had shown care for my daughters. I felt that they were always safe with him. This routine was to follow till their finishing year.

By now things were very bad at home. Everything Sarah said or did was a lie and even the girls were beginning to notice. Between puberty and familial atmosphere, Aisha was becoming extremely moody and had developed a temper. She was prone to flying off the handle in an instant. Rihana remained passive as ever, still internalising whatever happened around her. After me she bore the front of Aisha's explosive outbursts only to retreat to the sanctuary of her room. She kept herself occupied with brushing her doll's hair or writing. Often I found little notes full of pain and sadness but never personal. She was projecting her emotions on paper and there wasn't much that I could do. The more I tried to converse the less open she became. At least hugs and kisses were always there and never short in supply.

It was amusing to hear when the girls in Aisha's school tried to make fun of kisses and hugs from her dad every morning. She ordered me to pull the car right outside the school for all to see before asking me to get my ass out of the car. Then she wanted a proper hug and her kiss on the cheek for all to see and I loved every minute of it.

At times there was a problem with my time keeping. If I was ten minutes late there was hell to pay. If Seamus got delayed, she was on the phone and I knew the rest of the day would be problematic. She had become very temperamental and emotional but daddy was always there to take the brunt of it, with a smile. My back pain was getting worse and there were times when I difficulty in putting on my socks or shoes but I

204

managed like I had managed everything else. At least now I could be with the girls every evening, seven days a week. Now Sarah had upped the ante. She found a stray pup in Clarinbridge and brought it home. It was meant for Rihana. I had never seen a dog shed so much and it was not allowed inside the house. Sarah made daily threats that she would bring the dog indoors and even into our bed but Rihana resisted. She knew I did not like pets in the house. Eventually Sarah got her a kennel and Rihana paid for it. Sarah made sure of that.

Thankfully every week I gave the girls pocket money and they saved most of it. When driving the taxi I used to give all my leftover change to Aisha and Rihana. It wasn't long before they had saved a couple of thousand Euros each in their accounts. The girls would buy personal stuff from their savings and Sarah was always on hand with the spending. The dog became a great companion for Rihana. She talked to him in all her spare time and called him cheeky. He is still alive and keeping her company. Only a month or so ago Rihana paid two hundred Euros to have the dog's teeth cleaned. The lucky sonofabitch! No one ever cared to spend a dime on this old dog.

When I think of it and my experiences, possession of extensive knowledge of family law, its practices, various domestic violence acts, separation and divorce act, the various childcare acts and the practices of women support groups, two words come to mind, cope script. Cope script is well known to all family law practitioners. A woman is referred to a woman's refuge, where in turn she is referred to women who have undergone separation and then advice is provided on how to create alienation of children from their father, what tactics to use, how to instigate domestic arguments even violence, what allegations to make, how to utilise the services of the domestic violence unit whose first job is to remove a husband from family home and much more.

What brought this on, a voice mail message? There was a digital message for Sarah with tit bits of information and advice on which solicitor to engage in matters of family law. A gentleman was recommended who had destroyed many an innocent man's life and there always appeared a man protesting outside his office. He was friendly with a lot of judges, politicians, cops and the right people in the right places with aspirations of moving up into the upper echelons of the law society. It's never the one but always a pit full of vipers. Sarah had been making plans for separation, since when, I have no idea. All the cards were in play but I wasn't aware. The naivety of men in matters of family law often frightens me.

Her favourite methodology of physical abuse was to slam the door in my face and wait for reaction. The back of the bathroom door still bears hallmarks where she slammed it so hard in my face that my nose almost broke and the back panel cracked. There's a six inch crack in the door which I am sure still holds my DNA. The other was to scratch me with her nails especially when I was in the middle of changing clothes and then she would catch me unawares. Many a time I could not rest my back against the driving seat because of the intensity of pain. Often she drew blood which made my shirt stick to the skin. Once I had to stand in a shower to soak and remove the damn thing. I told no one till my GP noticed the scars on my back. That was the first time I had told anyone about what I was enduring. He was visibly moved.

Then my all time favourite when she tried to scratch my face or hit me and when she missed I could see the fear in her eyes. If ever I got hold of her forearms she would scream for the girls, especially Aisha and then cower behind them as if seeking refuge. Hollywood and sisterhood should be proud of her. I never hit back, ever. Once she told them that I had tried to strangle her even though I was trying to protect myself from one of her onslaughts. She was strong as an ox and whenever

206

she came at me she lunged. What else was I to do but put my hand out? Or would I be well advised to stand still and oblige the poor woman.

Please don't say hit back or I would have wished for the rest of my god forsaken life to be spent in hell and it would have felt like a reprieve. Hell is no competition for family law and its various enactments. Judges do make sure of that. The system wrenches your nuts, detaches them and next thing you find them hanging on a feminists rear view mirror as a keepsake. Every solicitor I consulted told me so while reassuring that I would lose my kids. They all concurred that I was fucked. The best legal advice ever and it cost nothing.

Electric World superstore had come to town and opened an outlet in Galway. For the first time in a long time Sarah wanted a job and applied for a vacancy. She got a job as cashier and began earning a wage. Now she would be gone for a week or two to Dublin, for in store training; I am going to Dublin tomorrow, was the notice and off she went. Children were always a convenience for her personal use and amusement and currently served no purpose.

We were living in a council house paying discounted rent as a low income family and now she wanted to hire a house keeper. She opened a bank account in her own name. The joint account was only convenient for her to withdraw money. To her dislike I closed the joint account and opened a personal account in my name.

Only god knew what she would do next. Forever she had talked about separate sleeping arrangements but never discussed or carried out her plan. Now the odd time Kate was found sleeping in our bed with Sarah. After a night out they would return home at three thirty or four in the morning and she was invited to stay. These night outs became a weekly and sometimes bi and tri weekly event. I got sick and tired of her games and one night stayed downstairs and slept on the floor for the next three years till our separation with only a carpet between me and the concrete floor while a blanket gave me cover. There was no central heating and I could feel the chill in my bones. In return she accused me of ruining her carpet which I had paid for like everything else in our house. My sincere apologies, the net curtains were bought by her mother as a house warming present.

Now Sarah was busy dragging the girls, whenever and wherever she wished. The mantra of her not being able to conceive and my retained ability to reproduce was always on stereo and our daughters were always within earshot. She took them on a holiday to Blackpool with her sister Kate and her children. I was neither informed, nor consulted or invited. The girls were told that daddy does not like going out with her and they had to get on and have fun in their lives. Then she took them to Kerry and again I was neither consulted nor invited. Upon arrival during the early hours of the night she found that the rental house was infested with cockroaches and proceeded to drive to Cork where they stayed in a hotel. These trips were becoming frequent and I was constantly being alienated.

When twelve approaching thirteen Aisha wanted to go to the Oxegen music festival and I would not agree. The event's reputation inhibits any half decent parent from sending their pride and joy to these festivities. Sarah organised everything and off she went. When Aisha became angry and rebellious, Sarah was always on hand to coax and fuel the fire. She wanted to go to Bar Cuba when underage and I protested but she went with her mother's blessing.

If Aisha wanted to go to concerts, Sarah accompanied her. I had no say in any matter while Rihana stood, observed and accompanied them. PAS (parental alienation syndrome) was in multicolour, on display, and I could do nothing. It's only now that the psychiatrist fools on DSM committee have agreed that PAS does exist and have decided to include it in DSM V. For decades they fought with Dr Gardener and denied that PAS existed. Dr Finch has an awful lot to answer for. PAS has been accepted in US family courts since the nineties. Ireland always remains a century or so behind the first world countries so there is still hope but some way to go.

At the age of fifteen Aisha was being dragged around town to find weekend work while I wanted her to get some rest. She was studying so hard and wanted to do well in her junior cert but Sarah could not give a shit. I still do not have an answer to Aisha's fear of her mother and need to comply. It reached an extreme when I would bring my daughters home, cook their dinner and hear Aisha telling Rihana not to eat as Mom will be cooking the dinner that day. Rihana was starving and did not know what to do. When Mom would finish work, no one knew but Aisha waited patiently. Everyone was being tortured but Sarah did not care. She had her games to play.

Aisha worked and studied fulltime while still getting excellent grades. I often wonder how she did not crack up. By now she was firmly under her mother's control. I was often accused by Sarah of keeping our daughters wrapped in cotton wool. Rihana was always treated as accompanied baggage and she followed Aisha to protect and support her sister. Aisha organised a girl's sleep over and Sarah told me that it was not appropriate for a man to be in the house. Aisha is uncomfortable with me being in the house, I was told. I slept the night in the pro shop, on the floor of course. Aisha rang me at close to midnight asking me to return home. I told her to have fun and stop worrying and assured her that I was ok. It was freezing as I lay under a pile of garments to stay warm. Every time I turned they rolled off me. I got no sleep but survived.

209

By now everyone knows that Rihana had suffered stress at birth and there appeared a problem with her teeth. They were crooked and protruded in different directions which made her self conscious. Upon consultation she was deemed old enough to visit an orthodontist. I knew probably the best professional in town and he advised that she would need braces. Discounted cost for me €4,500 as the normal rate was €5,400.

Sarah agreed to share the cost 50-50. The payments were organised in six instalments of €750 each. She contributed €375 once off and then refused to pay a cent more. That was the only payment she had made by the time we separated and refused to contribute a single cent thereafter. She was earning €28,500 plus receiving child benefit for both girls. My total income €9,800 and I ended up paying the balance of €4,125.

By now life was hell and at times I drove to the prom and stayed in the car park contemplating ways of taking my life. It was three or four in the morning when my fingers and toes went numb and I would sheepishly return home. Who would look after the girls? How will they cope? What will happen to them? A million questions would race through my mind and I would postpone the suicide research for another day.

For some strange reason Sarah began to sit with me and narrated stories from her past about her sexual conquests. This happened occasionally in the past but now was becoming quite the norm. To add insult to injury she bragged about admirers who visited her place of work and asked her out. Whether it was a fragment of her imagination or real, I have no idea but could not care less. In fact I often prayed that she would disappear with one of her fancy men and leave me and my daughters in peace.

Often she would follow me around the house stating that our marriage was a sham and what kind of marriage was it when we couldn't even have a decent argument. I bought a digital recorder, from Electric World of course and began recording these conversations because she always denied ever making such statements. I was left in peace for a while till she drew up another plan. She unilaterally decided to pay for the household shopping and I was allocated the care of all the bills. There were three exceptions, rent, coal and the phone landline. She needed the landline for her hour long conversations with her family. The shopping excluded meat, flour, rice and everything the family was eating for lunch and supper.

Then she embarked on a new project and began pestering me to take a mortgage and buy a house in the newly built estate across the road. What I did not know then was that she had been doing her homework before making a court application for separation. Not in a million years could I have imagined this woman to be so vile and evil. If we were to separate then I would be liable for the mortgage payments and most of her household bills while she would be awarded the custody of our daughters and appointed primary carer. This woman did not know the meaning of the word primary carer but family law does not give a rat's ass to rights and wrongs of married life.

I was also not aware that in 2002 Sarah had made an application in her sole name to the Galway county council for purchase of one of their social housing properties, if and when they became available. She had done the same with Galway city council. This only came to light when offers to purchase started to arrive through the letter box. By then Sarah was long gone and it was 2006.

In 2004 shit was to hit me in the face at my place of work. In the golf club I was getting news about Sarah's behaviour in the night clubs. One of the owners of a night club in Salthill knew me well and was keeping me updated. Sarah had met him while I was driving a taxi and he had remembered my darling wife.

The stories were often scandalous and mostly embarrassing. It began by accident as one member referred to this well bosomed blonde who was standing outside the shop window in the golf club. He had a story or two to tell about her. Then she was supporting a blonde look. Sarah walked into the pro shop and upon realisation that she was my wife, he left ashen faced without saying a word. Later he apologised profusely but was telling the truth. His stories corroborated what others had already told me and merely affirmed what others had been telling me for months. Then she had decided to embarrass me at work.

Just to add spice to this sad story there was a trip to the psychiatric department at University College Hospital Galway. By now the mental torture was playing havoc with my cognitive processes and often the brain refused to function. I desperately felt that I needed to do something to stop this mental torture, but did not know what. As it was a voluntary admission I was allowed to walk out at any given time. She accompanied me to the hospital and I think Sarah would have preferred if I had stayed there forever. Poor Sarah, they literally threw me out the next morning. Well they had no choice. How were they to know that Professor Fahy was acquainted with me and retained respect for me?

I had stayed overnight and the requested sedative gave me a wonderful night's sleep only to be spoilt by Professor Tom Fahy, one of the top professionals in his field of practice in this country, if not Europe. Sarah was present, probably ready to have me sectioned into psychiatric care for good. He asked his registrar, who let him in with his index finger pointed in my direction. Well he admitted himself voluntarily the registrar replied, sheepishly.

Tom started laughing. Who else has been talking to him, he enquired. The poor counsellor raised his hand. They all acknowledged in unison that they could not find anything wrong with me. He wanted to know what I was doing there. To save them further embarrassment I explained the whole situation to him. He put his arm around my shoulder and spoke to the people that were present. I shall not forget those words till the day I die and his words of encouragement were my saving grace. He pointed to his staff and said, This is Sam. He is the finest and most intelligent man I have had the pleasure of knowing. If there is something wrong with his mental state then we should all be incarcerated here.

Professor Fahy put his right arm around my shoulder and walked me to the front door and said, you are far too intelligent for most people. What takes you a few moments to comprehend may take others a lot longer and you will have to make allowances for them, and yet there is the chance that they may never comprehend what took you seconds or minutes to figure out. It's a gift and can be a curse. It's a cross you have to bear. Then he walked me out of the building with his comforting arm around my shoulder. The look of disbelief on Sarah's face was a treat to savour. Now Sarah had another enemy added to her ever growing list.

Despite all the shenanigans in our life, on New Year's Eve we usually lit a fire in the front room and brought in the New Year. This year Sarah went to bed as I sat with the girls. Pain was etched all over their faces especially Aisha's. She is a very emotional and deep thinking young woman and easily hurt. Forever the girls had made every effort to please their mother but always in vain. It later transpired that she had been planning separation for the past couple of years and had no inkling of playing happy families. In her mind she had already separated from me.

On mother's day the girls wanted to buy flowers for Sarah. Daddy can you please bring us to the florists, they asked. I brought them to my favourite florist and the staff was absolutely wonderful to my daughters. Every bouquet they suggested was out of their price range. The poor things wanted to pay but collectively only had €35. I knew the one they liked and told the staff to pretend it was cheaper. They looked so happy, but somehow I think Aisha knew that Daddy had pulled a stunt and her looks told me so.

We returned home to find Sarah in her night clothes on her way to the bedroom with a plateful of toast and a cup of tea in her hands. She nonchalantly took the flowers from Aisha's hands and proceeded upstairs. Aisha's looked ready to cry while poor Rihana looked so sad and deflated. We had still not had our breakfast as the girls had planned to start with mother's day flowers and then prepare breakfast in bed for their mother. I had the flour prepared for their weekend favourite, paratha and fried eggs with a hot cup of tea. It's an Asian delicacy which the girls got every Saturday and Sunday and thoroughly enjoyed. All three of us were quiet and I did not know what to say. The reassuring hugs and kisses were reluctantly received as I proceeded to cook their breakfast. As Sarah was busy upstairs with her culinary delights I cooked for us three.

We were ready to eat when Sarah's footsteps were heard coming down the stairs which made Aisha and Rihana apprehensive. As we took our first nibble Sarah appeared with her empty plate and a mug which she placed in the dishwasher without a word being said to return and utter the immortal words, hey guys where is my breakfast? Aisha began to cry while Rihana's head went down like a lead balloon.

She had lit the fuse and I exploded. I picked my plate full of food and promptly smashed it on the dining table with its contents scattering all over the place. I accused her of being a selfish and uncaring woman who did not give a shit about anything and anyone but herself. Before I could utter another word she turned on her heels and went upstairs to the bedroom. Still, they craved for a mother.

Now the threats moved up another notch and she wanted me out of my house. This became the weekly then daily mantra till one day she actually managed to shock me again. If you don't get out of my house I will call the cops and tell them that you sexually abused me. Thankfully she was not accusing me of rape. Don't forget for the past three years I was sleeping on the floor downstairs. Carpet was the living proof and it carried indentation of my torso. Immediately I picked up the phone and called 999, gave them my address and reason for the call; there is a woman here who wants to report an incident of sexual assault. Before I could proceed further she had grabbed the phone and slammed it down. Her face looked flush as she stared at me. She was very nice to me for the next two weeks. She even told me that she loved me. Strange enough she tried to do the same even after we had separated.

On her birthday in March of 2004 I bought her a beautiful bouquet and delivered by hand in front of her colleagues. Most of them knew me, including the General Manager. The women told her how beautiful they were, some felt jealous but all were happy for her and yet she looked embarrassed, very embarrassed indeed. At the end of the day upon returning home she accused me of embarrassing her in front of her colleagues.

Out of the blue she suggested mediation and I agreed. She had already made arrangements and I accompanied her. We got the mediated written agreement posted to us individually and three weeks later we had separated. The mediated agreement was for co habitation and not separation. She had taken both the written agreements and burnt them in the range. It was three years later when I found that she had been planning separation since 2002. It had taken her three years to bury the marriage till

215

all the tricks had been exhausted and we ended up in a family court.

The cancer that set in on that fateful night in 1989 had finally killed the marriage, if such a thing ever existed. I was to be free at last. It was a Saturday afternoon and I was sitting downstairs watching TV with my darling daughters when Sarah walked in and asked them to leave us alone for a few minutes as she had something important to discuss with me. They looked apprehensive, even scared as they left the room. Lately they had been most secretive which was most unusual for them. They went to the kitchen and put the TV on. Give me money and I will leave you in peace, she said after closing the door. Why should I give you money and where the hell is it supposed to come from, I asked. What have you ever done for me? I added. I never claimed that I have ever done anything for you, she replied. But you must have some money, I know you have money.

Damn right I did. All twenty three thousand and some change for a life's worth of work while £15,000 sterling hung over my head which I owed to my family. She said that she needed money to buy a house and would then leave me alone, in peace. So now she was acknowledging that she had made my life a living hell and would leave me in peace. How much money do you want? I asked. Give me 25,000 Euros, she said. How much money have you ever given me, I enquired. Well I never said that I ever gave you any money was her reply, as she stared at the floor.

If you leave the house I'll give you 10,000 Euros, take it or leave it, was my final offer. I did not wish to see this woman's face for the rest of my natural life. When will you give me the money, she asked. After you have left this house, I replied. Then she made another disclosure. She had already bought a house in Salthill and would move out next Saturday if I paid her. She was already in possession of the keys and the secret my daughters were hiding was finally revealed.

I'll leave the house next Saturday for the day, I said. Get your brothers to help take your stuff out and I'll have a cheque ready. Promise, she said and I did not answer. There were no appropriate words left in me to say to this woman. She was full of lies and deceit till the end. Another surprise waited. I went to tell the girls the plans for next Saturday and she followed me in. Don't worry girls; we'll make a girlie home and no men allowed. Now we can do what we like, when we like, she announced grandiosely.

They already knew but did not know how to tell me. The poor things looked in pain and lost. She had it all prepped and planned with them weeks ago.

I was always the last to know. Once a fool, always a fool, that's me alright.

Chapter Twelve

The poor fecker that is moi, thought that I would lick my wounds and get on with my life but another saga was about to unfold. The girls had agreed between themselves that they would spend equal time with both their parents. It seems everyone had been doing their homework, except me. When my head is stuck up my ass and no visible daylight, what am I supposed to see? I was just glad that there was no one there to bully me, treat me like dirt, and speak like I had no worth. The girls turned up in rotation. I picked them from school and dropped them at their mother's house in Salthill. During their time with her, they mostly took the bus everywhere or else had to walk.

There is another comical sting in the tail. Just when you would think this poor sucker is getting a break, there is more, a bit like Dallas. Bobby is dead, everybody knows it but then he is alive. A bit like that, except that I had no oil wells and was stone broke. The first Monday after separation she opened the front door and brazenly walked in. I and the girls had just sat down for dinner. They were in pain. Their eyes, their tone of voice, their whole body language was screaming pain. They dragged their feet, looked tired and appeared devoid of their beautiful smiles like someone had sucked the life out of them.

It seemed my darling daughters had lost their soul and zest for life. I still got the kisses and hugs but they would break my heart. A volcano of emotion seemed simmering just beneath the surface. I could feel their pain yet could do nothing.

Hey guys, Sarah smiled and cooed. Oh, dinner time, where is my dinner? Aisha's head was bent over her dinner plate and I saw a huge tear rise to the surface and drop in her dinner plate. Rihana looked at me, a little confused, a little bemused, a little angry but none of us said a word. Sarah walked to the cooker, lifted the lid and tweeted, oh Yum, mince and peas. It was Aisha and Rihana's favourite with freshly made chapattis and salad. Now there were no chapattis for her. The lonely tear that dropped from Aisha's eyes was followed by more droplets till it began to stream. The more she ate the curry the more there seemed in her plate. The tears were dropping and her head was almost touching her plate. I feel incapable of describing the pain that went through me. Rihana's eyes were welling but she is so cool that she had total control of her introverted emotions.

Sarah playfully took a piece of chapatti from Aisha's basket, sat down and began to eat. I was choking on my dinner and could eat no more. Aisha had come to a standstill and Rihana was barely able to chew her food. Then Sarah proceeded to do the same with Rihana's dinner, a portion of chapatti and cooing delight at the dinner. Me, Aisha and Rihana were sitting their motionless. This could not be happening and seemed unreal. It beggars belief yet there she was in her true element for all to see without an iota of care or remorse. With a regal wave she got up, kissed them both on their cheeks and said goodbye to the motionless girls. The time had stood still.

For the next ten days this routine was repeated. I felt emotionally numb and could not say a word for fear of upsetting the girls. They were already on edge and grieving. That was the last time there was supper for four in my house. This woman had spent her life sucking the life out of anything and everything precious to me. The girls were merely items of amusement and convenience for her just like the contents of her handbag.

One evening the girls informed me that she won't be gracing me with her regal presence. Her eldest niece Julianne had spoken with her as did her youngest sister Kate. Have you not done enough damage to the poor man already? Leave him alone, they had said in unison. My darling daughters had informed me.

219

They also told me that uncles Jimmy and Charlie were conspiring to sort me out. They had overheard a conversation in Clarinbridge. Now the rage was really beginning to build inside of me. All the pain and suffering was coming to surface and I was ready to kill any fucker related to this woman and I would start with the two fat bastards. I was ready but they never came.

Month of April, 2005 and I thought life had begun to settle down. Sarah turned up the odd time and could be heard talking to the next door neighbour. It wasn't that she was talking to her; she wanted the whole street to hear her. Life is wonderful, new house is brilliant and would proclaim how much she was glad to be out of hell, at last. This next door neighbour, we barely spoke to her. A single mother, two children, different fathers and she was living with her current beau. He is a strange man of limited vocabulary but could swear for Ireland in the Vulgarity Olympics.

She was described by Sarah and others in the local community as common as muck who only turned up when she wanted something, a bowl of sugar, a couple of onions, to use the phone for ordering her twice a week Chinese takeaway or a taxi. The couple went drinking every Saturday and Sunday night to return sloshed and paralytic with drink leaving a nine year old as a babysitter to care for their five and two year olds. This appeared a strange camaraderie in making. Sarah was ready and willing to tell anyone and everyone who would care to stop and listen about her new found emancipation and happiness.

She left Electric World to everyone's relief and started job as a manager at a video rental store. She got a pay rise, sold the car I had paid for and proceeded to buy a three year old car. Now she was earning in excess of 32,000 Euros p.a. and being paid child benefit to the tune of 3,500 Euros plus. Life was certainly agreeing with her. I was living a lavish lifestyle with an annual income of 9,360 Euros while taking care of unpaid bills that she had left behind. Now the threatening phone calls began to arrive. She threatened to report me to the cops claiming that I had stolen her car. Even though I had paid for both cars, she had them both registered in her name. Then the overdue bills began to arrive, including phone and house rent. Her name was on each and every one of them yet I had to pay. It was time to shut this lunatic out of my life forever. I told her to go to the cops and never to ring this house again. Then she made a habit of turning up unannounced to see our darling daughters while they stayed with me. For some ungodly reason they never said anything to her but gave out stink after she had left. To date this seems to be the norm.

Many a time when I rang to check about their welfare, they were found sitting in the car park outside her place of work doing their home work. Sitting in the car for an hour was the norm and at times stretched to an hour and a half. They were apparently hungry and tired but would not challenge her. If I had done the same, my life certainly would not be worth living.

Slowly some form of normality was beginning to prevail or so I thought. One morning in 2005 a hefty official looking letter arrived through the letterbox. These were summons to appear for a family law court hearing. Sarah was seeking a lump sum payment and weekly child maintenance payments. She wanted me to pay her in excess of three hundred euro per week in maintenance for the children and money for her upkeep even though the girls were spending equal time between the two parents and she was in receipt of children's allowance to add to her salary which was three times more than what I was earning.

She was pleading poverty and it was claimed that she was finding it difficult to make ends meet. She was the plaintiff and I was the defendant. I was required to inform the court registrar of my intent of contesting the application for maintenance. The letter read more like pay up or else.

Now I felt enraged. This abusive parasite and her flock had made my life a living hell for sixteen years and she wanted me to pay her for doing absolutely nothing but giving me the pleasure of her company. And yes she had hired a thousand euro suit as her lawyer. My first port of call was my friendly solicitors who all concurred that I was fucked. Their words not mine and yes they were able to afford a thousand euro suit too. Why? I asked. Well it's just the way it is, was always the reply, no matter who I asked.

How is this justified? I asked. Well it's the judges. They can do what they like and they were in unison again. This was my welcome to family law. I was still under the illusion that law is there for the people to seek justice in Tort and to serve with honour, dignity and equality. Not so, as I was to find out in later years. This rage was to consume me for at least a couple of years. Common sense, common decency and accountability did not and still do not exist.

Now I was acting like a Jack Russell terrier with a green chill stuck up its backside. I wanted to bite and bite hard but no one understood or wanted to understand. I had to decide what I needed to do and went to the citizen's advice centre where usually the staff is most helpful, knowledgeable and accommodating. I was led to a cubicle where an intelligent looking young man welcomed me and asked me how he could help. I began the story and knew within five seconds he had no clue with regards the subject matter. At least he acknowledged that no one there had the knowledge or capability to help me. He gave me the contact number for a woman who helped men going through separation. It took me more than two months to make contact with her.

A very regal Irish accent answered the phone. It was a mobile phone as no one ever answered her landline. I told her that for the past two months I was trying to get through to her helpline and no one had answered the phone. She ignored my question and informed me that she does not usually take calls but we could talk while she was waiting for a friend who she was meeting for coffee. I told her briefly about what I was enduring and asked what advice or help she could offer. She narrated her visits abroad to various conferences on family law and directed me to buy her CD's from her website as her contribution. But I need advice and what steps do I need to take, I asked again. Well we organise once a week meeting in the local church where men like you meet and you may be able to pick up advice from there. I was in Galway and she wanted me to drive to Navan where lost souls like me met without any professional guidance.

This is the best she had to offer. I told her that the man at the citizen's advice centre informed me that she is funded by the state to help separated men and what other help she could offer. She still had not answered any of my questions and I was becoming more desperate by the minute. Plus it was costing me money on the mobile phone which I could not afford.

I detect a foreign accent, where are you from, she asked and the regal tone had departed. Pakistan was the reply. Well you should go back to your country and sort out the lot of women there before you go complaining and asking questions. By the way I have to go, my friend is waiting for me. That was it and the call was over. The wonderful land of the caring appeared anything but caring by the minute.

By now I was so desperate that I even called woman's aid to be informed that they only dealt with women's issues. Every day they received two or three calls from separated men looking for help. It seemed no one cared about men and there appeared nothing in help for fathers undergoing separation. Men who had been destroyed were handing out advice leading to more destruction, especially over a pint or two.

In later years I learned that even men did not care about men. The next step was to go and meet with my local and national political representatives. Our two local members of Parliament, Messrs Padraic McCormack and Noel Grealish were most helpful in listening but knew little about the workings of family law. I pestered them for the next seven years till Padraic retired from national politics. He is an honourable man who seldom if ever let me down.

Noel tried his best but got frustrated at every step even though he was personal friends with the former attorney general, then minister for justice and a distinguished senior counsel, Michael McDowell and several other ministers. For some ungodly reason the subject of men, especially fathers, was deemed taboo. At least this little foreign made tractor was starting to pull some heavy weight trailers filled with manure.

Next stop was the mayor's office who was a practising barrister. She agreed to meet with me but later changed her mind and informed me that she would allocate me five minutes in the lobby of the city hall but could not discuss matters of family law, because of her vocation. But I rang the mayor, I protested, who supposedly represents the city and its residents. If I need a barrister, I will find one, I said.

That was the end of that conversation, albeit meeting. We had unplanned meetings thereafter, whence I talked while she busily looked for an escape route. This was my first lesson in politics and lawyers. They were good at neither but great at ducking and diving while protecting their fraternity and making money while the sun shone. This was also the first time that I had seen abuse of the civic office and the principle of priority of protection of their ilk than serve the public. As time went on I experienced the same with other lawyers in prominent public offices.

My education had begun in earnest as corruption, nepotism and dysfunctionality appeared the accepted norms as I progressed in meetings up the officialdom ladder. I met with senior civil servants, public servants, ministers, one or two heads of the state and another who later became the head of the state. All this was very educational indeed. Often I was described as being perceived as a threat to the system, as disclosed on numerous occasions by many a minister. In 2006 the system was to pull every dirty trick in the book to bury me and shut me out.

I returned to my friends who happen to be solicitors and received advice to seek legal aid. It had a reputation for being sympathetic to women's causes and men often complained of receiving inadequate representation which offered little comfort to my state of mind. I asked one of my friends, how much would it cost to hire a private solicitor? No one knew. Well it can be anything and the barristers never tell us how much they will charge till the case is over. It appeared that solicitors and barristers could do what they liked and charge as they like without fear of accountability. My education in family law had begun and lessons were being learned thick and fast. Why couldn't any lawyer tell me about their charges, after all section 68 of the Solicitors Amendment Act of 1994 clearly stipulates the disclosure of fees and its structures. This was year 2005.

Well no one ever pays heed to it, I was told time and again. Law Society governs the solicitors but never barred anyone from practice when found in breach of its own statutes. Flagrant breaches of law were common practice without fear of being held accountable. Now it appeared that the practitioners of law were the ones who did not have to abide by the law.

Having run out of choices my next stop was the law centre to seek legal aid. I was given application forms with instructions to return as soon as possible because there was a waiting list of two months and more for the assignment of a solicitor, if my application was approved. But my court hearing is in less than six weeks, I protested. Sorry but we are understaffed, under resourced, underfunded and under a lot of pressure. It seemed I was not the only entity with fear of being interred or going under.

I was also advised to apply for children's allowance as I was doing most of the work with our daughters and they were spending half the time with me. I phoned the child benefit office in Letterkenny. Holy God! The woman on the other side sounded indignant. The child benefit is for the mothers, she hollered down the phone. Excuse me, no, I said politely. It is for the primary carer and not the mother.

What's that? She asked. Well hold on the line, I better check, she sounded confused, god bless her. I have always thought that most public servants are born confused or else it's in their remit to keep the public confused as I was beginning to find, to my detriment. We'll send you the forms, fill them and return them, she stated curtly.

It felt like climbing multiple ladders at the same time. Legal, personal and political and at every corner there appeared a size thirteen waiting to kick me in the face. I still did not know what I had done wrong and no one bothered to tell me. Well it's just the way it is, was the common reply. Next I was advised to apply for family income supplement. I was applying and that is all I seemed to be doing, applying without getting anywhere.

I decided to visit our junior minister, Minister of state for Justice, Equality and Law Reform, Frank Fahey. I was told to make an appointment and I did. Then I was asked to put in writing the matter to be discussed and I did. On the day of the meeting the minister curtly informed me that I had misspelt his name. I had always thought that Fahy was spelt as stated but in fact it is also spelt with an 'e' in Fahey. It's amazing how quickly offence can be taken. When asked how to rectify this mistake, I was told it was my job to do my homework before looking for meetings with ministers.

This gem of wisdom I have always kept in mind. Now I always do my homework before meetings with anyone especially politicians. It is surprising to note how little they know about the workings of the state and the system that runs it. Anyhow I researched, looked everywhere and found the missing 'e' in Fahey and rectified my misdemeanour with regards the minister's surname. Audience was granted, sorry can't help was the answer and it's a matter of family law and will be dealt with in a family law court was the outcome of the meeting.

A year later I again met with the minister and he did try to help but to no avail. In the meantime he had also learned a lesson or two. The system appeared again stacked against men in law and in the government's social policy. It was the opposition from the system that irked and surprised the minister.

In the meantime life was as 'normal' as normal can be and I still had my darling daughters to take care of and finding some solace seemed nothing short of waiting for a miracle to happen. Soon I was notified about the date of my court hearing and an appointment was given with regards meeting with my solicitor. Ms Mary McIntyre was a solicitor in the law centre. She had joined the law centre because she wanted to help women suffering abuse at the hands of their husbands, I was informed.

She was courteous as she asked me to prepare notes of my married life. I had come prepared and readily handed them over. I was told that a week before the hearing we would meet and discuss the case. In the meantime she would study my notes to help prepare my defence. For the first time in ages I felt a little sense of relief and believed that justice would be served offering me some form of vindication at last.

We duly met before the case hearing and she advised me to take out the section about sexual abuse. The judges would only allow cases of sexual abuse committed against women. How can a woman commit sexual abuse? She asked. I duly removed the section. No questions asked. I felt I had to comply. Then she informed me that judges know what they are dealing with and a fair judgment will be made. There will be no lengthy hearing. Other lawyers had told me that I was going into a much fucked up system with the judges dead set against men. The judges may not even fathom what I was stating to be true. There seemed a conflict in legal advice on offer. (A suicide warrant if ever there was one needed!).

However, she acknowledged that she believed my notes and did not question them or any element of their truthfulness. She did not need or seek further information and expressed her opinion that no one could lie like that or else being a bloody good liar, I should become a politician. It was meant as a joke and I accepted it in spirit. But how would the judge know about the hell I had endured, without a full hearing. They know these things, was the reply. But how could they know? I asked again. They have dealt with hundreds of cases and you will be put in the witness box and when questioned, tell your story, but be brief, she advised.

All of a sudden I had a queasy feeling building in the pit of my stomach. This did not feel right and something was not making sense. I knew nothing about family law and its practices except that I needed to get on with my life. I had married in good faith to love, hopefully be loved in return and raise a happy family just like everyone else or so I had thought. How wrong one can be when seeking justice, I had no idea. All I knew was that the judge would hear my story and I will be vindicated. This was all I had to look forward to and it kept me sane, at least for a while.

I was settling down into a routine with Aisha and Rihana without Sarah's dramatic interferences, interventions, hysterics, threats or abuse. Most of the time the girls seemed lost and in pain and I was trying my best to make their days as comfortable as possible. The odd interruption came when Sarah phoned. She would have a conversation with Aisha as Rihana seldom had much to say. Then the fateful day arrived, the day of the court hearing.

Freedom at last, a thought crossed my mind. I was instructed to be at the court for 10 am, I arrived at 9.30 and there was not a sinner in sight. Panic set in and I rang the legal aid office, got no answer and the panic increased. I thought if the court started at 10 am then people would be there by now. Ten minutes later I phoned again and still no one answered. At five to ten someone answered the phone. Sorry I just wanted to check that I was at the right place, I blabbered. Yes you are, the secretary replied. But there is no sign of my solicitor, I whimpered. She will be there shortly. She is preparing for today's hearings, I was informed.

I did not feel comfortable to say the least. People had begun to arrive and it was getting busier by the minute while I stood there all alone. I saw some solicitors talking to their clients while others acknowledged my presence and asked my reasons for being there. I told them briefly about the hearing and they wished me good luck. Soon Sarah appeared pursuing a deep consultation with her thousand euro suit. They both looked content without a worry in the world and then disappeared.

There I was all alone, feeling uncomfortable and becoming a little angry. Where in God's name was my solicitor? I had never been to a court and this was my virginal experience and I was definitely not enjoying the foreplay, I can assure you. Then I walked into the courthouse building to acclimatise myself with the surroundings. All I saw was worried and stressed out male faces while women seemed comfortable and relaxed. It was an eerie environment. The men looked like they were facing the gallows while women seemed on a day out. Definitely a bad omen, I thought.

Everyone had company except Mr MaGoo, that's me. Who the hell did I have to call upon but no one? Then Sarah appeared as if she was walking into a theatre. Walking sheepishly behind her were my darling daughters, in school uniform. Poor Aisha walked up to me and told me that her mother had pulled her out of the classroom against her wishes. Dad this was not my idea, she said. Mum forced me to come. She appeared neither comfortable nor happy. Rihana stated the same. She seemed angry but had come down to keep an eye on Aisha and was always protective of her older sister. She knew that their mother could bully Aisha and somehow Rihana always felt that Aisha needed protection. I told them both not to worry and assured them that it was not their fault for accompanying her. I found a corner and stood around waiting for divine intervention. Sarah stood twenty feet away looking rather comfortable and regal. There was an air of triumph in her demeanour.

Rihana walked over to me and she looked angry. Well if Aisha wants to stand with her then I am staying here with you, she said firmly. In the distance Aisha looked most uncomfortable hence I asked Rihana to go and stay with her sister. She did not want to but I managed to persuade her to accompany her sister. I'll be fine, I reassured her.

I was still searching for my solicitor when there was a tap on my shoulder. She was there at last and I felt a little calmer. The judges usually do not start the case hearings till eleven, I was informed. Find a quite place where I can find you when our case is called. I found a secluded corner and told her where she could find me and firmly planted myself. My daughters had wandered away with their mother and I did not see them for the rest of the day. Despite the hustle bustle of the court it was one of the loneliest days of my life. I believe by then I felt detached from the world.

Around one o' clock my solicitor informed me that the judge had departed for lunch and advised me to do the same. I pointed out the spot where she could find me upon her return and once again sat down with a copy of the local newspaper to occupy me. Lunch was the furthest thing from my mind and to date I cannot describe the exact feelings and emotions I was experiencing. Isolation, hopelessness, bereavement, sadness, sense of loss and an element of anger somewhere in between but saw no clarity.

I sensed utter confusion inside my head and then a fleeting thought occurred that I would be better off dead. Pain had made me numb and death seemed a welcome escape. After all what control did I have over my life? There seemed no point in living. Somehow slowly the stray thoughts departed. I remained rooted to my spot and had no notion of moving for fear of losing my turn for the court hearing. I was not willing to take that chance. I needed vindication and today was the day as my life hung in balance.

Around three o'clock my solicitor approached to inform me that the judge had left early. The court clerk had informed her that the judge had to meet his wife for shopping and court proceedings were over for the day. The person who held the strings of my life had other priorities. This was my first taste of family law and of things to come.

The cost of hiring a solicitor was €500-1,000 per day irrespective of whether the hearing took place or not and the clients with their lives in limbo got screwed while his lordship went shopping. The same applied to the barristers and they all carried multiple cases. Judges enjoyed constitutional protection and appeared to be a law onto themselves without fear of accountability to anyone. The Irish constitution grants them complete freedom without interference from state or its officials, elected or appointed.

My solicitor had disappeared after informing me that she had a few things to catch up with in court and will be in touch with regards the next hearing. I had not eaten all day but food was the last thing on my mind. What mind, it had taken leave of all senses and I felt more lost and confused than ever. I was in a state of floating aimlessly, mindlessly and without focus. It seems I had no control over anything, including me. Somehow I got home and did not wish to be there. Hell I didn't know where I wanted to be. I had one strong and overriding desire, a wish to disappear forever as emptiness surrounded me. It felt scary and then my entire body broke into a cold sweat as I began to shiver. I brought my well worn blanket down and covered myself. I felt so cold. I have no idea how long it lasted till I fell asleep on the floor in the front room.

The next morning it all felt so surreal as I got up with a purpose but did not know what it was. At nine o'clock I rang the solicitor's office and got no reply. Quarter past nine I tried again and got no answer. I cleaned myself up and went to the court building for my hearing. There was no one there and it was locked. At ten o'clock I rang the solicitor's office and the secretary answered. I informed her that I was at the courthouse building but it was locked. What about my hearing? I asked. The solicitor was on three weeks leave and will be in touch upon her return, she informed me.

Then who is going to represent me today, I asked. We will contact you in due course was the reply. Still I was none the wiser. I took it for granted that the courts worked same as everyone else, 9 to 5 Monday till Friday. I spoke to a gentleman opening the court building and asked him about the next court sitting. He informed me that the court would be sitting the next day. By now I had decided to represent myself and needed no one to fight my corner. The way I had been treated thus far left me with no faith in the system.

I had to start work at twelve which took my mind off the day's proceedings. I was at work but my mind seemed elsewhere. It was in a constant state of turmoil but somehow I made it through the day. After all I had tomorrow to look forward to and had little time to prepare my case! I was there next morning at 9 o'clock sharp and raring to go. The first people to arrive were the cops with men in handcuffs. This was strange and a little confusing but I decided to wait. The motley crowd from the day before was nowhere to be seen. I waited in the distance. An hour or two had passed and still no sign of Joe public. Just cops and then more cops and in between an odd solicitor or a barrister appeared.

Now this was totally weird and I was beginning to feel very uncomfortable indeed till I saw a friendly face, a barrister I had known through golf. He is an absolute gentleman. Good morning John, I greeted him with a smile. What are you doing here? He asked. I briefly told him what had transpired in the last forty eight hours and listed my experiences. At first he laughed his head off before realising that I did not know my arse from my elbow with regards case hearings and court sittings and then he looked genuinely concerned. He took me aside and explained that that day was the criminal court sitting. Family law hearings took place every three weeks and my solicitor should have explained to me about the family law process and its workings. Suddenly my heart sank and I felt deflated. I did not think that I would make it through the next three weeks. He promised to speak with me later, and left. I felt like a real dumbass and a complete idiot. Now I was completely lost. There was no wind left in my sails and I felt dead on the inside. Why, I have no idea. I could barely walk. For the first time I felt too tired even to contemplate suicide.

I looked at the courthouse building with a sense of sadness. It is a beautiful structure designed by Sir Richard Morrison in 1812. It had recently been restored to its previous glory reminiscent of a time when the land was ruled by law and order of a more oppressive and exclusive nature, almost like family law. The Brits and Black and Tans were here then. Abuse of power, crucifying of the innocent and impoverishment of the natives was the norm, almost like family law. The above could be seen as applied in the practice of family law in the 21st century; a stray thought crossed my mind.

My experience thereafter and the knowledge gained were to vindicate the above statements. Except this time the cruel experiences were being forced on the natives by the natives, especially the industry of law.

Today the courthouse stands as a tribute to that age long since gone. It decides the future of those who seek justice under the remit of the family law and were to be destroyed forever; I was to learn sooner rather than later. Men, women and juveniles face the discipline of the criminal code as set out in legislation and limited by the constitution while fathers, mothers and children face life-changing judgments from untrained and uninterested judges where 'prescriptive' judgments are handed down with prejudice usually against men, especially fathers. Sweet Jesus! I was giving myself a lesson in history and teaching law better than the Law Society and King's Inns put together. Most lawyers I knew concurred that in family law judges hate men. One court clerk made a startling disclosure that some of his colleagues had taken to drink because they could not emotionally cope with the judgments current judges were dispensing. Men do not get favourable judgments was beginning to sound like an understatement. By virtue of being a man I was about to be condemned in the family law courts without a single black and tan in sight.

Then I wished more than ever that someone would help me end my miserable existence. Anything and anyone to help me achieve the end of my existence would have been most welcome. I just did not and could not care anymore and no one cared about me, or so I felt.

I was still working at the golf club. Some of the members had heard about my predicament, how I do not know but were most sympathetic and concerned. Some extended invitations to me and my daughters for their family outings, which I politely declined. Others were ready to appear as my character witnesses and these were kind offerings but none could soothe my traumatic existence. I never told anyone the whole truth merely that I was undergoing separation. A fact repeatedly came to the fore that men knew nothing about family law and only what they had heard in snippets from others. The only common consensus was that men are screwed in family law. This was just what I needed to hear whence cometh the day of deliverance!

I was busy researching family law, family law act, divorce act, Irish, UK, US and the European precedents in law by ECHR (European Courts of Human Rights) and ECJ (European Courts of Justice) and the Irish Constitution from A-Z. There is something comical about the Irish constitution. It is widely reputed that 80% of its content in 1937 was prescribed by the Catholic Church. Pray tell me who forgot to mention the word father and his role within the family? Straight away women were given a

235

huge club to wield in all family law processes and no dumbass noticed.

The day of reckoning beckoned and I arrived in my casuals, holding a plastic shopping carrier bag which contained all my documents. The building was packed to the rafters and lemmings were plentiful! The ground floor had no standing room and even the forecourt was crowded. By now I knew the routine. I met with my solicitor, found a nice quite corner and waited for the bell to toll. I had learned my lesson from my first appearance and today I carried two newspapers and a magazine to keep me occupied.

There existed nothing in the world but me. I noticed no one, acknowledged no one and spoke to no one. It was my doomsday and I had to stay focused. I was informed Sarah was in the building and the thousand euro suit had done a lot of home work with her. News travels fast in legal circles. During the day my solicitor approached me three times to consult with me. They were demanding €300 a week for Sarah and my daughters. What would I like to offer? She had asked. Nothing, not a cent I told my solicitor. I had informed her earlier in the day that I was not interested in any consultative process but only the court hearing, in front of the judge. Well I have to inform you about whatever communication they make with me, she stated.

I had decided that if I did not get justice on the day I was going to exhaust every legal process, through circuit court, high court and whatever it took and I was adamant. She left only to return with the news that they would settle if I agreed to pay for the upkeep of my daughters but without payments for Sarah. Tell them to go to hell, I blurted. Tell that scumbag suit and his client that I will see them in court and no more deals. I was ready for the bastards or so I thought. Lunch came and went and soon it was four in the afternoon before my solicitor returned.

She looked worried. I don't think we will get a hearing today, she said. The judge is ready to go home and there are case listings ahead of us, she informed me. I am going to see the judge and it's today or never was my stupid reply. I had no intention of returning to this shithole ever. I had committed no crime, I was guilty of nothing and yet I felt that I was being treated worse than a criminal. I ranted as I began walking towards the door where the court sitting was taking place. She looked genuinely worried. Let me see if I can have a word with the court clerk. But she still advised me to think about a settlement. What bloody settlement? Why does no one listen? She returned within five minutes of leaving. The suit had made an offer. They were willing to settle for one cent.

Not a cent, I hollered and I knew that the suit was within earshot. Sarah was snuggled neatly beside him. For some reason, for the first time they had looked rattled. She is not getting another cent off me, ever I told my solicitor. I was standing right next to the entrance to the court room, ready to barge in. My solicitor entered the courtroom with the intent of having a word with the court clerk and she told me to stay put. A few minutes later she emerged. She had spoken to the judge and we were granted twenty minutes and no more for the hearing. I checked my watch. It was ten minutes past four.

The suit ushered Sarah in followed by my solicitor and me in her tow. For people who are not aware of family law hearings, they are held 'in camera'. People present are the judge, court clerk, two legal representatives, plaintiff and the defendant. Then the court is closed and no one is allowed in. Whatever transpires in court cannot be disclosed outside of the court or else there are harsh penalties. Whatever is said and done is hushed by 'in camera'.

Breaching its compulsion to remain dumb in respect of all that is said and done in the courtroom is to commit contempt of court and face six or more months' imprisonment in addition to or alternative of a potentially crippling fine. Learning about family law was my ongoing education. I learned later that these penalties only applied to fathers. Mothers were seldom punished and the court orders were rarely enforced against them. That fateful day the word 'Teflon Mum' entered my vocabulary.

As I entered the courtroom I saw the judge perched high above us mere mortals, devoid of expression or emotion. The poor court clerk sat there looking knackered. He probably had listened to enough crap for the day. And then walks in this schmuck with his legal aid lawyer to face the thousand euro suit and his regal client. What a bloody contrast that was. I must have looked like Mary Antoinette about to meet her maker. First thing I noticed was a nod of acknowledgement between the suit and the judge. Court clerk did not seem interested and probably wished to be somewhere else. The suit proclaimed his intent of represent Sarah while my solicitor made her acknowledgement and the circus began in earnest.

Someone had dressed Sarah and did her makeup Hollywood style. A sombre face, immaculate looks, demure in appearance and the damsel carried a look which cried for sympathy and help. The stone faced judge looked at her like a lovesick cow. Oh yeah now he shows emotion, the fecker, a thought crossed my mind. I am screwed was the only other thought that I could muster and then began to comprehend the meaning of getting fucked in family law. I was about to be gang raped but just did not know how it would happen.

The suit announced the calling of Ms Sarah Boggles to the stand. The judge looked interested and the court clerk could not be bothered. The judge's eyes followed Sarah to the witness box. Jesus, by now even I was on her side. This creature was crying help me! The court clerk rose wearily from his chair and

238

walked over to the witness box. I swear he was dragging his feet and his arse was not far behind him. I actually felt sorry for him. The suit proceeded to neatly put down three rows of A4 paper and straightened them into piles. He appeared very organised indeed and it was most impressive.

I glumly looked at my scruffy plastic shopping bag with its contents and then glanced in the direction of my solicitor. She seemed pre occupied and in a world of her own. I hope she is thinking hard, to god I hoped and prayed. I soon came out of my stupor as it was time to pay attention. The suit had straightened his tie, buttoned his jacket and was standing tall and erect.

Do you swear to tell the truth, the whole truth and so help you god, said the court clerk. I do was Sarah's reply while she held the Bible. The judge smiled sweetly at the suit and asked him to proceed. I became invisible. This theatre was firmly under the suit's control from the very beginning and slowly even I began to foretell my future as the proverbial horse's backside. The opening was gripping, enthralling and exhilarating. Sarah was leaning forward ever so slightly as if in pain and then she winced.

Bravo, what a wonderful opening and without the utterance of a word and then the suit began his oration, Judge my client had a surgical procedure done two days ago. I would request the court to acknowledge her effort in making this appearance in such traumatic circumstances. She has suffered enough and would like this experience to be over as soon as possible. It was a wonderful opening and I almost applauded in admiration. From now on I was to sit on my hands and watch classic theatre with awe and admiration. Now I knew how the thousand euro suit had acquired his nickname. The feckers had come well prepared to get me hanged. The performance was brilliant, the opening statement encapsulating as the judge leaned towards Sarah looking worried. I could visualise Sarah sitting on his knee telling her story and then he would kiss it better. As for me, I felt fucked. I may as well have walked around this court with my pants around my ankles having made their lives easier.

Are you ok Mrs Anjum? The judge enquired with concern. Do you think you will be able to continue today? We are fine judge. We would like these proceedings to be over as soon as possible as my client needs to go home and recuperate, piped the suit. The cute hoor never missed a cue! The judge acknowledged with a sympathetic nod and then he stared at me with looks to kill as a cold shiver ran down my spine. I want this over by five, he ordered.

I had one look at the court clerk and a message was received. I think it said you are fucked mate and another one for the books. He did not look up till Sarah's theatrics had concluded. Obviously not a great fan of the theatre, I thought. The suit walked regally towards Sarah and thus began my character assassination, one strip at a time. He was talking and I was watching the clock as minutes ticked by. At exactly ten to five he finished with his witness.

This guy is good, I had to acknowledge. Sarah had done her home work well and was getting her money's worth. The suit had begun in a dramatic fashion with a worried expression. Are you ok Mrs Anjum? Are you comfortable? Is there anything I can get you? No thank you she said in a barely audible voice. I had never heard a Rottweiler whimper before. This acting was wasted in this shit house. It needed a bigger auditorium packed to the rafters with spectators. Wow, brilliant, fucking brilliant. Even I wanted encore. The judge was leaning forward, his chin firmly planted in the palms of his hands with elbows resting on his huge table. He was all eyes and ears.

Well Mrs Anjum, said the suit with flair as his left hand rested in his pocket and right arm extended, how are you coping with your financial difficulties? He occupied the centre stage and slowly looked towards the judge. With great difficulty, she whispered. He pays me no money and I can barely make ends meet. The lying bitch! I had seen her statement of incomings and outgoings alongside her statement of means. This was presented a few minutes before entering the court and I had noted exaggerated claims of expense which I had duly pointed out to my solicitor, who assured me that she would deal with the discrepancies.

Phone bills in excess of €100 per week, instalments for her new car and necessities that were more appropriate for a family of millionaires rather than one like mine. She had three holidays abroad in the past nine months and was now claiming poverty. The judge was peering intently at the statements, his glasses perched on the tip of his nose and he looked in deep thought.

So you are telling this court that your husband has not paid you a cent since your separation, the suit enquired in a grandiose fashion. That's true, she replied. It seemed that she was having trouble withholding her impending need to laugh. This was rehearsed, well rehearsed indeed. Within your marriage did you ever know what your husband earned? He asked. Never, was her reply. Did you ever know how much money your husband had?

No, she replied. So what you are telling this court is that you never had any knowledge of your husband's money affairs. That's true, she said. He never tells me anything. This woman had open access to my account and its details. She opened my bank statements before I arrived home from work. She had twice gone to the building society to have bank drafts made in the sum of €5,000 each and collected them. I had visited my building society the next day to sign for them. The manager and the staff knew me and would accommodate Sarah knowing that

I would turn up the next day to bring matters to order. This was vulgarity at its best.

You may recall my daily habit upon returning home, walk to the kitchen, take off my watch, take out my wallet and car keys and plonk them next to the microwave. This was my every day routine for the past twenty and more years which is still in practice. And this woman was telling everyone that she never knew the contents of my wallet when in reality every time she needed money she got it from my wallet. I was getting angry and asked my solicitor to question her lies. When it's our turn, she replied.

This facade seemed to go on for ages till the suit had exhausted his script. I was expertly portrayed as a good for nothing ogre. Judge I think my client has had enough and I am done. The suit announced with an air of arrogant satisfaction before returning to his seat. As he walked past me he glanced sideways and smirked.

Mrs Anjum would you like a glass of water, the judge was heard asking. No thank you judge, Sarah meekly replied still occupying the role of a damsel in distress. I was left with ten minutes to drag my sorry ass to the witness box, get sworn, cross examined and led to the altar for my hanging. All this had to be performed in ten minutes. All through Sarah's performance not once did I get a sideways glance from my solicitor.

Now it was my solicitor's turn to question Sarah. So you said my client never gave you a penny, she began. That's right, was Sarah's reply. She did not sound meek anymore and even the court clerk lifted an eyebrow. So who paid all the bills? my solicitor asked. Well he paid some of them, was the reply. And your socialising, who pays for that? She asked Sarah. I do, with my money, Sarah emphasised. So you can afford to go out twice and three times a week and yet you are strapped for cash.

Would you like my client to pay for that too? She asked. Judge this woman can go out three times a night, stay out till early hours and is short of money, she addressed the judge.

I did not like this line of questioning. I stood up and corrected her that Sarah usually went out once a week, sometimes twice and would not return till 3.30 or 4.30 in the morning. The judge was not amused but I had felt the need to correct the facts. The next five minutes of questioning was a pile of rubbish which said nothing about her role within the family and the duties she had performed within the family. Everything said and done thus far did nothing but portray me as a gobshite. Even I would have convicted me by now. Sarah was excused and my solicitor sat down. Sarah moved so gingerly that I could visualise the judge offering her a wheel chair for transport.

Why did you not question her about her behaviour within the family, her treatment of me or her contribution to the family? I asked my solicitor. The judges know and they have experience is all she said. To this day I do not understand what she meant. I desperately felt the desire to get out of there and seek a new trial or else I was screwed.

Now it was my turn in the witness box. I picked up my plastic shopping bag and walked to the altar, sorry witness box. I got nothing from my solicitor in either a sideways glance or an acknowledgment. Slowly yet deliberately I sat in the witness box. I had a trapped nerve in my lower back and could feel the onset of a headache. I took out my bottle of water, two tablets from my shopping bag and washed them down.

The judge did not look amused and I really could not give a flying fuck as I got ready for my funeral. Sarah was sitting in the back benches looking smug as she stared at me and smiled. I turned my gaze to the suit. He was fiddling through his stacks of A4 sheets. The court clerk came over to ask me about my religion and then handed me a worn out copy of the Quran. I repeated the same to tell the truth and nothing but the truth and he retreated. The suit calmly opened the buttons of his suit jacket, a sheet of paper in his hand and walked towards me. He looked intent and very serious indeed.

Why won't you give your wife money'? He barked. Why should I? I asked calmly. Because she is your wife, he reminded me. And I am her husband, was my retort. The suit was not amused and glanced towards the judge. But, she is your wife, he repeated. And, like I said, I'm her husband but, what has that got to do with anything? You're supposed to pay her money, he barked again. What for? I asked. Because she is your wife, he replied once more.

We have established the fact that I am her husband and she is my wife, so is that what we are going to do for the rest of the day. I asked, slightly amused. You'll tell me that she is my wife and I'll tell you that I'm her husband. Judge can you direct the witness to answer my question, he pleaded with the judge. Well judge as soon as the honourable counsel asks me a question I will answer it. Please tell him to stop making inane statements and pretend they are questions, was my contribution to this farce.

This appeared to light a fire under the suits backside. He paced the floor like a headless chicken struggling to get the beak out of his backside. Then he changed tact! Why don't you work full time, was his next question. I have to look after my daughters, I replied.

But you can work full time now that you are sharing them with your wife, he quipped. Yes I would as soon as things have settled down and a job becomes available, I replied. My back problems do not allow me to work long hours. And what's wrong with your back, he sneered. Are we to believe everything

244

you say? This man was beginning to piss me off but I had realised by now that he was digging a hole for himself. All I had to do was help pass the shovel. I rummaged through my well worn plastic bag and pulled out two letters from two eminent orthopaedic surgeons who were treating or had treated me regularly for the past seven years for sciatica. I looked at Sarah and her demeanour had changed. She looked worried. Maybe she realised that she had been less than truthful with her counsel. Suddenly the court clerk seemed interested in the proceedings. I handed the letters to him for deliverance to the judge and then they were passed over to the suit. He did not seem impressed and his hands began to tremble.

These prove nothing, he said unashamedly before handing the papers back to the court clerk. The court clerk looked amused. Even the judge's demeanour seemed quizzical.

I see that you work as golf professional, the suit enquired. No as a trainee PGA golf professional, I corrected him. For the first time the judge spoke to me and asked, what is this PGA? Professional Golfers Association, judge I answered respectfully. They train golf professionals. The suit did not enjoy me hogging the limelight. So you give golf lessons, he quickly interrupted. Yes, probably once a week or maybe every two weeks, I replied.

So you are well able to play golf but don't want to work, he sneered. No when my back feels good I can play golf but if the nerve gets trapped and inflamed without warning, then I am crippled. This can happen without forewarning, I informed him.

But surely you have to show your clients how to hit a golf ball? Yes if the need arises, which is seldom, I replied. So you want us to believe that you do not have to show your clients how to hit a golf ball and yet you can teach them to play golf, he asked innocently. Well you don't have to cut people every day to show your students how to become a doctor, do you, I asked. My response made the court clerk laugh and even the judge's face showed a wry smile. My solicitor sat there passive. If I did not know before, then I knew now that I was on my own.

The suit returned with a new sheet of paper. So what is it that you do at home, he asked. What I am asking you is that what else is it that you do? I gave you the answer before as to what I do. Why can't you be more direct with your questions, so I can give you the answer you are looking for? I don't do mind reading, was my retort.

Ok I'll make it simple for you, he seemed to jeer. So now you think I am a simpleton? I answered in the same tone. He looked at the judge. The judge laughed as he directed me to answer his questions. Judge, I'm doing my best. All he has to do is ask me a question and I will give him an answer, I replied innocently. The Judge looked at the suit and asked what question do you have? Do you have any questions for him? Yes, Judge, the suit replied. Please ask him the questions then. Mr. Anjum, please comply with the questions, the judge directed. Judge, I'll do my best, I promised.

So let me rephrase that, he offered. You are married, he asked. Whoopity do, this man is a genius; I thought and had no idea where he was heading. I think we have established that fact repeatedly otherwise I wouldn't be here. He looked at the judge and the Judge just threw his hands up in the air. The suit turned around and asked me, what would you like me to do? Be specific. What is your question? I asked. What do you do in your family environment? He asked. Every twenty four hours? I asked and he replied, yes.

I get up at six o clock in the morning, I go downstairs, I put the plates on the table, I take out the frying pan, then the bread and then the butter. When the alarm goes off I hear my daughters go to the bathroom one after the other. When they are finished in the bathroom I go and brush my teeth, shave, and answer if nature calls. While I'm in the bathroom they are getting dressed. I spoke slowly and deliberately. Are you with me so far? I asked and the suit gave me a dirty look as I continued. I don't need too much detail, the suit retorted. But this isn't too much detail, I corrected him. Usually by five past seven they are dressed. I brush my teeth, I shave then I get dressed. They go downstairs and prepare their school lunch while I cook the breakfast.

Their eggs have to be the right temperature, they can't be too hot nor can they be too cold. Their toast has to be warm and lightly buttered. While they are having breakfast I make them a cup of tea, then I sit down and have breakfast with them and then I take them to school. The suit looked infuriated.

Twenty to three their school is finished and I collect them and bring them home. They sit down and organise their homework while I make their tea. Then it's time for their homework and I get on with my chores. When the dinner is ready my wife joins us and sometimes contributes by setting plates on the table. Then we all eat. The girls watch their favourite programmes like Buffy the Vampire Slayer and Angel in the front room while Sarah goes upstairs for the evening and watches her favourites like Eastenders, Coronation Street and desperate housewives plus any current soap. After watching their programmes the girls return to their homework. My eldest daughter studies late into the night and suffers recurring headaches. I rub her head and try and put her to sleep. Rihana goes to bed before Aisha and then it's my time to settle downstairs. This can be eleven or two o clock in the morning.

Does that cover my twenty-four hours? I sounded angry and continued my rant. Oh, sorry I forgot to tell you that in between I put on the washing and do the ironing. There is the odd occasion for replacing buttons and stitching and repairing garments. I do have a sewing machine. Did I miss anything? I asked the suit.

Your honour will you please tell Mr. Anjum that this is not a game? He pleaded with the judge. Judge this is my life and not a game, was my reply. He asked a question and now I am answering it. If he does not like the answer, he should not have asked the question. I am sure he has done his homework with his client, because I hear he is very good at prepping his clients. The judge threw his two hands up in the air again and exhaled.

I brought to the suits attention that his client had her head firmly planted between her knees while she stared at the floor. And should she be looking at you? He sneered. Did she tell you that I sexually abused her? I continued and he chose to ignore my question.

So you claim to do everything around the house and pray tell me what is it that my client does, he asked sarcastically. After all she is only a mother. Why didn't you ask her when you had her in the witness box, I replied. I glanced at Sarah and she looked like shit. Even the judge looked in her direction and did not seem happy. The suit had not given up yet. What else is it that you do? He was back talking crap, again.

Well I do DIY, all the painting, decorating, household repairs and anything else that needs mending. Now the suit was looking exasperated. I don't know whether he was angry with me or with Sarah. May be he felt blindsided and for once it was not my fault. He turned towards me and repeated his question, and what else is it that you do? Well what else would you like me to do? I asked.

Can you just answer my questions, he thundered as he turned towards the judge seeking divine intervention. You may continue the judge waved to the suit.

So can you answer my earlier question, the suit asked once more. Judge I have no more job descriptions left, I said while ignoring the suit. The suit looked at the judge, the judge looked at the court clerk and I looked at everyone. They all had a smile of their faces bar Sarah and the suit. He was almost frothing at the mouth as I heard him mutter a curse under his breath.

Now I was enjoying myself and the court clerk was wide awake. Five o' clock had long come and gone. The suits hands were shaking so badly that he managed to knock his three neat bundles of A4 to the floor. He was busy collecting the papers when the judge asked, have you any more questions for the witness. Just one minute judge, he replied. His papers now looked a mess as he plonked them in a heap on his table. He was thinking and I decided to help.

Well you forgot to ask me about the sexual abuse, I reminded the suit. What sexual abuse? The judge asked quizzically. The suit looked fucked, well fucked indeed. His mouth was wide open. Well judge Sarah forgot to tell this court that I have sexually abused her, I volunteered. Now everyone but the suit saw what happened next. Sarah's head had disappeared between her knees. This was the fastest surgical recovery anyone could ever have witnessed.

Suit had no further questions, my solicitor had no further questions, I had a million questions but no one willing to answer and it was close to six. At five to six the judge made his ruling. No child maintenance payments were to be made by either party and joint custody was granted. The suit literally jumped out of his skin with indignation. Judge we will appeal this order, he almost screamed. The judge had turned and started to walk and the suit was talking to his fast disappearing backside.

The appeal never happened.

I stood up gingerly. By now my back was killing me and the head felt fuzzy. I promptly emptied the contents of my shaggy plastic bag, medicines, papers and plastic bottle in front of the witness box turned around and walked out of the court room.

My solicitor asked me to wait for her and I waited in the forecourt. She apologised for the delay and told me that we would meet before my judicial separation hearing. She was late coming out because while watching the proceedings, she had literally wet herself. Then she wished me good luck for the future and walked away.

A few months later the suit lost his life. He was in his late forties, loaded with cash and looking forward to climbing the ladder in social and legal circles. While drunk at his birthday party he tripped and banged his head against a table. He did not make it through the night. It was politely suggested that I killed him. I still remember his parting shot. If you are that good a parent then why the fuck don't your daughters live with you, he had sneered. May you rest in hell is the thought that often crosses my mind but then I remember the pain of being separated from my loved ones and I cannot wish ill on anyone.

Why, because I claim my love for my children and I am sure he was loved by his family. I shall let God be a judge of all our demeanours because my pain might cloud my judgment and I cannot allow that to happen. All I feel is sadness and nothing more! That was my first and hopefully last district court hearing of family law; I had hoped or maybe wished silently. The story did the rounds in legal and social circles. Everyone seemed amused and many wished they were a fly on the wall.

But my nuts were about to be wrenched even further. The system and its dysfunctionality bordering on criminality were to pursue me further. I went home and sat down quietly. There was no sense of justice or vindication. All of a sudden my life seemed empty and without purpose as it was spent looking after my family and now it was gone. I put on some music and played somewhere over the rainbow, one of my favourite songs. It had always been a source of comfort as I played on repeat and the tears began to well up. It seemed like I had cried for hours and after ten or more replays I had had enough.

Life had to go on and I went to collect my daughters from school. They were unusually quiet and seemed lost. We travelled home in silence. Aisha was so tired that twice she tripped over herself. Rihana was her quiet self never revealing her thoughts. One Friday we sat down and talked. Aisha was finding it difficult to cope with four days on four days off routine and her sleep pattern was in tatters. I found it difficult to suggest that they stay with one parent till Friday and the long weekend with the other. They both looked relieved. I think they felt torn between two parents and loyalties were stretched to the extreme.

From now on they decided to stay with their mother from Monday till Thursday evening and the rest was mine. At least now they will be settled and happy, or so I thought. While they stayed at their mother's house, I visited every evening. The first time I went to visit them Sarah walked towards my car. Aisha and Rihana immediately stood between her and my car blocking her approach. Leave him alone, they said in unison. They looked determined and angry as Sarah appeared to be taken aback.

I just want to talk to him, she whimpered. Well he does not want to talk to you, they told her. She slowly returned to the house. The next day she approached me again and invited me to have a look at her house. I told her emphatically that I had no wish to ever speak with her or to enter her house. Before she could answer the girls had appeared. Leave daddy alone, Aisha roared and Sarah left. We sat in the car and talked about the day's events. They seemed calmer settled down. Hugs and kisses with warmth were returning. One evening Sarah rang to tell me that she still loved me. I barely managed to put the phone down before running to the bathroom and emptying the contents of my stomach. Will this ever end; a thought had crossed my mind.

This is the very same woman who had made my daily life a living nightmare and yet there she was proclaiming her love for me. On one of my visits to Sarah's house Kate came over to apologise. She like the rest of her family was not aware of the extent of my pain or the damage my marriage had suffered.

The family assumed everything as Sarah never told them anything and she truly looked sorry. Sarah's niece, Jimmy's eldest daughter expressed the same sentiments. They both acknowledged that I sounded and looked much better since the separation. If only they knew the hell I had endured for seventeen years.

Many a time Aisha expressed her wish to come and live with me if I could get a different house. There were too many painful memories in this house for both my daughters. I could barely manage this house never mind moving to another. Other times she asked, Dad we used to be so close, what happened? She appeared sad and tearful but I had no answer. How could I? I did not even comprehend the question. The only thing I knew for sure was that my daughters had entered my heart from the time they were born, never to leave.

Chapter Thirteen

Now I had to sort out my own life which started by getting the bills transferred in my name. I also contacted the local council housing section for the transfer of lease in my name. There was another drama in the offing. I was called to a meeting with the housing officials. One of the officials was Pottymouth Pat whom I had met previously at a couple of public gatherings organised by the city council. She appeared a most odd character devoid of manners or etiquette. At the meeting I was tersely informed that I owed the council money in rent arrears. Even her colleague was shocked at her demeanour and the tone of her voice. But I have been regularly paying my rent and the statement shows that actually it's the council that owes me money in rents overpaid, I protested.

I had the statement in front of me. The dumbass was reading the statement incorrectly. I was over €400 in credit, as her colleague pointed out. She looked confused and angry at the same time. This does not matter she uttered. I have the annual rent assessment forms here and your name is not included on those forms for the past three years. Hence the lease in your name is illegal, she stated categorically.

Excuse me, I said. I have been living in this house for the past ten years and the lease was in joint names till we separated. If you look at the original lease you will see that since the house was built, I and my wife signed the lease as tenants and since our separation we came to the housing office and Sarah signed over the lease to me in front of your official as per her instructions. Pat's colleague pulled the stack of papers towards him. This woman has shit for brains it seemed. He looked over the papers and appeared sympathetic. Well who filled in these forms, he asked. It's always done by my wife. She has been filling them since we moved into the house. You should be able to compare her handwriting, I replied. Pottymouth looked confused and everything she said made no sense. Her colleague asked her to stay quiet. He brought the papers over to me and we both went through the assessment forms. The first eight years Sarah had filled the forms but then the handwriting had changed. This was Rihana's handwriting.

It later transpired that Sarah had dictated the details for Rihana to fill in. Poor Rihana was fourteen and none the wiser. How was she to know what her mother was up to? Any way the matter was settled, the lease was perfectly legal when Pat threw another spanner in the works. You still owe the council over two thousand five hundred Euros in adjusted rent. What adjusted rent? I asked. We have reassessed your rent by including you in the household for the past three years. She had a valid point. But this assessment should apply jointly, I protested again. You will have to pursue her for her half of the liability and she has committed fraud, I added. Not my headache, she retorted. You have the lease now, you have to pay or we can annul the lease, she replied. She took out the calculator and worked out her figures. After subtracting monies the council owed me I was lumbered with a bill for €2131.36 in rent arrears.

Lately I have taken legal advice to take the council to court and currently discussing the matter with my legal counsel if the moratorium allows. In 2005 I was emotionally and physically drained without an iota of fight left in me. I got up and left the meeting and settled the outstanding amount in later months. Now I wish that I had nailed the woman's sorry and incompetent ass to the pole outside the city hall building.

This reminds me of the time when the Irish government had decided to sell Eircom and its shares were offered for sale to the public on the open market. Like a lot of people I had purchased over ten thousand euro worth of shares in my, Sarah and our daughters names as an investment. Within three months of purchase I was advised by a financial adviser to offload them as soon as possible because they were about to take a nosedive. Sarah refused to sign. They were her shares, she had insisted. Two weeks later their worth was sixty percent of the price I had paid. Then she had signed the forms after a loss of €4,000 was incurred. This money I had intended for our daughter's college education. It was constantly coming to my awareness that not only was my marriage an emotional loss but a financial disaster at the same time. Her contribution at any given time was either negligible or nothing.

In 2005 I came across an article in the National Independent newspaper about a fathers group based in Tallaght, Dublin and I decided to give them a call. A most amicable guy called David answered the phone. We had a chat and he disclosed that Minister for Children Brian Lenihan was scheduled to officially open their centre the following day. I was invited to the event in Dublin for the 7 April 2005.

The minister was due to arrive at 11 am and he asked me to be there early. I got up at 5 am the next morning, tidied myself up and headed for Dublin. I was willing to travel anywhere and face the devil to help change this god forsaken system. I got there an hour early but got to know the guys. They all seemed well meaning while David Carroll showed me around the place and introduced me to his fellow directors, David Whyte and Eamon Quinn. Ray was out there somewhere he said. They had four directors and appeared a well organised team. David asked me if I would like to say a few words at the event and I said yes without hesitation.

The moment of truth arrived and the minister appeared. As they were entered the building I was hastily introduced to Ray who was with the minister like a blue bottle hovering around stale fruit and buzzing. As he walked past me he muttered, who invited him pointing in my direction. I had never seen or met

255

with this man before. David Carroll told me not to take much notice and we proceeded to the hall. There was a good mixture of people in the crowd. I was invited to sit with the minister and Ray flanked him on the other side.

Minister was eloquent but never addressed the issues on hand in his presentation. It seemed a very prettily wrapped Christmas box with nothing inside and then I was invited to speak. I could not stand up as my legs suddenly refused to budge. I remained seated and began to speak. I felt detached from my surroundings till I noticed a black line of mascara running down a young woman's cheek. She was sitting in the front row. Then I heard a man begin to sob while a couple of middle aged women wiped away a stray tear or two. I have no idea of what I had said and thanked them all for being there and offered my gratitude to David Carroll for inviting me.

Then Ray spoke from the soap box and soon it was all over. We began to filter out in the open for tea and biscuits as I walked out to the main entrance. I felt empty and had no appetite. Then people approached me and started to shake my hand while commending my speech. Before long I was surrounded by ladies who wished me the very best as they went for tea. The minister approached and asked me about my crusade while briefing on the complexity of the system and how it had to be dealt with one piece at a time. Then he wished me good luck and left.

There was a shy looking gentleman staring from a distance. When all had cleared he came over to shake my hand and proceeded to give me a warm hug. Today for the first time I heard what needed to be said, he whispered. You spoke for every decent Dad in the country, he added. He was a lecturer in University College Dublin and had endured hell at the hands of his former partner with no end in sight. He hugged me again and promised to be in touch before disappearing in the distance. We spoke thereafter and he reiterated that my words had provided him with some solace. He went to write a research paper which is currently on my website.

Then events at work took a nasty turn. One evening a gentleman turned up at the pro shop and requested courtesy of the golf course. The professionals are allowed to afford courtesy to fellow golf professionals at the discretion of the head professional. All else is decided and informed by the club secretary or its committee. There were no instructions left in the shop for affording courtesy to this gentleman. I politely informed him of the club policy and also that I did not have the authority to say either yes or no.

He became very angry and informed me that he was playing golf courses around the country for a charity and seemed highly indignant. The office was closed and I could not contact anyone. I politely told him that I will see if the course ranger was on call as I had neither the authority nor discretion. Then he became abusive and now I was the recipient of racist abuse in one of the top golf clubs in the country. His parting shot advised me to get back on the fucking banana boat that had brought me here.

The course ranger was found, he played the course and I did not see him again. The next morning there were committee members rushing around and I heard that a meeting had been called. My boss was called to attend. Upon his return he was raging and wanted to know what had happened. I narrated the whole story. The bastards! They are trying to put the shit on you. Just stay out of their business. Golf clubs and their feckin committees, he was seething. He agreed that I had done nothing wrong. Just stay away from them, he repeated.

The news had travelled and one of the junior members Patrick asked me the reason for being upset and I told him. Within twenty minutes his dad appeared in the shop. He is a renowned practicing solicitor and one of the club members. He had always made time for me and offered to take my case against the club and the jackass who had abused me. Then the proverbial shit decided to hit the fan. Alan, the boss's son asked what happened and I told him. He was livid and now he wanted to speak with the club secretary. This was quickly turning into a circus.

My solicitor wrote to the club demanding an explanation and the club tried to pass the buck by saying they had no responsibility towards the on goings in the pro shop. It was the head professional's headache. In the evening the club captain arrived in the pro shop in an inebriated state accusing me of telling lies against a gentleman of good character and bringing the club's name to disrepute. He ordered me to withdraw my statement or else I would seriously have to rethink my position within the golf club.

While this went on I was searching for an office space with the purpose of opening a support group for separated fathers. One of the local golfers, Dick Pryce was in the pro shop discussing the above mentioned event and the subject came up during our conversation. I told him that I had discussed the matter with two members of parliament, deputies Noel Grealish and Padraic McCormack and Noel had promised to get me a rent free office from one of his friends for a period of six months till I was able to stand on my feet. I had not liked the office because it was too posh.

Who else have you spoken to? He asked. I had also spoken to a wealthy local property developer who also happened to be a club member. He had promised to help but three weeks later told me that his association with me would be bad for his business as it's always women who choose the house and this would be detrimental to his business. Dick seemed angry. He asked me to come down to his offices on Tuam road and promised me an office on the terms Noel had offered. The office needed cleaning and a lick of paint but was available. He empathised with my cause and promised to help. It was later disclosed that Dick's younger brother had been screwed to the tune of a couple of million Euros in divorce settlement while he was left destitute and penniless with massive debts.

After work I went to see Dick to look at the office on offer. This was July of 2005. The office was cluttered with broken furniture, rubbish and really dirty. Well you can clean this up and have it for six months rent free, he offered. Then we signed an agreement for twelve months from 1 January 2006 till 31 December 2006 with €5,000 payable at the end of twelve months. Now I had an office for eighteen months and spent two weekends, cleaning, washing and painting before carpets were laid and it looked like an office. I paid for everything.

My boss was away for the weekend and letters were going to and fro when on a Friday I went to work at 0945 and Alan, the boss's son blocked my entry to the shop. He said that there were two gentlemen there who wished to speak with me. Two gentlemen, one of whom I recognised from the local Salthill police station came forward and informed me that an allegation had been made stating I had stolen a set of Callaway golf clubs from the shop. Its total cost €399.

I was dumbstruck and looked at Alan for an explanation and none was forthcoming. He had been called to the course secretary's office and shown a video of me leaving the pro shop with a set of golf clubs which were given to me the previous day by Jason from Wilson sporting goods. He, like other suppliers was regularly giving me golf clubs for trial and feedback but they were not available on the open market.

Alan why would I take a set of poxy golf clubs from the shop when I have left thousands of Euros worth of golf clubs in the shop that were given to me, I asked. He did not volunteer an answer. There was something strange going on and I needed to get to the bottom of it. He demanded the front door key which I promptly handed over to him. I asked the cops to call Jason and verify my statement which was duly confirmed. The clubs Alan claimed I had stolen were nowhere to be found. I took the cops to my car where I always kept my golf clubs. My personal clubs were always supplied and custom fitted by Mizuno. They were looking for a set of Callaway's. I asked the cops what else they would like me to do. They told me that unless Alan could provide proof the matter would be closed. Well he could have hidden them anywhere, how about his house? Alan piped.

I asked the cops to accompany me to my house and they politely declined. There was no need and they considered the matter closed. I insisted that it would help me a great deal if they were to do as I asked and they reluctantly agreed. Alan followed us to my house. I opened the front door and asked the cops to search whatever and wherever they liked while I waited outside. Alan wanted to go in and I warned him that I would kill him if he dare step inside my house.

The cops told him politely to go away as they took details of the allegedly stolen golf clubs and entered my house. For the next hour and a half they went through everything, including chimneys, loft, bedrooms, under the beds, in the wardrobes, the garden shed and found nothing. They were thorough and professional. Then they appeared and told Alan that nowhere in my house were his alleged clubs and the rep had verified my story of the clubs I was seen taking out of the shop the previous day.

Alan's face was in a state of shock. It looked like he was about to have a heart attack. The cops gave me their business cards and asked me to come to the station the following morning to make a statement and then left. Alan was long gone.

I arrived at the police station the next morning for my interview. There was no interview. The cops had called me to the station to explain and apologise for the events of the previous day. They also advised me to pursue Alan through court and seek damages. They had also spoken to one of their superiors who had vouched for me as a gentleman worthy of anyone's trust. They were willing to appear in court as witnesses and assured me with a handshake as they departed.

I suppose every cloud has a silver lining. I called my solicitor and informed him of the day's events. He was livid and ready to sue both the club and Alan. It seemed in his opinion that the club had got to Alan and advised him on the course of action to take in order to get rid of me and save the club hassle. They had gone through the club CCTV and found me leaving with a set of clubs which became a perfect premise for the day's events. I never claimed that Alan was the sharpest tool in the box.

On Monday I returned to the clubhouse and went to see my boss. I had always held my boss in the highest regard. He appeared upset and wanted to know what had happened. He got angry and called his son useless and everything else under the sun. What can I do, he is my lousy son, he said. He should have waited till I returned he said dejectedly. The committee got to him was his opinion.

The club had no contract with my boss and Alan was told to toe the club's line or they would be required to vacate the pro shop as they did not have a written contract with the golf club. Now everything was becoming clearer. The club had pressurised the idiot into making an ass of himself. I decided to call it a day, picked up my belongings and left. It was impossible for me to continue to work in the shop after all that had expired. I only wished to remove my personal belongings from the workshop which were stored in black bin liners.

My boss gave me a letter of recommendation, two weeks pay and I was gone till I received a call from him a couple of weeks later asking for a meeting and we met in the car park at the golf club. He was emotional and in tears. He pleaded with me that Alan had a young family and two little kids. He had always treated me well and asked me to withdraw the court proceedings against his son.

Please don't destroy my son's life, he pleaded. I promised Sean that I would instruct my solicitor to withdraw the case against Alan. He was most grateful and looked relieved. He had always been like a father to me. What else could I do? He gave me a hug and handed me a bundle of notes. I refused to take his money. Please take it for your cause, he said as he placed the money in my hand and left.

My solicitor was not agreeable. He wanted me to punish the club and Alan for what they had done to me. I was exhausted and had no fight left in me. What little energy I had was spent looking after my daughters and the office.

I instructed him to close all matters and left. He advised me to think again, carefully. I had made up my mind and this chapter was closed. I had to move on. I really needed to pick up the pieces and get on with my life.

While working at the golf club I finished work at six and headed for the office where I worked till eleven maybe midnight. Now I could dedicate all my time to 'the cause'. Separated men were coming from all corners of the country. I catered for their needs when my daughters were staying with their mother. Life was hard enough without taking on a new project but someone had to do it.

Chapter Fourteen

Now most of my time was spent answering phone calls from men suffering hell on earth. They needed to speak to someone, anyone who could relate to them. I got a low call number which cost me a small fortune in later years. I thought surely these guys would help in the long run. Suddenly poor Panda comes to mind as he eats, shoots and leaves. I was about to meet a lot of Pandas, thousands of them, all dressed in tri colour.

In the interim I was back annoying Messrs Frank Fahey, Noel Grealish and Deputy McCormack. After my last meeting with minister Fahey I had phoned an accountant friend of mine and requested registering a company under Fathers for Justice, Equality and Law Reform. Well I had told the minister if he and his department won't do their job I will do it for them. They were big words and no money.

I returned to his office in 2006 with a begging bowl. We had two meetings and in between I phoned his department in a state of distress while offloading my story on a poor woman who dared listen. She was most kind and sympathetic. She informed me that our ministers were scared of women's lobbies and support groups. They could have whatever they wanted but there was nothing for men. Men were hopeless at fighting their cause and they were clueless and useless, she added. In later years the same was repeated a thousand times and more and her statement was vindicated.

I brought the original proposal back to the minister's table. I had the company registered; application made to the Inland Revenue for granting of charity status and was back looking for financial assistance. Can you please help find some money for my office, I pleaded with the minister and he promised to look into the matter. Thankfully my accountant friend in his wisdom had discarded the title of the minister's department and had it renamed Fathers for Equality and Justice Limited. I was granted charity status in February of 2006 but still had no money.

At our next meeting I informed the minister of my achievement. He looked a little surprised because usually it took a lot longer than two months to get a company registered and obtain charity status. Not only that but I had managed to table several questions in Dail Eireann (Irish Houses of Parliament) and obtained figures relating to funding provided for women's support networks. It was twelve million euro plus rising while allocation for men stood at ZERO.

I also informed him that his department had just approved the funding for the appointment of two part time outreach workers based in the local charity COPE. They run the local women's shelter among other projects and help run a shelter for men suffering from alcohol and drugs dependency. The cost of part time outreach workers was €32,995 for Galway and €28,995 for Tuam. They went around knocking on people's front doors after men had left for work and questioned women on how their partners behaved towards them. They were giving them lessons in what constituted domestic violence and how to deal with it.

Soon thereafter I started to get calls from irate women complaining about these 'Bitches' and advised me to do something about them. Like a lot of things in later years I was being voluntarily allocated unpaid portfolios without a penny's worth of support from Joe public.

The meeting with the minister went well and he promised to pursue the matter of funding. A fortnight later I was called to the minister's office and he looked furious. Let's go to my private office, he said and I followed him. His personal assistant Claudia was present and the door was closed. He paced around the floor and looked extremely angry. He had made a recommendation from dormant funds of €30,000 in funding to my charity and was furious because his request for funding was turned down and he needed answers. The secretary general had never turned down the minister's recommendation before this incident.

Any ideas? He asked. I had plenty of them but didn't want to share. They would sound unbelievable, even if true. The only one that came to mind was the former attorney general, then minister for justice and a distinguished senior counsel Michael McDowell. He was minister Fahey's boss. I had been a vocal critic of King's Inns, the Law Society and their hierarchy which not only protected incompetent law practitioners but were complicit in their heavy handed dealing with clients. Especially the barristers whose fee structures are seldom disclosed and they went around national universities lecturing law students in the benefits of becoming a barrister.

Their tag line was that when they became a barrister they had reached the pinnacle of society and could charge as they pleased. All they had to do was turn up for the court hearing. I had repeatedly accused the Law Society and its members of unprofessionalism and incompetence without accountability to anyone.

The law society had over 20,000 outstanding complaints against solicitors on its books. Blatantly and persistently they were found in breach of section 68 of the Solicitor's Amendment Act of 1994 and thus far none had been held accountable. I was beginning to point out the flaws in legislation and its conflict with the constitution and European law and had already been told that I was disliked in the inner circle and should desist from tabling questions in Dail Eireann. Alongside I criticised the autocracy and hypocrisy of judges in family law and their incompetence, inconsistencies and ignorance in dispensation of family law, abuse of power, procedures and judicial discretion.

In the interim my phone was tapped as I was informed by some members of our police force who were sick and tired of the arrogance of Minister McDowell and the way their department was being treated. And here was I, a penniless foreigner, naturalised Irish national taking on the might of the state and its corrupt and dysfunctional faculties with empty pockets. Well minister I don't know what to say is all I could contribute in wisdom.

The secretary general has promised to give me in writing his reasons for declining my request, the minister stated. Let's give it two or three weeks and see what happens and then we parted. A fortnight later I phoned his office and they were waiting for the written reply. I rang again and they were still waiting. I rang the justice department and got through to the finance section. A young woman whose name I cannot disclose told me that the reply was being prepared but the ministerial file requesting funding allocation for my charity had disappeared.

After resigning her post she made further disclosures about other corrupt practices and felt compelled to resign her post. This was 2006 and when in 2010 another minister requested the discovery of the very same files, they still could not be found. Needless to say not a penny materialised in funding.

Now it was the turn of local councillors and I knew most of them. I sent them emails and phoned them personally. God bless the thirteen of them who turned up in my office except my friendly former mayor, champion of all things good and my friendly barrister Ms Catherine Connolly. Her younger sister Collette was present. The two sisters collectively served on more committees than their male counterparts, were forceful, resourceful and more potent than their male counterparts put together.

The Mayor Brian Walsh was a most amicable young man in his early thirties, full of energy, wit and wisdom. They needed to know why I had called on them and I told them; the family law, its practices, its impact on men's mental health, the rates of depression and suicide among males, their exclusion from government social policy and their exclusion from the Irish constitution as fathers, so on and so forth.

One of our councillors was a practising family law practitioner. He concurred whole heartedly with my sentiments and stated that family law and its practices should be dumped in its current form and started from scratch. But alas the vested interests were far too powerful. Councillor Padraig Conneely was unusually quiet. He is renowned as the most charismatic character in local politics and a fierce critic of establishment. He appeared eerily quiet.

Two motions were passed in my office; to seek help for my cause and second were an acknowledgement as me being the only person ever to keep Councillor Conneely quiet for so long. Both motions were passed unanimously but neither materialised. At the end of the meeting best wishes were bestowed and the councillors departed after tea, coffee and refreshments.

Councillor Connolly stayed for a while and made the disclosure that still stands true. Irish men are good for nothing when it came to their issues and women had fought hard to gain power and will not let go of it easily.

I returned to answering calls from separated Irish Dads who had nothing more to offer than their tales of woe and I did the best I could. I set up a basic website which developed over time and within six months of its inception was receiving in excess of 40,000 hits per month. Ten to fifteen calls per week came from around the country before the ex pats from U.K, the rest of

Europe and North America began to call looking for advice on matters of family law. Every penny I had was spent on my daughters and paying the office bills while I survived on two egg sandwiches a day.

To help raise funds, I decided to organise a golf tournament with the help of a dear friend, Roger Griffin. Declan Cunningham from Golfstyle was most generous with his support in provision of prizes as were the reps from golf companies. Barna Golf Club looked after me thanks to one of its directors, Mr Pat Donnellan, an all Ireland legend in GAA.

Roger and his family have always been there to support me through thick and thin, as Seamus Langan proved a friend indeed. I probably owe my life and what little is left in sanity to these two friends. Prizes worth €12,000 and more brought in a princely sum of just over €3,000. This became an annual event for the next five years till I felt emotionally, physically and financially drained and got tired of doing all things single handed. Pandas never came to help.

Once again my good friend Jason from Wilson came to my assistance. He hired me as a technical consultant for sports trade shows and demo days. It paid handsomely and promptly which enabled me to put money aside for my daughters and the rent for the office which was due at the end of the year 2006. I had kept Dick Pryce informed of my financial dilemmas at any given time. His answer was always the same; you are doing good work, don't worry about the money. I trusted him till the end of 2011 when he changed his tune and tried to sue me for back rent.

My good friend Mark Sturdy of Golf Glider called to see if I could do some work for him. He makes electronic golf carts and it would help him a great deal if I covered his repairs and warranty this side of the country. I needed money and it was a no brainer. Now I was repairing caddy cars, counselling free of charge, studying, researching, dealing with politicians but most importantly, I never neglected my daughters. They always came first and often surprised me with a visit to the office. It was always wonderful to see them. They were both working at the weekends. Aisha got her marks and entered university to study corporate law and Rihana was at the tail end of her secondary school year.

Whenever I phoned Aisha was found walking to or back from the university, whatever the weather. Rihana had the same routine even though she was working in the evenings and did not finish till half ten or eleven at night. The news of attacks on women was rife and sexual assault and rape seemed daily news. And my darling daughters were walking home.

Sarah's house is over five miles from mine. Aisha's university and Rihana's work were equidistant to Sarah's house. Every evening Rihana worked I decided to collect her from work and dropped her at Sarah's house. Aisha was more independent, seldom did she ask or took a lift. I believe she was angry with the whole world and especially me. The rage was beginning to surface.

Since separation my phones were on 24 hours a day, just in case my daughters needed me. Many a time a neighbour would ring to tell me that my daughters were standing outside their mother's house, crying. To date I have not been told why. She had no friends and now no one in the estate wished her acquaintance.

The calls from men began arriving at all hours of the day, especially after pub closing times. They were in tears and lost as they sought perfect solutions that did not exist. They had no understanding of the complexity and dysfunctionality of the family law system which is heavily entrenched in the mother's corner. Multiple Pandora's boxes were being opened with consequential nightmares. I still did not realise that I was being sucked into a black hole. The more I helped these men, the more they took with nothing offered in return. It only took me seven years and a bit to figure out the adage of a man being like a panda.

Now Sarah pulled another stunt and a letter from the department of social and family affairs arrived on my doorstep. Somehow Sarah had claimed and was being paid lone parents allowance. Seldom were fathers given custody of their children. A mother's rights to her children are deemed inalienable and enforced in legislation, constitution, judicial discretion, jurisprudence, Supreme Court precedence and application of family law in Ireland.

The letter from maintenance recovery unit stated that as Sarah was being paid by the department they wanted me to reimburse them. I picked up the phone, rang their office and demanded an explanation. Public and civil servants are not very good at explaining their actions. Instead they prefer to shut you out, because they can and who is going to challenge them? It had to be this muppet of course.

Next stop was deputy Padraic Mc Cormack's office which resulted in questions for the Minister for Justice and the Minister for Social and Family Affairs requiring a written answer to the question;

- If and when a civil or public servant can overrule a court order?

I already knew the answer, never. A court order can only be over ruled by a superior court. I possessed a court order stating that I did not have to pay a penny in maintenance.

Now Padraic wrote a letter to the department while I phoned their head office and was passed from one officer to another. I could visualise headless chickens ducking and diving while singing; oops we did it again. I like many others went through Britney phase plus the tune is so catchy but I could not catch one of these elusive feckers.

They fucked up again. Oops, I was about to quote Miss Britney Spears once again. A two page reply to a member of parliament full of garbage in sections and sub sections stating how and when they could bypass law and a court order. Then a letter arrived from the local office of department of social and family affairs. Mr Michael Spade, an investigating officer was looking for an appointment to visit my office and enquire about my financial affairs because it had been reported to him, by my wife, that I was making loads of money by fixing electronic caddy cars.

I picked up the phone, gave him an appointment while informing him that I will be in his office first thing in the morning. I also asked him to have all his questions and paper work ready for I did not have time to waste. I asked him about his time of arrival at his office. He said 9.30 am and I disclosed my intent of being there at 9.25 and then put the phone down.

At 9.10am I knocked on his door and walked in. I apologised for my early arrival and asked him what he needed from me. Please take a seat Mr Anjum, he directed me towards an empty chair. He had a file sitting on his table and pulled out a letter. It was my wife's handwriting and a newspaper snippet of an advert giving my contact number for repair of golf caddy cars. My wife had written a two page letter inclusive of the newspaper clipping.

He wanted details of my earnings. I refused to comply. Do you have any other questions, I asked. He had none. Who gave you the right to investigate me without substance? I demanded to know. Well we are paying your wife and have the right to claim our money back. She is not my wife and that is why she is not living with me, do you understand that, I asked him. He nodded.

If you want to pay her, that's your choice and not my headache. Do you know that I have a court order stating that there is no order of maintenance against me, I asked the dimwit. She did not tell us as you can see in the letter, he said sheepishly. By now there were two of his colleagues peering through the door. He got up from behind his table and walked to close the door after telling them that all was in order. Well we have to act on information provided to us, was his solemn reply. This man was dumber than a dumb ass, god bless him. So what do you want to do now, I asked calmly. We will have to investigate this matter further, he said. Well you do that and if you ever come near me, ever again, you will regret it for the rest of your life, were my parting words. I never heard from him again.

I had more business to attend to with the senior civil servant who had written the letter of explanation to Padraic. I rang her and her secretary informed me that she was out of office but will return in a couple of days. She was pregnant and was off sick for a couple of days. A week later I got a call from her secretary requesting that I hold the line as Ms Mighty would like to speak with me. I enquired about the contents of her letter and she replied that she stood by the contents of her letter and did I have a question for her. Yes as a matter of fact I have, I said very politely. Do you only hire mindless idiots to work in your department and what are you going to do with regards to my query, I asked.

She sounded indignant. I do not have to listen to you calling my staff names and what query, she barked. Your letter, are you standing by its content, I asked. Well I am standing by the letter sent by my department, she replied. So what you are saying is that you and your staff can over ride a court order, I asked very politely. Well I never said that and if you do not like the contents of my departmental letter then take us for judicial review. I was not referring to the departmental letter but in fact the letter you wrote, signed and posted for the attention of Deputy McCormack. Would you like me to read the contents of the said letter, I asked sweetly. I heard a hundred litres of air sucked in a millisecond before she put the phone down.

I am stubborn as a mule and dumb as an ass and simply don't know when to quit. In my quest for justice I was still hell bent on fighting the system with not a dime to my name. I contacted solicitors and narrated my tales of woe, took out the letters and asked how much they would charge. One lady who later became a dear friend agreed to take my case free of charge. She was aware of my work and wanted to help. Now all I had to do was find a barrister with balls. Those were her instructions. In this fraternity men with balls are a rare breed. I asked Ann how much could a barrister cost for judicial review? €10,000 upwards depending on how much the state wants to fight and the length of time it takes for the case to conclude, she replied.

Now my hunt for a barrister began. Without money no one seemed interested. A snippet of Ann's advice hit home. Find a newly qualified barrister who wants to make a name for himself and is not yet influenced by the inner circle. I had an open and shut case with proof in black and white. All I needed was a wig and a gown and instead found a procession of clowns, aplenty.

A friend of mine's brother, Brendan had just qualified as a barrister and I rang him through the Bar council. I left a message for his attention and he duly returned my call. Barristers can only take cases through a solicitor but he agreed to meet with me for an informal chat in Galway and we met. He was meeting a few friends for lunch in McSwiggan's in woodquay and gave me ten minutes. I showed him the letters and explained the basis for seeking judicial review. He seemed excited like a goose ready to lay a golden egg.

Let's get it moving, he said. From now on we will communicate through your solicitor. Now go and find one a sap, he said. I already have, was my reply. I believe by now he felt half a dozen golden eggs ready to escape his orifice. Do you know any senior counsel who will work pro bono, he asked and my answer was no. Don't worry, I will find one, he assured me. I left him to savour his lunch. It felt good as I left the restaurant. This will help change this fucked up system or so I thought. The pressure seemed to have eased as I walked to my car in a fairly happy mood.

I sensed someone was staring at me but did not know who. It is a narrow footpath barely wide for two people to pass and instinctly I turned around. The person who had brushed past me was Sarah. She was walking away yet looking over her shoulder towards me with a very confused look. My wife had just walked past me, brushed past my shoulder and I did not recognise her. Surely this was a good sign and I was over her. Feeling happy and quietly content, the rest of the hell was forgotten as I returned to my normal days being a daddy to all with nothing in return except compliments and best wishes. All the dearest would depart till the next time they needed me.

Next day Noel Grealish's secretary rang to ask me to come to Noel's office. At the time I was very angry with politicians. If he wants to meet with me he can come to my office, I replied. The poor thing was taken aback. Let me talk to Noel and I'll call you back, she stammered. A few minutes later the phone rang. She had spoken with Noel and wanted to know my address. I duly obliged. Half an hour later deputy Grealish was sitting in my office. Noel is an honourable member of our parliament and there he was looking so embarrassed.

Sorry Sam it took so long. The Minister for Justice Michael McDowell has agreed to meet with you. He will be debating with Sinn Fein to reclaim the tri colour in National University of Ireland Galway in a few days time. Can you make the meeting? He has allocated half an hour for your meeting and bring one or two of your clients if you like. Bring the camera and we can take some pictures with the minister, he offered. I thanked Noel sheepishly and he left after a warm handshake. One minute the state gave me every reason to kill myself and next it was meetings with the ministers.

I invited two of my clients, John McGuire and Pat O' Hindenburg, a retired army sergeant to accompany me. Then I asked a young lady from Carrick on Shannon whose brother was enduring the hell of family law if she would like to meet with the minister and they were all happy to oblige. While John and Pat's cases were run of the mill, mother gets children, keeps the house, gets child benefit, maintenance payments and both were paying through the nose, Mary's brothers case was slightly different.

He was an unmarried father in his early thirties who had been granted interim custody of his children. It's extremely rare for an unmarried father to get custody of his children. It transpired that his former partner had severe psychological problems hence he was granted custody of his children. Her parents had warned him that they had money and would not rest till they found a judge favourable in getting their grandchildren back. Some years later they succeeded in their objective and children were returned to their mother. The sad part is the young man was suffering from incurable cancer and passed away two years later. The children were not allowed a visit to their father's funeral.

The evening of the meeting arrived; I gathered my guests and gave them instructions on protocol. The minister had allocated

5.30 pm for our meeting and was due for 7 pm in NUIG Galway for his debate with Sinn Fein, 'To Reclaim the Tricolour'. Noel came to inform us that meetings were running late and we would be called soon. At five to six we were called to find the minister for justice sitting flanked by Deputy Noel Grealish and two female members of his staff to his left and his private secretary to the right.

I sat opposite, facing him with Pat to my right and John and Mary to my left. Noel introduced me to the minister and we shook hands. Then I introduced my guests and asked Pat if he would like to speak with the minister first. That was a bad move on my part. Instead of sticking to his problems with family law Pat began narrating his life story. I had warned them all of time constraints yet Pat got busy outpouring his sorrows while the minister frowned. I nudged Pat several times but to no avail till Noel virtually told him to shut up. John had little to say and Mary was brief with her story. Then the minister's attention turned to me. He has a reputation for being arrogant, brash and condescending to say the least.

So what is your problem, he literally barked. Not a good start, I thought. Pat had made us look like a bunch of prats and now I was supposed to argue the case of morons. Instead of talking about my personal life I went straight for my problems with judiciary and law practitioners. His face was rapidly turning red. And what's your problem with them? He asked. I talked about fathers rights or the lack of them, incompetence in practice, lack of knowledge of family law, inconsistencies in application of law and court orders, reluctance to enforce court orders against mothers, safety and barring orders on tap, lack of jurisprudence and lack of accountability to mention but a few.

He was slightly taken aback and the look of derision had waned. And what's wrong with family law, he asked. He did not look happy. I recited the constitution and lack of recognition of fathers within family, lack of practice of equality, legal precedents, reluctance of successive governments in setting up dedicated family law courts, so on and so forth. His eyes had narrowed. By now he knew that I was no schmuck. He is a senior counsel after all. He opened his top collar, loosened his tie and hence began a discussion. There was no way on god's earth that I was going to be beaten, at least not that day.

Noel repeatedly informed the minister that they were getting late for his next engagement but the minister was busy arguing with me. At ten to seven Noel managed to pull the minister away and informed him that they had to go, now. The minister sat back in the chair, exhaled, buttoned his top collar, straightened his tie and stood up. He extended his hand across the table and offered a meeting in Leinster house to be organised by Deputy Noel Grealish. Let's continue this discussion over lunch, were his exact words. I acknowledged to await Noel's call and looked forward to the said meeting. It never happened. Every time I called Noel, I was told that the minister had a very busy schedule and was having difficulty finding time in his diary. Eventually I tabled a question in Dail Eireann asking the minister about the meeting and when it would happen. Using privilege of the house the minister replied in writing stating that he had never met with me and no such meeting was ever offered. I have sworn affidavits in hand from two of the three guests that came to the meeting and I am sure the honourable counsel's staff can jog his memory with regards the truth of the matter.

Many a time the former minister has since been invited to debate with me but sadly has declined including the occasion in 2011 when NUIG Law Society organised and invited him to debate on matters of family law. Initially he accepted the meeting but four days before the debate he excused himself stating clash of dates in his diary. I was later informed that initially he was not aware of his opponents name but after acceptance of the invitation my name was mentioned which necessitated the excuse. Only god knows the truth.

The word 'deadbeat dads' was in vogue with the media, especially fuelled by the then Minister for Social and Family Affairs, Seamus Brennan. After verbally bashing fathers for years, in 2005 he made a statement in the Irish Examiner stating that fathers will be given equal rights in law. That pig never flew.

In 2010 the current Minister for Communications, Energy and Natural Resources, Pat Rabbitte in an interview with Olaf Tyrannsen which was published in The Hot Press magazine stated that he found it unbelievable that the matter of unmarried fathers and father's rights had still not been resolved. Now I find it unbelievable that he is a minister in government and not a dickey boo. This response has been consistent from successive ministers and governments with regards fathers rights and matters of family law.

Having returned to my world there was a letter waiting from my solicitor and I went to meet with her. She had a half moon smile on her face. At last someone is willing to fight your corner, she said. Brendan had confirmed his acceptance in writing to represent me, that I was known to him and he was offering his services free of charge. He was going to engage a senior counsel and will be in touch shortly. At last, Ann exclaimed. Now we were both happy.

Soon our local papers expressed interest in their wish to speak with me and subsequently articles were published in Galway Advertiser and the Galway Independent. It was soon followed by Limerick and Cork. Galway Independent did a full page profile and one of my letters got published in the Irish Examiner. It was not long before a journalist from Connacht Tribune phoned me. I made time and she arrived with basic questions in matters of family law. She said that this subject was more appropriate for a national daily and would write a small article which was duly published in The Times on page four.

The very next day on 13 July 2006 RTE news came to my office. I got more than fifteen minutes on the evening news and things looked better than they did before. Now I turned my attention to the national and international media. It started with RTE, TV3, Sky news and all the national radio stations but no one expressed an iota of interest.

Then I decided to write to the director general of RTE with regards equality of coverage and received a written reply assuring me that the principle of equality is and will be applied. When contacted, a researcher from Gerry Ryan show informed me that the show did not deal with issues such as father's rights and family but advised me that it would be more appropriate to speak with someone of the calibre of Marian Finnucane or Pat Kenny. Guess what, I rang them both and got passed from pillar to post till the producer of Pat Kenny show, Pat Costello came on the line.

She was most professional and gave me a listening ear. She thought it was an excellent idea to speak with Pat and acknowledged that I was the first person who appeared decent, knowledgeable and appropriate for the show. The schedule for the show is organised six months in advance and if I were willing she would try and move the schedule around. Does a Bedouin need an oasis? I agreed immediately. I told her that as soon she was ready I would make myself available.

She promised to call me the next morning and seemed very excited. I received a call the next morning and her tone appeared strange, reserved and almost frightened. She explained that she had to consult their legal department as per practice and was strongly advised that if I were to say anything in breach of *'in camera'* RTE did not possess enough funds if litigation was to ensue. I assured her that I was fully aware of the principle of *'in camera'* and the discussion on air would ensure that the said principle was not breached. She still seemed unwilling to pursue this conversation. After a few minutes it was agreed that she would try and include me in the next schedule of programmes. I have not been able to contact her since that conversation despite having been put through to her extension on numerous occasions. The sound of my voice and name ensured disconnection of the line. She was not willing to speak with me anymore.

Now my attention was turned to Galway Bay fm and Keith Finnegan. Keith is a highly respected broadcaster and CEO of the radio station. He organised the time and the interview took place. He was astonished to hear my narration of family law and its practices and the live broadcast ruffled a lot of feathers.

After my live on air talk with Keith Finnegan I received a call from one of Ray's friends. There was a woman on the phone who had chewed his ears. No name given but claimed to be a friend of Sarah's family and was disgusted that men like me were allowed in their organisation and proceeded to call me everything under the sun. But she gave no name. I asked him to call Ray and find the phone number on his calls received database. I told him how to check for the number and he promised to call me back with the number.

It was Sarah's home line. She had told Ray that I was scum, a useless husband, a shit father and for the next forty five minutes abused me and threatened to sue Ray's organisation for god knows what. Ray never got a word in edgeways which is most unusual. You were married to this woman, he exclaimed. Yup, is all I could mutter. Thus began Sarah's abusive and threatening emails through my website and contact us pages. The first stated, how does it feel that your daughters don't ever want to see you again? Hurt, but I did not pay much heed as I was well used to her abuse.

2006 was coming to an end and I owed rent for the office. I had managed to save some money from my stints on the trade shows and had to borrow some more from a dear friend of mine to cover the monies owed. I went to Dick to pay my rent. Where did you get the money from, he asked and seemed genuinely concerned. I like to pay debts, I replied. I also informed him of my intent to close the office as I could not foresee help coming from any corner. I put €5,000 on his table which he pushed back towards me.

I don't want your money. You are doing good work and let me see if we can help you raise some money, he said. Have you got any friends that can help us raise some money for you, he asked. The only name that came to mind was Mr Billy Rooney, a local businessman and an absolute gentleman. He was always kind to me and considered a pillar of the society. Ok let's get together and see what we can do for you, he said. I still insisted that he keep the money and left.

I regularly checked with Ann to see if there was any joy from Brendan. She had spoken with him and reassured me that all was in hand. A few weeks later I was informed that she had sent the case file to Brendan but since had not heard from him which was most unusual. She asked me to try and get in touch with him because the moratorium only allowed six months for the case to be filed in the high court and we were running out of time. I tried to get in touch with Brendan through every avenue possible but to no avail. He had simply disappeared from the face of the earth. I think they got to him, Ann said one day and I knew exactly what she meant. After all this is a very closed system and it knows how to protect itself. They simply shut you out.

The dance of a thousand veils has become my favourite expression when describing the system of government. A nation that prides itself on family values allowed over a hundred thousand children to disappear and left a few more open to abuse. What did I expect? The very same system was still in play with little fear of accountability. Now I had to find a barrister, quick. I spoke with Dick. Don't worry I will speak with my brother in law who is a barrister and has written a book on family law, he said. He felt confident and told me not to worry. This was Friday.

He came looking for me on Monday and did not look too confident. I spoke with my brother in law and scared the shit out of him. He has been practising for only two and a half years and this will ruin his career if he were to take on my case. He had also informed Dick that no one in their right mind would represent me. It would mean curtains to their career.

I suggest you forget about it and get on with your life, Dick added. It's not going to happen. You are on your own, he said before leaving my office. I picked up the phone and rang Sunday Business Post. They have two barristers who write on matters of law. I managed to speak with one of them. He listened to what I had to say before telling me that he was not a practising barrister any more but advised that I should not let go of this case.

Then it occurred to me that I knew a barrister who was recently appointed a senior counsel and had recently been through a separation and divorce. I rang him and we had a lengthy discussion. He told me that in his divorce proceedings he was financially wiped out. If he were to take my case his career would be over. He also told me that word had gone out for no one to touch me with a ten foot barge pole or else. He further advised me to search for a senior counsel who had made his money and had a bone to pick with the system. My fears were confirmed and this was the end of an open and shut case. Justice is blind but no one had ever warned me about it being so corrupt.

Life was progressing as normal and no help ever came from men. For the first time in this country professional qualification in counselling was approved and I duly enrolled on recommendation of my good friend and mentor Mr Jim Byrne, an eminent counsellor. It will give you more credibility, he advised. This was a four year B.A in Counselling and Psychometric testing. Concurrently I was studying for a diploma in community education while running the office and tending to my daughters needs on a twenty four hour basis. They always came first and my spare time was spent chasing politicians and the system.

Sarah was busy repeatedly telling Aisha that because of me, her future would be ruined. Who would hire her? She did not have a chance in hell of ever becoming a solicitor or a barrister. Aisha was becoming aloof and withdrawn and always looked tired. One early morning I saw her standing outside the shop where she worked. She appeared half asleep as she leaned against the glass window, waiting for the manager to arrive and open the shop. I shed many a silent tear. The next day I went to see her. I was always weary of going near her work place but this day she looked so proud as she introduced her daddy to the staff and put her arm in my arm as she took me for a tour of her domain.

I don't know who felt more proud, her or me. I guess she was. Her face lit with joy and she wanted me to take something as she wanted to buy a present for me. It's a young people store and what could I buy? They had nothing to suit an old goat and I had everything I needed standing right next to me. We settled for a hug and kiss. She was studying and working hard and it was her final year before pursuing an LL.B. Rihana had finished high school and I went to her graduation. Aisha was there with her mother and asked me to join them. She had no clue about how much I despised this woman and could not stand the sight of her never mind sit next to her. I spent the entire session standing at the back of the hall recording Rihana's graduation.

Towards the end of the afternoon she recited a poem which she had written specially for the occasion. There was not a dry eye in the hall. It was sad but absolutely beautiful. My darling daughter wrote words which pained my heart and I could have exploded with pride and pain. There hung raw emotion in the air. The principal told me that he was sad to see the last of my daughters leave. He felt sad for he probably would never see the likes of them again. The respect between us was always mutual and acknowledged and then it was all over. My daughters were ready for the adult world. Rihana was heading for town to celebrate with her friends. I emptied the contents of my wallet for her pleasure.

2007 had begun and I was busier than ever but there appeared no sign of help on the horizon. Then two silly things happened. I got the phone bill and tears began to roll down my face. I had no money left, not even to pay the office phone bill. This was the final straw. I got up quietly, looked around the office and very slowly, yet deliberately walked out of the office. This was not the way I had envisaged this to end.

It was over. I used the rear entrance of the building and walked out for the last time and felt nothing. Oh shit I did feel something. My feet were soaking wet. I had stepped in a puddle but it wasn't raining outside. I got into my car and removed my shoes to find water inside them. My socks were soaking and I began to shiver. It was freezing outside. I lifted the shoe and turned it over to find the sole had cracked from one side to the other. I looked at the sole of the other shoe and it too had cracked. I felt ok till the laughter began. It felt so funny that I laughed some more till the tears began to stream down my face. I was taking on a powerful and corrupt system and could not afford a pair of shoes. Now that was funny. Alas! It was time to go home.

On the way home is Golfstyle a shop owned by one of my golf buddies Declan Cunningham. He comes from a wealthy family and had always been good to me. I decided to call in and say goodbye. He had always helped me with my golf tournaments. I pulled up outside and put on my soaking wet shoes and regained my composure. Hey Sam, how is it going, Declan greeted me as I entered the shop. Fine, I replied. Would you wait in my office for a second? I have something for you which I have been meaning to give you for ages, he said. Cheers, I said and proceeded to his office. My world had come to an end and I neither wished nor wanted anything and just wished to be home.

Sorry about that, he said as he entered the office and proceeded to open the top drawer of his desk. He pulled out his cheque book, wrote something, signed it and then handed it over to me. It was in the sum of €250 and my phone bill stood at €238.98. Give me another month or so and I will do the same again, he chirped. Tax donations and whatever, you know. Now if a few people could do that won't you be alright, he asked. The fool did not know that I was already feeling alright. I muttered something in gratitude and he told me to fuck off and keep up the good work. Now go on you have work to do, save some lives, he waved cheerfully. I shook his hands and fucked off, back to my office. Took off my shoes and socks and did not finish till close to midnight. I felt no cold and there seemed nothing but hope as I got on with what I had to do and what I had set out to do.

The next morning I bought a pair of black shoes for €9.99 and polished them vigorously till they looked a €100 worth. The radio was on and I heard it on the news. The Law Reform

Commission was launching its Third Programme of Law Reform and coming to town. Its first sitting was scheduled to be hosted by the faculty of Law at the National University of Ireland, Galway. I googled their contact number and then picked up the phone. A very polite voice asked if she could help me. Yes please, I replied in my best English. Can you give me a little information about this Third Programme of Law Reform? Oh, I will transfer you to Mr Charles O'Mahony. He is the organiser and our senior researcher. Thank you I said meekly.

An educated voice appeared on the other end asking how he could help me. I told him who I was and needed information about the Third Programme of Law Reform. He was very accommodating and gave me the relevant information. The Law Reform Commission sits every eight years and invites submissions from anyone and everyone. Then the recommendations are prepared and presented to the government. 70% of their recommendations from the last programme were brought into legislation, he informed me with pride. Can I address the Law Reform Commission, I asked. He advised me to prepare notes and would ensure that I got five minutes to address the panel. Thank you I said in my best Paddy, Pakistani Oxford English as the phone went down. I felt excited. Patrick, a client in need of help was present and looked excited too while offering to accompany me. The next two weeks are a blur.

The fateful day came and I could not wait to put on my good suit and tie and waited patiently for six o'clock to arrive. The conference was scheduled for 7 pm sharp. I was there at six thirty to acclimatise myself with the surroundings. My palms were sweating profusely and the collar of my shirt felt damp by the time I got into Aras Moyola. Thankfully Patrick met an acquaintance and we felt a little comfortable. I looked for Charles O'Mahony and soon found him. He was very polite and accommodating as he briefly explained the process and wished me good luck.

Members of the Law reform Commission were waiting for the arrival of the former Supreme Court justice and current president of the Law Reform Commission, Mrs Catherine McGuinness. Soon there was hustle bustle and I saw a diminutive lady with a distinguished smile appear. There was something special about her. Her smile seemed warm and welcoming yet I felt in awe of her. She appeared simple yet elegantly attired.

She was special, maybe even regal with an aura around her. The press photographer was called and pictures were duly taken. Then we were ushered into the hall. Alongside Patrick I crept to the back of the hall. The front rows were occupied by black suits, some with stripes but all looking legal. The law practitioners always look like morticians and possess a certain look about them.

I was nervous with a stomach full of butterflies. My hands were shaking and I had them firmly clasped around the piece of paper with my neatly typed notes. Patrick looked comfortable and without a care in the world, which helped. Then the proceedings began promptly with a speech and Madam Justice was welcomed to the NUIG. My first impression of Madam Justice McGuinness held true. Her voice was clear, oozing intellect and honesty which forebode anyone for making an ass of himself and here was I, the proverbial schmuck. Suddenly I did not feel very comfortable.

The format of the proceedings was announced and two mobile microphones were made available to the floor. Cameras were ready to record while the proceedings were being held *'in camera'*. It was a slow start and I listened and observed. I knew that I had to say something, just did not know how or when.

287

After twenty minutes I was beginning to get bored. Is this the best they have to contribute is a thought that crossed my mind. It was very basic in nature, especially in matters of family law. My courage was beginning to build and confidence grew by the minute.

I knew a hell of a lot more than these utterances and then my hand shot up. All eyes turned towards me. I paused and then I saw that by now familiar smile of Madam Justice, full of encouragement and I began to read my script. I was very wary of my five minutes. I could feel my hands shaking and my voice trembled with emotion. I had difficulty focusing on my words and then heard my echo which sounded slow and deliberate yet clear. I believe I saw Charles nod and also knew that I had Madam Justice's attention as she was looking directly at me.

I could feel the heat rising in my cheeks and little beads of perspiration appeared on my forehead and then I began to speak with fluency. Somewhere in the distance I heard a sigh. After the initial five minutes it was just me and the world ceased to exist till I had finished speaking. Charles was smiling and Madam Justice seemed in deep thought. My knees gave way as I began to sit down. Well done, very well done, I heard Patrick acknowledge.

There was a pause which seemed to last till eternity. Thank you Mr Anjum, that was most eloquent and wonderful. Now any questions from the floor, Madam Justice sounded pensive yet inviting. Nothing! Again she invited questions but there was nothing but silence. People sitting at the table seemed a little nervous and confused. Sideways glances were passed between the panel as a few words were exchanged. This is most unusual because we still have a lot of time left. Is there anyone who would like to contribute or say anything? Madam Justice's enquired as her eyes scanned the audience.

Slowly a gentleman carrying crutches who was sitting behind me stood up. Madam Justice I believe that I speak for majority of my colleagues when I say that the earlier speaker has already spoken about all issues that we came here to address plus much more and there is nothing relevant left for us to say. He gave me a gentle tap on the shoulder and sat down. Madam Justice announced that this was most unusual and brought the proceedings to a much earlier close than expected. Charles was walking hurriedly towards me as I slowly got up and headed for the exit. Madam Justice would like to speak with you and lets have some pictures taken, he said.

Madam Justice was most cordial and complimentary. The press photographer could not be found and I took my leave. I was enduring a roller coaster of emotions and needed time out. I had met a lady. It had been two decades and more since I had last thought of someone as a lady. What an evening, what an experience and what a memory. Another pleasant surprise awaited me. The next morning I received a call from Charles O'Mahony requesting a detailed transcript of my submission. I promised to send it before the end of the day and duly obliged. Charles was once again most complimentary and relayed best wishes from Madam Justice.

26 March 2007 had brought some rays of sunshine on an otherwise dismal looking future. I was to hear from Charles again. The second sitting at University College Cork was uneventful and he invited me to the final submissions to be held at Dublin Castle.

I duly attended, picked an argument with John Bowman who was chairing the floor and had the pleasure of listening to Justice Kirby a retired senior justice from Australia. He was the guest of honour and a most knowledgeable person with a wicked sense of humour. When questioned Madam Justice McGuinness and Justice Kirby duly acknowledged that law was always at least fifty years behind in time. They added that judges are there to apply law and not impart justice and sometimes did that poorly. I had no more questions left. At the end of proceedings I had a quick word with Madam Justice McGuinness and Justice Kirby before bidding goodbye to Charles not knowing that this relationship was to last another four years.

Three years running I was nominated for the Mayor's Awards with the highest number of nominations but did not manage to win once. I suppose such is life. Annual golf tournaments were a social success but made little money and the finances were tight as I struggled to keep the office open.

I was back in the loop searching for funding when Family Support Agency kindly agreed to grant me €2,500 per annum for the years 2007 and 2008. It was better than nothing but the flow of clients was forever on the increase. The service was still free of charge to encourage men in seeking help but no one wanted to help me. Eight to ten phone calls a day were coming from around the country but no offers of help.

Aisha's 'debs' was on the horizon and she was busy shopping. Spending money was Sarah's forte especially when it belonged to others and she took Aisha trawling around the country. Eventually Aisha found a dress that she liked and I paid for it. She found shoes to match and I paid for them. She found a matching handbag and I paid for it too. Total cost came close to six hundred Euros. I did not get to see her dressed even though for days I had my camera and flash ready. To say I was gutted and heartbroken would be an understatement. Alas, I am only a man and a deadbeat Dad at that. What would I know?

Then I had an epiphany. I wanted to organise a fashion show, 'Dashing Dudes and Dazzling Dames'. Friends loved the idea and a friend of a friend Ms Julianne Gray agreed to help organise the show.

The local councillors were on the catwalk.

The county councillors were on the catwalk.

Former county and city mayors were on the catwalk.

Parliamentarians were on the catwalk.

Galway United footballers were on the catwalk.

All Ireland winning Hurling under 21's were on the catwalk.

Provincial rugby players were on the catwalk.

Every shop in town had made dresses, suits, casuals and shoes available. One of country's leading singers was on the catwalk and brought the house down. TG4 recorded the show for future broadcast. It was acknowledged as one of the best fashion shows ever.

Guess who forgot to support the event? Everyone turned up except men. The show was successful as PR exercise but I suffered a financial loss of €6,000. Thus far the picture did not look very rosy for men but they still expected perfect solutions to their imperfect fiascos.

Then I sought a meeting with the HSE West Health manager. She was in control of €292 million worth of budget. A friend of mine Peter, who owns one of the biggest accountancy firms in town, accompanied me. It was a very good meeting. She wanted to know my personal story which compelled me to open this office. I narrated the event with the social worker in the U.K and my experiences of separation. She acknowledged my sentiments and the need for the service on offer while adding that they didn't do that kind of thing anymore. She was referring to the forced removal of children from their father to foster care. She stated that I could do with €180,000 and would refer me to some other funding sources. This was the month of November 2007. Three weeks later we met again. The secretary general had knocked the application on its head and no explanation was given. When asked, I told Peter about the outcome. He was astonished to hear that the application for funding was turned down. As far as he knew it was or would have been approved.

We had more meetings thereafter, she recommended a different approach, referred me to a consultant to prepare business plans and I was another €1,500 out of pocket without any money ever coming my way from the HSE West. Something very strange was brought to my attention. I was informed by a lady who worked in the HSE that gossip was doing the rounds and there were pockets of women who had labelled me a misogynist and anti single mothers. Their grapevine was working at a ferocious pace to suffocate me and my cause.

Then one of my clients from Alcoholics Anonymous asked a strange question. One of his fellow alcoholics was a social care worker from the HSE. Did I know him? He had asked. Upon given his name and description I acknowledged him as a very good golfer and a friend I held in great respect. Well he is no friend of yours, he responded. His sponsor, his wife had accused me of pushing Joe back to alcoholism. I was sending too many men to social services and they could not cope. Hence I was being called every name under the sun. I never knew Joe was an alcoholic. Husband and wife also disclosed that I was a no good golfer and not qualified as a counsellor even though at the time I possessed two degrees in psychology and counselling and a level seven diploma. It seemed a lot of people out there felt they had to undermine me for whatever reasons.

A week later I had a meeting with the Minister for Health Mary Harney and Deputy Noel Grealish was present who made strong and passionate representations on my behalf explaining what I had undertaken and achieved. The Minister agreed to look into the matter but promised nothing. She did ask me a question. Was I going to change the culture of Irish men? My reply in jest stated that I could probably raise the dead but would not undertake the impossible. A week later I got a call from deputies Grealish and McCormack to inform me of their forthcoming meeting with the department of health officials and felt hopeful of acquiring €90,000 in funding. The minister's personal secretary was to accompany them

The minister's personal secretary requested an input from the health manager of HSE West with regards appropriateness of the need for funding of my charity. It was not long before I received two irate calls from the said deputies. My friendly Health manager had torpedoed the funding. Who was pulling the strings and from where, no one seemed any the wiser. Men were still coming with harrowing stories of despondency and hopelessness and I kept the doors to my office open.

The Deputies got me €9,000 from the lottery funding but were extremely disappointed with the outcome of the past three years of hard work with little to show for it. They acknowledged that there seemed powerful opposition to my cause but could not put their finger on it. They could do no more and I accepted the sad fact with resignation.

A week later the government announced €25,000 for the local cat's home in Galway. A little more was allocated for the local dog pound. By then funding for women's causes by the HSE stood at €15,000,000 and more. Domestic violence against women and rape crisis networks were doing good business. Men could go and fuck themselves was the general consensus.

Then a close professional friend came to know about my office and its work. He knew Minister Brian Lenihan personally and offered to make representations on my behalf. He had also previously held an office next door to the minister in Leinster house. Two days later he told me to stop frightening people in power or I would never get funding. I was making people in the corridors of power extremely uncomfortable. And stop tabling questions in the Dail, he had advised.

Later in the day I received a call from my darling baby sister who lives in sunny California. She felt sorry to tell me that Dad had passed way. He had visited the hospital for his annual check up and they had advised him to stay overnight as it was too late for him to drive home. They had given him a clean bill of health. He did not wake up the next morning and had died in his sleep. I cried at night and went to the office in the morning to listen to other peoples woes but no one ever listened to mine. After three days I had no more tears left.

Sarah rang to offer her condolences and I promptly put the phone down. Then she rang my sister I to pass her condolences. She also informed her that I had given her no money upon separation but she still loved me. By the way what would be my share of inheritance, she had asked.

My neighbours were mostly single mothers and their children decided to have some fun at my expense. Their favourite pastime involved standing on my rear garden wall in a queue, dropping their pants around their ankles and urinating into my back garden while I was away at work. The future did not look bright for Irish fatherhood.

One day a spark plug flew past my head missing my right eye by an inch or two. Then there were the occasional eggs thrown at my kitchen door and some hit the rear wall and bedroom windows. I could not remove the stains from the wall and still see them as a memorable gift from the youth who would be tomorrow's parents. Three of these young men currently occupy residence in the juvenile detention centre. This reminds me of Margaret who lived a stone's throw away. She was a single mother of three sons and a daughter. The eldest boy and the youngest girl had different fathers. The middle two were sired by a father and a son so now one brother was the uncle of the other. The eldest was thirteen and brought home a twelve year old girl friend to live with the blessing of his mother and they were co habiting till the brood decided to break into my shed in broad daylight and steal my tool box, lawn mower and everything else they could lay their hands on.

I had had enough and rang the general manager of the HSE, city hall and the cops to rectify the said matter. A senior social worker was allocated to the family with intent of sorting out their mess. Within a fortnight the mother had disappeared with the children, never to be seen again.

My good friend Pottymouth Pat from the city hall had decided in her wisdom that despite all the shenanigans I was experiencing no action was required till I decided to install security cameras around my house. Dear Ms Pottymouth promptly sent me a letter threatening eviction. Single mammies around my estate including my next door neighbour had claimed invasion of privacy. The mayor was involved and eventually the matter was brought to a satisfactory conclusion. Then there was the occasional letter containing literary filth left on my doorstep. Ms Pottymouth duly noted that it was not important and worth investigating while her colleague was horrified and undertook to pursue the matter further.

Now there was the occasional visit from an eight year old girl and her six year old brother looking to borrow a cigarette. Their mother suffered alcohol dependency and the kids virtually looked after themselves. The girl soon graduated to alcohol before her tenth birthday and became a regular client of the local constabulary. Over 90% of my estate was occupied by single mothers.

2007 was ending in a sorrowful state with little peace in the office or at home. I went to see Dick and repeated what I had stated previously. I think it's time to close the office and I have had enough. The state wants to bury me and men won't help. I think it's time for me to move on. He told me to hang in there for a while. He wasn't charging me rent and all I had to do was pay my phone, electricity and management charges. I thanked him for his benevolence and decided to hang in for another year. It was 2011 before Dick's real intent became apparent.

I sat in the office on Christmas Day and took calls from suicidal and despondent separated fathers. I had my usual two fried egg sandwiches with me. At least I did not go hungry. Year 2008 began and on the 1st of January I found a letter in my mail box. It was a bank holiday and there was no post delivered the day before. It carried incorrect address and some god fearing soul had delivered it to my office on New Year's Day.

My divorce hearing was due in a couple of month's time and thankfully I had nothing left for Sarah to try and get her smutty hands on. I wearily plonked myself down and opened the letter. I was holding a €1,000 cheque. One of my clients in Shannon had convinced his colleagues to fund my charity that year and they had all agreed. Over 80% of his colleagues were female, God bless 'em. That was my third donation received in three years from over 2,500 clients who had visited my office. The ones who had phoned must have been three times as many if not more.

Now Dick was becoming a frequent visitor to my office. He always had some business proposal on the go. Alongside seven partners including his younger brother, he was contemplating building a 4000 unit villa development in Bulgaria. The plan included building of two signature golf courses bearing Nick Faldo's name.

I spent three months working on the proposal and organised a meeting with Nick Faldo's advisers. The figures quoted £750,000 each for the signatures or £1.25 million each for Nick Faldo's design. The project soon fizzled out. Secretarial duties were ever growing and the preparation and sending of regular letters and faxes to his legal advisers in France, the UK, Hong Kong and USA were becoming the norm. Because the office was given to the charity for free, I felt obliged.

Whatever gifts I received from my friendly golf reps, I promptly handed them over to Mr Pryce as I barely had time to scratch my ass never mind play golf. There was a four hundred euro worth of Taylor Made rescue wood, the staff golf bag as used by Padraig Harrington, Titleist golf balls, handmade Scotty Cameron Putter, golf attire and much more to the tune of over €4,500 euro.

Then I proceeded to organise and pay for the signage to his building, over €700 in cost and in between was asked to make contacts with various businesses and ministerial offices to organise and accommodate meetings for him. This was only the beginning and much more was to follow suit. As a benefactor he decided to organise and chair a fundraising committee which did not manage to raise a dime. He proposed gifts of fully electronic golf trolleys to future benefactors which were to cost me over €600 each. He is still using one of them while he gave the other he gave to a friend from whom he was seeking personal favours.

When I was invited to a fundraising dinner with a minister, he wished attendance and brought his wife with him. I paid for them both and got them seated next to the minister. If I were due a meeting with a minister, he wished to accompany me and ruined them all by his incessant touting and search for ministerial favours. Then he wanted a franchise for solar powered waste bins and asked me to contact the company in the US because he was getting nowhere with them. I spoke with the people in the U.S. and organised a meeting with their directors. His brother accompanied him to the meeting but the venture never left the ground. At the same time he was involved in the distribution of pharmaceutical drugs and we had consultative meetings. It transpired that he wanted me to contact international charities offering them surplus drugs as a donation.

I rang most of them to learn that many European pharmaceutical distributors were using this donation process as a scam to dump out of date drugs in third world countries due the high cost of licensed disposal. Thereafter he wanted to donate worthless shares to my charity to the tune of €60,000 for tax write offs. I politely declined. There was an ongoing problem with his younger brother John's divorce proceedings and the caring older brother sought my assistance.

It started with his brother's court appearance in Tralee, county Kerry. Summons had been issued for his arrest in lieu of non payment of maintenance to his former wife. He had made a multi million euro settlement in divorce but the state of economy had left him penniless. He had been left incapable of putting more than four euro of petrol in his helicopter, speed boat, Humvee, sports BMW coupe or his BMW sports motor bike and barely had enough money to feed him.

I spent over three months counselling, sorting through his legal papers, visiting the court in Tralee, dealing with his new girlfriend and then it transpired that he could not get legal representation. He owed over two hundred thousand euro in legal fees and his previous lawyer would not release his files.

Dick was worried that his 'baby' brother may be contemplating suicide and I was to become John's counsellor, legal adviser and chaperone.

Every day Dick barged in, plonked his ample backside and demanded news of his brother's welfare but never gave or volunteered to give his brother a penny. John did not trust Dick and advised me the same. To Dick's irk their mother helped John in small measures which was draining his impending inheritance.

Dick decided to fire his management company because he did not like their attitude and they did not like Dick's bouncing cheques. Now I was hoovering the corridors, keeping the communal kitchen clean, doing minor electrical repairs, fixing doors and hinges alongside catering for other demands such as procuring confectionery machines and dealing with the company. I was also his software and business consultant and felt obliged because I had an office free of charge and was trying to save men from desolation and at times suicide.

By now men were handing over notes of their impending and planned suicides. In between I was chauffeuring Dick whenever his car went out of action. Then I became his involuntary letting agent. There were daily reminders in text of the said demand. Surprisingly no one wanted to rent his offices and most of the building was empty bar three offices as no one lasted more than a year or two. Then there were his own personal problems and I was expected to be on his beck and call dreading the text stating, when you have a minute can you come to my office.

One day he looked worried and asked me for a loan of six thousand Euros for a friend who was in hospital having suffered a massive heart attack. I was almost penniless and where would I find such money. Listen you can have my guarantee. He badly needs the money for a few months and if he does not pay I will reimburse you in maximum six months, he promised.

I went to a business friend of mine seeking help and he handed over the cash, no questions asked. This was at the end of year 2009. In April of 2010 he called me to his office and asked me to be seated. He was busy signing cheques and handed two of them to me. I need €2,500 today and it's very important. I have deposited a cheque from Royal Bank of Scotland in the sum of ten thousand euro to my account which should clear by Monday. Cash these cheques on Tuesday, he said. I got him the cash, again. And I will have your other money soon, he reassured me.

I went to the bank on Wednesday and asked my friend across the counter if it was safe to lodge the cheques in my account and he looked worried. There were cheques bouncing left, right and centre from Dick's account. He advised me against lodging the cheques as there were less than ten Euros in the account. I returned to seek Dick but he was on his way to Monte Carlo and met with me a week later. I told him the story about his cheques and he went ballistic. There are thousands in my account and the bank must have made a mistake he insisted. I told him there was no mistake.

He promised to clarify facts and return to me with an answer. He came to see me the next day and informed me that the ten thousand euro cheque was sent to the wrong account and the bank was busy rectifying the matter. He assured me that he would have the money next week. Next week came and he asked me for the cheques as he was going across the road to the bank to collect the cash. He did not return and thereafter he became elusive. Two weeks later I managed to get hold of him and asked for the return of monies as promised and he offered to offset them against my rent. This was the month of September in 2010. What rent, I asked. Well times are bad and I

300

can't give you anything for free, can I. This is strictly business, he replied.

In December 2010 I finally decided to close the damn office and get on with my life. Not so. Mr Pryce had other plans. He tried to sue me for back rent. On Christmas Eve I closed the office and put everything in storage. I have had enough. In 2011 letters arrived from his solicitor threatening my fellow directors with litigation and he visited my home to threaten me with dire consequences. In return he received a police caution. According to his estimates I owed him €20,000 but he would settle for €4,000. The case is pending in court and I will ensure that his ample ass is nailed firmly to the cross. I have promised myself this treat.

John Bowler's wise words echoed in my head. God help anyone who under estimates me. Walter Mitty just did.

Chapter Fifteen

Four years had passed and I had instructed my solicitor to file for divorce proceedings. I wanted this cancerous growth cut away from my life forever. I advised her with regards preparation of a deed of waiver as in Irish family law proceedings are interlocutory, hence never ending. When signed by both parties, the deed of waiver brings matters to a close. This time Sarah was being represented by a female lawyer from the law centre with pronounced sympathy for women and their portrayal as victims.

Customary written nonsense was being exchanged and I needed an end to this vulgarity. I advised my solicitor for the need of a signed deed of waiver signed, preparation of a transcript of the court hearing and a deed of divorce. I reminded her of her promise of a full hearing when separation proceedings had commenced. I wanted my day in court and wished to expose the scum for what they really were. This was my final hoorah.

A letter arrived from Sarah's new found feminist solicitor friend demanding an explanation with regards my request for a transcript of the proceedings. I was curt in my reply and told them it was none of their business. Within a week they responded offering me nullity of marriage. Three months prior to my hearing I was aware of a case where nullity of marriage was granted but the father had to apply for legal guardianship of his son, as if he were an unmarried father. His expensive and high powered lawyers had cost him his rights of guardianship and joint custody of his son at a princely sum of just over €9,000 for the days hearing. The judge had erred in principle and abused judicial discretion but no appeal was lodged as by now the client was broke and in debt.

Yet I was being offered a settlement which meant my marriage never existed and the past sixteen years of hell were a mere illusion. It's a great deal my solicitor advised but I was past taking advice from anyone, especially lawyers. My communication was crystal clear. I wanted my day in court and wished no more communication with the other side. From the onset I was promised a barrister, good in reputation and competence. On the day of hearing he turned out to be a good for nothing peacock strutting around with his beak firmly stuck between the cheeks of his buttocks

Sarah's solicitors made their usual demands for a poor woman in need of money and all I needed was a full hearing. I was advised to claim recovery of €10,000 obtained by Sarah through duress. She was already working overtime on the girls narrating her tales of sorrow and suing her for money did not seem such a good idea. She had already promised Aisha her home as her inheritance. I believe that Aisha already thought of her mother as a victim. She had little time left for me and mostly stayed with her mother. Pressures of work and study were narrated and lack of availability of time was often mentioned. She was drifting away and I could do nothing but watch from a distance.

Exactly one week before the divorce hearing my solicitor rang to inform me that the other side were willing to withdraw all their claims if I would consent to a no contest divorce and sign the deed of waiver. In return there would be no hearing and no transcript of the proceedings. Tell them to go to hell and see you at the hearing, I replied. I was instructed to be present at the court for 9am and I made sure that I arrived for 8.30.

From the onset something did not feel right but I could not put my finger on it. The penny dropped only after the proceedings were over. From start to finish the entire case had been a set up and shut me out. A full hearing and a transcript would have made an ass of the legal profession and its practices. I had bet my friend Ann that a stunt will be pulled on the day of the hearing and then it had happened.

I met my peacock on the morning of the hearing in a little corner room with no privacy and an open door with people constantly peering to check its occupancy. Sarah stood on the fore court looking nervous and flanked by her sisters. And there was I, standing alone as nothing had changed in that aspect of my life.

My peacock informed me that he had studied my case and will be making strong representations. After five minutes of chat I knew that he barely knew the basics of my case and I felt my temper starting to rise. Mr Peacock, I said with controlled politeness. I was promised a full hearing. Is the person here to take notes of the proceedings? I asked. I have to consult other clients and I will see you in court, he said before walking off without answering either of my questions. I had been landed with a limp dick which no amount of Viagra could cure.

My solicitor approached me and briefly told me about the oncoming process. I feel like I am about to be shafted, am I? I asked but received no reply. The judge has a full listing of hearings and he does not want time wasted. We will be in and out. As our case is all said and done, no contentious issues, maximum fifteen minutes and it will be all over, she said. Hence the judge wanted us in first. What the hell was this in and out? A one dollar fuck with no frills or strings attached. My head was in a spin and all my plans were being flushed down the legal toilet. The feckers had pulled a stunt and there was nothing I could do or so they thought.

At five past ten on that glorious grey and miserable morning I was led into the court room of the circuit court. I saw Sarah to my right with her solicitor facing me as her barrister faced the judge. I sat at the back of the court observing my solicitor gazing at the table while my five foot six inch peacock faced the five foot two judge. The stage was set as I looked around and found

304

a woman fiddling with her pens and a pencil case while a clip board perched in her lap ready to take notes. A thought occurred as the judge entered the courtroom, all of five foot two and looking serious with intent. I had studied many of his case histories and he seemed fair and competent. He also had a reputation for being strict on principle.

All rise, a voice boomed. I felt proud of my peacock as he shot up with zest like a greyhound on meth. Sarah's barrister was a dowdy woman with a quarter in brains, little intellect and sixteen plus stone on a five foot eleven frame and looked like a grizzly in an ill fitted dress. One look at her and nothing appeared in sync. I had waited four years to get vindication and now they had me exactly where they wanted. The court was called to order, the judge made a short speech, the lawyers bowed in courtesy and the proceedings commenced.

The grizzly stood up and addressed the court declaring her intent to represent Sarah and proceeded with the narration of her case. Then Sarah was called to the witness box. Oh feck. Nothing had changed from the district court to the circuit court and another circus was beginning to unfold. Poor Sarah's sufferings and lament were being muttered. Grizzly is neither good at representations nor as a speaker. To put it mildly, she is pure shite as a barrister. She read her notes like a misfiring tractor and tried to paint a picture of poor Sarah, a woman scorned and wronged. All this time the judge sat glaring at me and not once did his stare move. I was about to get fucked over for the second time with little to say in the proceedings.

Sarah poured her tale of poverty and sadness. She forgot to tell him about her multiple holidays abroad, holidays at home, yearly change of car, lunches in cafes, late nights, socialising and not making a cent's worth of contribution towards our daughter's upkeep and general well being. But it was repeatedly iterated that they were living with her. No one cared to mention that I was still looking after them and paying for their debs, their holidays, their orthodontist and much more. It was twice mentioned that I was making no maintenance payments. The Judge was still glaring while Sarah nodded agreement with mama bear and her narrations of woe. I knew the feckers had aced me again. I was beaten by both sides, her's and mine. When they finished, the judge asked why there was no maintenance order and advised Sarah to seek maintenance from me. Why didn't Shorty ask me? I would have answered his question. The friggin peacock and my solicitor were too busy staring at the floor. They forgot to tell the judge that both my daughters were paying their mother for board and lodging.

Divorce was granted but I was left sitting on my ass. No one had bothered to call me to the witness stand. I noticed the woman on the left was busy scribbling and a thought entered my head. I shot up and spoke directly to the Judge seeking leave to address the court. Sarah looked nervous, grizzly bear looked stupefied, my solicitor's head jerked and I saw the peacock wipe imaginary sweat from his forehead and the judge did not appear amused.

Counsel did you advise your client about court procedures, the judge spoke curtly to the peacock while completely ignoring my request. Yes Judge, the little prick said to the littler prick as his forehead almost touched ground on its way to kissing the judge's backside. I stood my ground. Judge I have the constitutional right to address this court. The little fecker knew that I would not let go. I was invoking my constitutional rights and would not let anyone stand in my way. He frowned and directed my peacock to advise me.

Before my peacock could open his mouth I told the judge that I wished to address the court and this time my voice boomed around the court room. I have a full day of hearings and I don't have time, the judge spoke to me directly. I only need five minutes judge, I replied. He looked exasperated but gave a reluctant wave for me to proceed. OK Mr Anjum what would you like from me, asked his bloody worship. An acknowledgement on record that this court is wholly incompetent in its function as a family court and not fit for the purpose it is set for. The judge appeared a little shocked. He looked at my peacock and the peacock told the judge that it seemed like I had made up my mind and there was nothing he could do. Not once did my solicitor bother to look at me.

OK Mr Anjum, you have this court's acknowledgement, the judge stated. I was busy looking at the young woman scribbling away. Judge may you please repeat what you have just said, I requested. The judge looked directly at me and stated that I had the courts acknowledgment that it was not fit for the purpose it was set up for.

I turned on my heels and walked out of the court. I had my divorce and now the world could go and fuck itself. No one had stood on my side, never mind helped. Hopefully this was the end of a sad, ardous, torturous and a long journey.

It was all over now.

Chapter Sixteen

Life was beginning to settle and Rihana was still sticking to her schedule. Aisha had drifted away. After finishing work on Saturday's she went out with friends. She told me that she liked music and dancing but could not tell when she would make time for me. She was finding her independence and had at times intimated that she would like to get her own apartment. This frightened me and then there was Rihana's welfare to consider. The two sisters had been an immense source of support for each other.

I was scared of the thought of my nineteen year darling daughter having endured the traumatic experience of family breakdown being out there on her own. I managed to convince her to stay with her mother who was seldom home.

Life ambled along as I picked up the pieces and tried to rebuild my life. One day Aisha rang me and she was hysterical. Sarah had hit Rihana as per her custom and Rihana had kicked her mother in return. Rihana had warned her mother that if she were to ever hit her again, she would kill her. She was sick and tired of her beatings and was not a child any more. Rihana was seventeen years of age. I often wonder and torture myself with the thoughts of my contribution to their lives of hell. One day when angry, Aisha yelled and accused me of keeping her and Rihana wrapped in cotton wool. Whatever that meant I accepted the accusation. I was becoming accustomed to her yelling by now.

Then something else happened that drew my attention to the workings of the police domestic violence unit. I have a next door neighbour in his early thirties who allegedly is related to a notorious criminal family in Limerick. At the best of times he is a pain in the ass and not the most sociable of characters but a simple hello and the odd civility were usually exchanged.

One evening after picking up Aisha and Rihana we returned home to find his rubbish bin blocking our driveway. This was a weekly occurrence and this person is not the tidiest of people. His bin was filthy and never washed. As I tried to push it away, the slope of the driveway made it roll sideways and the empty bin keeled over. I parked the car and went inside my house with the girls in tow. They had barely put their bags down when there was a loud knock on the front door. I asked Rihana to answer while I put the groceries away.

Dad there is the man from next door and he wants a word with you, said Rihana and she looked intimidated. I walked to the front door and the little fecker all five foot seven of him invited me to step outside so he could sort me out. His face looked redder than a baboon's backside before he broke into a tirade of abuse. It was racist filth in all its glory. As I stepped outside he turned around and ran back to his own door while continuing his oration.

Rihana was standing behind me when Aisha appeared in a flash and ran past me. I had never seen her so angry. She was ready to take him on. The little shit sniggered and I went inside to call the cops. In the meantime Sarah had phoned and during their conversation Rihana had discussed the recently occurred events. Ten minutes or so later the cops arrived soon to be followed by Sarah. Then it all became a farce.

There appeared two female and two male cops. I busy was explaining the events to them when Sarah proceeded towards the front door. I told her not to go inside my house. In an instant the female cop leapt towards me. It's her house who are you to stop her? She literally spat the words out while frothing at the mouth. This is my house and she is not allowed in, I informed her. The male cops were taken aback at the ferocity of this female cop. I heard Sarah tell her that she did not live here

309

but had come to see Aisha. This woman was six inches away from my face and still raging. She glared like a Rottweiler on heat till her colleagues physically pulled her back and asked her to walk away. I asked for her name and she refused. The other cops asked me to let it go but I reported the matter to the superintendent anyway. I was later informed by one of her colleagues that she was a member of the police domestic violence unit and it was packed with female Rottweilers nationwide, he added remorsefully. The very same had been narrated as an experience by many a male client who had visited my office. Aisha thought better of it and decided to go with her mother, just for peace, she had said before giving me a hug and walking towards her mother's car. Rihana came over and decided to accompany her sister. I did get my hugs and kisses before they departed.

Then another event was to follow. I was sitting in the front room watching TV with Aisha and Rihana when noises were heard outside the front door. It was around eleven in the evening.

As I stepped closer to the door it transpired that there were people trying to break into my car. I slowly went back inside and asked the girls to call the cops while I proceeded to open the front door. As I turned the outside light on, I heard the running of footsteps. There were three youths running away, two boys and a girl. She was the daughter of a single mother who used to be my next door neighbour. She was in Rihana's class and a one time friend till she started to bully Rihana. One shithead decided to stand his ground, about twenty yards away from me. Did you call the cops, I yelled at Aisha as she returned a blank look.

I took off my glasses and shouted at her again to call the cops before walking towards the smartass, all of seventeen maybe eighteen years of age. He put his fists up and jeered, you can't touch me you fucking Indian bastard and proceeded to try and

310

hit me. Before he knew a thump had landed on his chin and he stood there dazed. I could hear Aisha bawling. As I turned towards the house, the gobshite landed a punch on the back of my head and ran. Aisha was in hysterics and could barely talk. Rihana informed me that my yelling had upset her. The more I tried to apologise the worse she seemed to get. As she calmed down, she had decided to go back to her mother's house and Rihana followed. Slowly my daughters were drifting away from me and I could do nothing or so it seemed.

In the meantime Rihana had disclosed that my snoring could be heard around the house and was keeping her awake. I made contact with the local hospital and got an appointment with the ENT specialist who always had made time for me. He made several suggestions including surgery. The adenoids could be removed but mine were massive and blocking my windpipe. At my age this procedure was considered risky to say the least.

I managed to convince him that I needed the surgery. Dr John Lang is an absolute gentleman and a highly skilled and well respected surgeon. While there I asked Dr Lang to have a look at my sinuses. They had been causing me breathing problems for the past few years. He shoved a camera up my nostrils and found narrowing of the pipes to the left of my forehead. This could have been a contributory factor to my snoring problem and migraines, I was told. I asked him to perform both surgeries at the same time. He refused and advised that they had to be done separately.

I pleaded with him and told him that my exams were due, my sister was coming to visit me from the U.S. and poor Rihana needed a good night's sleep. Eventually he agreed to perform both procedures at the same time. The date was set for Wednesday following week and I had to present myself on Tuesday no later than ten in the morning. I duly arrived with my books and research papers and I studied all day as the exams

311

were due to begin the next Monday. Mr Lang had been kind enough to have this pauper have a single room all to himself. Usual cost for the room was €550 per day plus surgical and medical expenses. Only god knows what the bill may have been if I had been asked to pay. Comedy was to follow as the registrar accompanied by a surgical nurse came to give me a going over. He was a most amiable chap from Nigeria. So you are having your adenoids removed tomorrow he said cheerfully while he took notes. We have to make arrangements for your adenoid procedure tomorrow and how are you feeling.

What about my sinuses? I asked. Oh may be another time, he said casually. No it's all being done tomorrow and I have discussed it with Mr Lang, I informed him. Impossible, he exclaimed looking slightly cross. The nurse did not seem amused either. I asked him to consult with Mr Lang. Oh he would, he said in a state of disbelief. Any way I had my books and papers to keep me occupied and also had exams to look forward to. I was dearly looking forward to seeing my darling daughters. I missed them terribly.

The next morning Mr Lang came with his team and explained the procedure to me and his team. The poor registrar looked at me as if I had landed from another planet. I think the interaction between Dr Lang and I was a bit intimidating for him and now he was giving me undue respect. Dr Lang left with the promise to see me in the theatre. I do not recall meeting him the next morning. They had managed to put me to sleep before he had arrived at the theatre. I saw him after surgery as I was being wheeled to my room. For some reason Dr Lang was laughing. Usually he is a very serious guy. In fact the whole surgical team was in fits and I was none the wiser.

Then the porter began to narrate my antics while I was under the influence of anaesthetic. When the anaesthetic is administered usually they ask the patient to count up to ten.

312

This applies to normal patients and then it was me. After seven I had started to tell jokes and others had picked on it. While Dr Lang was busy operating and taking lumps out of my throat the other feckers were amusing themselves by asking me for more jokes.

It had started with golfing anecdotes, on Dr Lang's prompt of course. He was digging deep into my throat with his scalpel while I dug deeper into my repertoire of cheap jokes. He shoved something up my nose to scrape my sinuses and I kept talking like a midget on helium. It must have been a sight. At least I had kept them entertained. The best ever was the porter's summation.

After cleaning up Dr Lang arrived to give me an update of my operation/s. He still had a huge smile planted on his face. In between trying to resist the compelling need to laugh he informed me that he had to dig deep into my throat to remove flesh. As the wound could not be bandaged I would experience clumps of blood, and bleeding for the next three or four years, he explained. Excellent, I said and thanked him profusely but probably not enough. People like him had always given me the will to live and hope for future.

Morphine was available on drip, just in case I felt pain and pain killers were made available on demand. I won't say more about his kindness for fear of embarrassing him. A gentleman indeed but for me he was an angel in disguise. The rest of the staff was absolutely brilliant too. No amount of money could buy the care I was given. University College Hospital team were absolutely brilliant from start to finish. If I wore a hat I would salute them, repeatedly.

Then pain was followed by more comedy. A middle aged motherly looking nurse walked in with a glass of water and a plate carrying painkillers with instructions that I had to take one

313

every one hour on the hour. I wasn't able to swallow a drop of water never mind the bloody pain killers. My throat had closed with swelling leaving me unable to speak. She pointed to the tablets while I smiled and pointed at my throat signalling that I did not want the tablets, because I wasn't able to swallow them. She insisted that it was Dr Lang's order. I told her that I was not in pain, in my finest sign language. I took the glass of water and sipped gently which nearly killed me. Like clockwork she turned up every hour on the hour and I gave her the same answer. By now we had our own sign language going. By six in the evening she had made six trips and did not manage to get a single tablet down my gob. She appeared exasperated and worried at the same time. God bless her.

She threatened to call the doctor and duly carried out her threat. Now it was two against one. Now the doctor looked worried. I should be in pain he said. He looked at me quizzically when I said that I was not in pain. I bet he was counting the marbles in my head or the sheer lack of them. I assured him that if in pain I would call the nurse. Ok maybe you could do with some morphine drip he suggested. No thank you, I said. The poor nurse looked like she was about to have a canary. She stood there dumbstruck while the doctor left to consult with Mr Lang.

Then I was left in peace. He was probably told to leave the stubborn fecker in pain till he yells and needs a shot up his backside. Anyway I was left in peace till my buddy Roger turned up with his wife Collette. They are the most caring of couples who had become my surrogate family. Roger asked questions, Collette did the fretting and I did my unique sign language in between gulping and trying to utter one word at a time.

I was managing the pain till the same poor nurse turned up with a slice of toast and a worried look. She probably would have preferred to see me across the yard in the psychiatric unit. Now she wanted me to eat. I took a nibble and pain shot across my forehead, through my shoulders and ran down my torso till disappearing through various orifices. She asked me to try again. I told her no, in a firm yet inaudible garbled tone accompanied by my sign language.

The poor thing looked close to tears and left the room leaving the toast on the side table. Roger got a great laugh while Collette scolded him playfully. Then lo behold the door opened very gently and Aisha's head peered from behind the door. She walked in quietly with Rihana in tow. For the past couple of months I was beginning to feel let down by my daughters especially when crippled with back pain. It took me more than twenty minutes to get dressed as my back was in spasms and left me in agony with no one around. I felt angry with them and did not tell them about my operation. They were getting on with their lives and I did not seem a priority in their scheme of things.

My love for them had not diminished but I felt angry and let down. I smiled and managed to drag my sorry ass up before giving them them a hug and a kiss. They looked very nervous and uncomfortable. Rihana had tears in her eyes while Aisha remained calm and composed. I was barely able to speak and they did not stay long as they had arranged to meet with their mother. I handed Aisha money for their taxi fare and then they were gone. I did not see them for another fortnight till Leyla arrived from the U.S for a six day holiday and the girls offered to accompany me to Shannon airport.

Roger and Collette left soon thereafter and I read some papers, cried a little and eventually went to sleep. The next morning breakfast arrived and I took sips out of the teacup but could eat nothing. I did try and chew the toast which pleased the poor nurse no end. Then Dr Lang arrived and I asked for his permission to go home. He looked horrified and told me that I had to stay till Friday and I told him that I had no intention of staying that long.

Eventually we mediated and agreed that I could go home on Thursday and return to his clinic on Friday. Somehow I made it through the day and tried to focus on my exams. Many a time I felt tempted to get up and leave but thankfully I didn't. My clothes were under the close supervision of the nursing staff and I could hardly leave wearing a hospital gown.

I asked my friend Seamus to collect me first thing the next morning and he duly obliged. On Friday morning I turned up at the clinic and was told that they had never seen such quick and clean healing and all was progressing better than expected. I was given a clean bill of health with instructions to return fortnightly. I went home to change and visited the office. I needed to catch up with work and study for my exams. I was back working seven days a week with no time to recuperate. Exams came and went and I received honours in my results.

Leyla arrived and Aisha and Rihana accompanied me to collect her from Shannon Airport. The warmth that existed between me and my daughters was beginning to diminish and I was none the wiser. My throat was still sore and oozing blood but somehow I managed. It was good to see my darling sister. She had endured an eighteen hour journey with three stops. She hugged and kissed her nieces who seemed nervous but behaved impeccably. We got home and the girls stayed for a while before leaving. Won't they stay with you? My sister asked with surprise. They have things to do and are busy with their lives, I replied nonchalantly. I did not wish for Leyla to see my pain.

Aisha had conveyed a message from her mother to Leyla. She wanted to meet her for coffee. Leyla was horrified. She could not stand this woman never mind speak with her. I asked her repeatedly to leave me out of the equation and then decide if she would like to meet with Sarah, if only for her niece's sake. It was neither good nor a comfortable proposition. Leyla made some new disclosures. Over the past few years Sarah had been on the phone to Leyla telling her about her abusive brother who would neither look after his daughters nor his wife. She had also accused me of being violent towards her.

Leyla had not told me for fear of hurting my feelings and she also knew that I did not discuss the shortcomings in my married life with either family or acquaintances. Leyla had a most pleasant stay but left in pain realising that neither of my daughters had stayed to look after me. If only she knew half of what I endured and had lived to tell this story. She enjoyed my cooking, appreciated my housekeeping and begrudgingly admitted that I was a better cook than her and our mum and would give the best of female housekeepers a run for their money. The week flew as she returned home to the U.S. Aisha and Rihana accompanied me to see her off.

In the latter half of the year I was invited to a distinguished law lecture at the National University of Ireland, Galway. Baroness Hale of Richmond was the guest of honour. She had written many a book on law and a year later was appointed to the first ever Supreme Court in the U.K. Madam Justice Catherine McGuinness was sharing the floor and I felt compelled to go.

At the time I was visiting community centres in Limerick and had to cut my schedule to attend the lecture. Mr Geoffrey Shannon, probably one of the most eminent legal scholars was in chair. This was the best gathering of legal minds one could wish and I had plenty to learn. I learned nothing except how condescending and conceited Baroness Hale appeared and how the industry of law have created a little world of their own. At every given opportunity indulgence was apparent till questions and answers. I waited and then I waited some more till

Baroness Hale answered a question pertaining matters of family law and the role and rights of fathers.

Her answer stated that men had changed very little as fathers and only now they were beginning to do a little cooking and ironing and had a long way to go before parity could be restored in family law. She also advised the gathered audience of law students and practitioners to focus more on family law as a lucrative career. Women having had generous court settlements were becoming financially independent and would soon be pursued by men seeking financial settlements.

It was the only growth industry in law, were her words of wisdom that I remember. It was heartening to see Madam Justice disagree with most of her sentiments and emphasised that the primary concern and focus should always be children. Geoffrey Shannon nodded but did not utter a word. My hand shot up as I wanted to ask a question. As the microphone moved towards me Geoffrey looked perturbed. He quickly gathered his wits and pointed out that there was time for only one more question and directed the microphone towards a lady who was retiring from the law department and invited her to speak. The young lady with the microphone looked confused as my hand was still up in the air. Geoffrey called the name of the lady and pointed to her position among the audience with forced humour while my hand stood upright seeking divine intervention. I got up and left the auditorium in disgust.

At every step of the way, the Law Society, the Bar Council and the state were doing everything within their power to shut me out and succeeding. Men were still wandering around like witless lemmings and their contribution amounted to nothing.

I wrote a fathers prayer and sent it around to government departments, media, and the government buildings and especially to members of the Senate and Parliament before putting it on my website. My website received 48,995 hits. The text follows:

A Fathers Prayer

'Oh Lord forgive me for I have sinned. I did not know any better thus became a Father and for this sin I have suffered. I pray that you the most loving and the most forgiving will grant me absolution, for my sins.

Oh Lord help us, for us the meek have no one else to turn to. Afflict our former Taoiseach with the curse of marriage, again, and drag him through the dark corridors of family courts where he shall receive enlightenment from the not so enlightened Judges.
Please God show our press the true meaning of freedom of speech, for they sadly not know the difference between, the 'Right speak, and the 'Freedom of speech'.

Oh Lord hear us, we the mere mortals and the meek seek what is our right and not what these sad creatures of the dark afflict upon us. Save us and deliver us from the clutches of evil, which you shall find in the Golden Pages, under the title of Government Departments.

Oh Lord hear us and deliver us from the not so wise monkeys, who have never known what to do, what they do and what they are supposed to do.

Oh God show them the light and the path to the local Courthouse, which will show them the error of their ways, after they have been 'Judicially castigated', 'Financially castrated' and emotionally crucified.

Oh Lord save us from The Taoiseach, The Justice Minister, The Minister for Family and Social Affairs, the rest of the Ghastly Ghosts and the Crooked Apostles, for the opposition is too weak to fight for the weak and the weaklings. Help remove them from Dail Eireann, for there, they do not belong.

319

Please God help us and deliver us from the practitioners of all things that are not dear to us. Can you please stop them from making things dear that are dear to us?
Oh Lord save us from the politically constipated, judicially antiquated, greed motivated, PR related and the spin dictated.

Oh Lord we humbly beg thee for your protection. 'Us the Lemmings, the intellectually deficient, the politically correct and the ones who no one seems to give a toss about.'

Oh Lord save us'.

Amen!

A labour Member of Parliament called back and he was incandescent with rage. How dare I desecrate and denigrate our highly respected politicians and institutions of government, especially our Taoiseach, he demanded to know.

This man had more hot air than a balloon aircraft and flew higher than a kite on speed. Then I had a word with Senator David Norris. He knows all about institutionalised racism and vulgarity. He is a proponent of free speech and equality in law and life. He became the first openly gay politician to the ire of the church, the state and the nation.

The very church that was bonking our children with the nudge, nudge, wink, wink attitude of the state while the nation stayed in a state of denial busily sweeping their crap under the carpet while attending the Sunday mass.

Nero fiddled while Rome burned.

Chapter Seventeen

In 2009 I had the media's begrudging attention and law graduates were attending my office in search of some insight and practise in matters of family law. My first advice was to dump the knowledge obtained from their books as it would serve little purpose in their practice of family law. The LL.B graduates are a rare breed and feel superior to their fellow graduates having self appointed to the pinnacle among all faculties in the university. They feel special. My comments were not taken too kindly but in ensuing years they returned to acknowledge that my earlier statement bore truth.

Then came post graduate students seeking assistance with regards research in psychology, social sciences, family law and social work. Some of them sent me their completed theses for comment. I offer my thanks to them for giving me credibility and further insight to their field of study.

One instance comes to mind which holds fond memories for me. A lady who in later years was to lecture in family law approached me with regards her PhD research. She was very sympathetic to the cause of fathers and their rights in law. While we talked she asked for something that I had written on matters of family law. I had a copy of my submission to the law reform commission on hand. She read it and asked if she could hold on to it.

At the end of our meeting she disclosed that she had proudly brought a published research article and she had wished to present it to me but after reading the content of my written submission she felt like her article was written by a school girl. I was honoured to accept her compliments alongside her published paper. Some of these occasions provided affirmations of my competence and knowledge which was refreshing. A question comes to mind, why are men so reluctant with acknowledgments and take things for granted? I offer my humble apologies for my temporary loss of memory and transgression.

Two men offered their services; actually one offered his services at a discounted salary of €50,000 per annum while the other tried to force me to employ him at a very manageable salary of €35,000 per annum. They both wanted to help me, my cause and fellow men. Neither possessed a primary degree or an iota of common decency.

Then there was Kevin who was thinking of committing suicide. His legal bill had escalated to €23,000 and he was left penniless despite earning in excess of €70,000 per annum. The deal being proposed by his solicitor would have left him with less than €100 per week for his sustenance. I sat with him to help prepare his case and advised him to fire his solicitor. He was scared but I convinced him to present the proposal to the court. The judge signed the order while his wife's counsel shouted outrage and threatened an appeal in the high court. Kevin was ecstatic and came to the office to hug me and brought me a present of a ½ litre container of milk, half a packet of chocolate digestives and a small box of tea bags as a thank you. He promised to return and help with my cause never to be seen again.

Then a former client started turning up without any formal appointment till one day I told him to stay away from my office. He was the first person to tell me to do my job and sort his mess out. I would refer to him as Sligo Paddy. He carried three cell phones, drove a fairly decent car and had jewellery dangling from his wrists but never left a penny for the charity's cause. He was an unmarried father with no access to his child and needed me to sort out his legal mess. He went around the offices block disturbing other businesses while demanding to know where he could lodge a complaint and get me fired. God bless the Sligo Paddy.

Then I got a call from a PR guy in U.K whose wife was putting him through hell and he was being constantly let down by his solicitor and barrister. To their disdain, upon my advice were fired by their client and he rang me as he danced in the rain. The judge had agreed with my proposal and he was ecstatic while crying and dancing to the amusement of the passing crowd. I did not hear from him again. There was much firing of the legal teams and I was busy evaluating and preparing cases with good outcomes but was slowly becoming disillusioned with men.

One of my volunteers Sophie, an honours graduate in law was becoming a real asset. She is bright, intelligent, committed and extremely caring. The poor thing came to interview me for a local newspaper and stayed till qualifying as a practising barrister. The poor mite paid for the sins she had not committed yet. I could not have done without her. She helped everyone, men and their extended families and especially the not so bright fathers. While she imparted invaluable legal advice free of charge, men spent their time viewing and evaluating her assets. From the uneducated to the highly educated, this was the common denominator. They failed to understand that it's the big head on the shoulders that is used for thinking and not the small head below the waist.

At last something good happened. Since last year I was paying myself a princely sum of €150 per week. It gave me sustenance and my home bills were paid. Family Support Agency had initially allocated a €2600 p.a. grant for counselling which increased to €4500 in following years and I had to declare a wage. Hence the princely sum of €150 per week.

In the meantime every charity in the country including woman's aid, rang me looking for a donation. Somehow they had got hold of my home phone number and rang all hours of the evening, persistently. They must have mistaken me for a philanthropist notwithstanding that men came, took and left with what little I had. The only solution was to have my phone line disconnected.

And then came some good news. A solicitor friend of mine had clients who had bought a sprawling estate with the intention of building a boutique hotel and a golf course. They were in serious trouble with so called professionals and getting nowhere in a hurry. On numerous occasions they tried to hire me as a consultant but I had turned them down. I was too busy saving men from suicide, depression and self destruction. Once again they came looking for me and my friend pleaded with me to see sense for my own sake and help her clients. Then she threw the curve ball. It would also help me pay my bills and try and save even more lives.

I agreed on the condition that I would work in my own time and the charity would always take precedence. They paid me €20,000 for my troubles which provided enough money to buy a decent pair of shoes, put some aside for my daughters and still have some left for a rainy day. All of a sudden I felt wealthy, could buy groceries, pay my phone bills and treat my daughters even nicer. A huge weight had lifted off my shoulders and I could do the job standing on my head. My daughters seemed happy and by now I had trainee solicitors and barristers as volunteers who were capable of answering phones. 2009 also saw me obtain my second degree and a level seven diploma.

Father and daughter had conferrals at the same university on the same and following days. Aisha looked excited and extremely happy having received a Diploma and a Degree on consecutive days. A few minutes later I heard someone talking in Irish and to my surprise found Aisha in deep conversation with her lecturer in Irish. My baby had become a young woman and in the recent past I had missed her so much. There was no time for tears just joy to behold. Some people knew me and came over to offer felicitations including some of her lecturers which made Aisha cross. Why can't you be my dad for one day, she moaned. I apologised and promised to make it up to her the next day when she graduated again. I invited Aisha and Rihana for a meal but they had made plans with their mother. The next day was Aisha's special day as she received her degree in corporate law.

I went to my favourite florist and stood there for the next half hour designing a bouquet to befit my darling daughter. I believe that I surpassed myself. By the time flowers, colours and their arrangement was finished the staff admitted that they had never seen such imagination and beauty. No they were not referring to me. I wanted the next day to be special and placed €1,000 in an envelope and pinned it to the bouquet.

Next day I donned my best suit, matching shirt and a handmade silk tie specially bought for the occasion. Aisha did not want a professional photographer and designated me the job of taking her pictures. The conferral was wonderful and my daughter stood out a mile. Rihana came and stood by me all through the proceedings as I felt prouder than any peacock. I took pictures in the hall, in the quad, on the forecourt and by the river till we ran out of locations. Then her friends came to meet with me. Aisha looked so proud. Then I came crashing down to earth. I had planned to take her and Rihana out for a surprise meal but they had made plans with their mother. After a hug and a kiss they left to meet with their mother. It seemed I held little importance in their lives as I drove back to my office.

I was invited by Deputy Padraic McCormack to a Fine Gael conference where the current Prime Minister was due to speak. Deputy Enda Kenny was on the soapbox and in full flow with rhetoric focused on health service and lack of beds. I waited patiently for questions and answers and held my peace. When the time came, I called for the microphone and duly welcomed the great one which woke Padraic up. He had fallen asleep as the great leader spoke. I asked him simply that when in power what changes he envisaged bringing to family law. The gushed look he had carried throughout the evening disappeared faster than the knickers on a cheap hooker. After a pause that seemed to have lasted till eternity, he replied. And as I was saying we will increase the number of hospital beds when we get to power and he continued with the rhetoric. He was back on the soap box as if my question never happened.

Then I was invited to a fundraising dinner with Minister John Gormley. He was the leader of the Green Party and an absolute gentleman. He was beginning to realise that the greens had gone into shark infested political waters with the mighty Fianna Fail whose fall from grace in 2011 was nothing short of spectacular. Vengeance is mine, said the Irish populace.

Dick Pryce wanted a meeting with the minister and I invited Mr Pryce and his wife to join the minister and made the introductions. The minister looked exhausted while Mr Pryce talked business. Thereafter I had several meetings with the minister and his fellow cabinet members. He tried to help but neither funding nor government support was available while the rate of suicide and depression amongst Irish males rose to an all time high. It seemed no one cared about Irish males, especially Irish men in power.

Then Deputy McCormack tried to organise a ministerial meeting only to be told by the minister for social and family affairs Mary Hanafin that the issue had nothing to do with her department and refused to attend the meeting. The next day she appeared on the front page of Irish Times declaring that absent fathers earning €18,000 and less were not paying a dime in child maintenance. It was a blatant lie. I had clients on social welfare of €185 per week paying €120 per week while sleeping on their mother's couch. Others had court orders for maintenance of €180 per week with €5 left for sustenance.

I knew the world of politics was dirty but never could have imagined the ferocity with which filth was being peddled. The meeting with ministers took place in Leinster house. It was shocking to see how little ministers actually knew about the workings of their departments. How much money do you need was the collective question from three ministers. €180,000 to run three full time offices in Galway, Cork and Dublin, I replied. Is that all one minister exclaimed. My civil servants earn more than that.

The meeting was most amicable and ministers seemed relaxed till one asked the fateful question. What do you think is wrong with politics and the workings of the state? Too much foreskin, too little foresight, I replied in haste. Thus endeth the meeting. They promised to help but no monies were ever made available. Men still came in droves seeking solutions while I became disillusioned with the male populace.

With 2009 coming to a close, I had once again made up my mind to close the office. Then a little miracle happened. In my life these events always happened when I was ready to take flight. Sophie got a call from a young lady called Ann. It appears that her brother who lived in the U.S had separated from his wife and had to fight long and hard to gain meaningful access to his children. Ann wished to help the charity as we helped fathers in trying to maintain a decent relationship with their children. She along with two female friends wanted to help and wished to organise a charity fundraiser.

By now my faith in men was long gone. I gave Sophie permission to speak with Ann and did not give the matter a second thought. Then another call came and Ann requested the charity's account details. I felt uncomfortable but obliged. The three girls managed to raise over five thousand Euros by the time I became aware of their lodgements. They wanted nothing in return, absolutely nothing. Time and again sisters helped their brothers and every time I was down a woman came to help me and my cause. I offer my gratitude and heartfelt thanks to all of them. Only gods knows where Irish men would be without their caring sisters. There was still hope and I could wish for a lot more but did not want to tempt fate.

Chapter Eighteen

Sophie became an asset with a mission. One minute she was approaching the media, next organising clinics and workshops. Men still forgot to turn up. In her spare time she chased the politicians. I shudder to think if god had made her a Jack Russell terrier; the hospitals would be full of chewed ankles and politicians on stumps!

She made time for the hardest exams of her professional career, the law society FE1 entrance exams and passed. Then she passed her bar exams and in between she found time to impress a visiting judge or two and won a scholarship to the U.S. Then she chased the newly appointed minister for Equality who later became a friend and the second esteemed lady in my life. It was the Minister for Equality, Integration and Human Rights, Mary White.

Deputy McCormack had come to the conclusion that the state would rather see me dead than alive and described minister Mary White as a lady who did not suffer fools lightly. It beggars belief that he still advised me to meet with her. The country was entering dire economic straits and ministers were not easy to get hold of. Sophie took on the mission with bravado. At a national conference, Sophie chased her around the hall and then she chased her some more. Whichever way the poor minister turned, Sophie stood next to her.

Not only did she accede to Sophie's request for a meeting with me but also granted her two minutes to address the national conference. If it were me, I would have resigned the ministerial position and run for the hills of sunny Carlow. Sophie could intellectualise anyone into submission. She narrated law like a parrot and ran around like a ferret, gnawing and chewing reference books and journals. My advice is not to mess with her. She is pretty as a picture, looks like a pistol and fires cannon balls. She is twenty nine years of age, looks fifteen and my advice, don't fuck with her or you'll wish that you were born a eunuch. Brains and beauty are a dangerous mix.

At my meeting with the minister I felt slightly overawed. She was the teacher and I simply answered her questions. I believe I got good marks. She asked basic questions and I dragged her into the quagmire of legal and social policy. She was patient and I was determined. As she felt annoyed, I became more annoying. God love her as she must be a saint to put up with me. And all this time the terrier behaved as if butter would not melt in her mouth. The bitch!

Minister Mary White promised to help and visited my office in the June of 2010 where she met with some clients of the charity and appeared visibly moved by the stories on offer. True to her word she went around the country and met with separated fathers. She wanted to find the truth for herself. She appeared in a state of anguish and wanted to put things right. She did dutifully what she promised with passion, pride and care. This lady cares deeply, I can assure you.

She is a Trinity graduate, a passionate speaker and loves nature but most of all happens to be a wonderful wife, mother, daughter and a precious human being. She also makes time for friends. An absolute treasure!

Whenever she spoke about separated fathers I could sense and feel the pain within her. Then appeared the million dollar question, what to do next? A ministerial meeting inclusive of Social and Family Affairs, Justice, Health, Community affairs and Education departments was proposed. The minister and her parliamentary and private secretaries chased the ministers and their staff with vigour. If there is anything more slippery than an eel, it's a politician. As soon as the subject matter was disclosed they became invisible.

330

Minister White asked for help and Deputy McCormack responded as he always did and duly delivered the newly appointed minister for Social and Family Affairs. We ended up with three ministers and a senior public servant with plenty of tales of poverty within government departments.

Minister Pat Carey came across as a warm yet quiet and reserved gentleman. I often wonder what made him enter the world of politics. There was no money to be found. After much deliberation minister Pat Carey left with no promises but to see how he could help. Minister O' Cuiv was himself, something offered and nothing delivered, minister Mary White pledged €10,000 which was matched by the Family Support Agency.

On 16 November 2010 I held a press conference in the Merrion Hotel, Dublin. National media was invited and they duly obliged. The charity launched its charter for family law and Minister White was present alongside one of the best family law practitioners in the country. Then Questions and answers were held. Every matter pertaining family law was duly discussed and answered. It covered the legislation, constitution, legal and judicial practices till questions were exhausted.

I was done and there was nothing more left to say. Sophie had invited fellow trainee barristers from the Kings Inns who found me threatening and intimidating. It was not my tone, my choice of vocabulary or my demeanour but the knowledge that I possessed and presented, I was informed later. I often wonder about the standard of guidance and training as provided by the Law Society and the Kings Inns when a schmuck such as I could intimidate the cream of their crop.

Minister Carey kept his promise and in December 2010 I was informed that €20,000 was allocated for an outreach worker and €30,000 for a counsellor plus €10,000 for travel and stationery. I was required to take care of office rents and all other bills.

On the 21st of December 2010 the Law Reform Commission announced its launch of Legal aspects of Family Relationships from its offices in Ballsbridge, Dublin. I was driving to the Law Reform Commission offices when my phone rang. I told the caller that I was driving and would call him later but he insisted on continuing the conversation. He belonged to a men's group in Waterford and had a client from my neck of woods who needed urgent help. He told me to ring him because it was my job. I disconnected the call and he rang again. This time I had decided that I had had enough of the pandas and the phone rang out.

It gives me great joy to state that Minister Mary White was the guest of honour for the proceedings at the LRC. As always the event was organised with professional competence and the staff were wonderful. Justice McGuinness was as gracious and welcoming as ever. The evening went spiffingly well. Madam Justice mentioned my name in her first line of speech which was a moment to cherish. One aspect of my journey was nearing end when a memorable event occurred which I shall savour for the rest of my life. Minister White strode across the floor with open arms and gave me the most wonderful of hugs to the amusement of the gathering. I felt safe, I felt wonderful and I felt alive. Some journey, eh!

The journey home was a nightmare with snow covered roads, abandoned cars and four hours to travel three quarters of a mile to reach M50. It took a further four hours to get back to Galway. Eight hour journey which usually took two but I was glad to reach home. I felt a little pensive, a little sad but glad that it was all over for now. My lonesome journey was over.

Ladies and gentlemen I shall bore you no more. You have your life to live and I have mine to search. In the meantime I bid you farewell for now and hopefully return with a better story. Till then be good to yourself and to others; a simple goodbye is all I have to offer.

The End

In 2011 I opened two new offices in Carlow and in Dublin. Minister Mary White officially opened both the offices and I felt honoured. The money allocated for the counsellor, that is moi, after tax, PRSI and Universal Social Charge disappeared in the rent and bills for the said offices. I was left with nothing but a sore back and hundreds of tales of woe.

By now I had had enough of men, mostly looking for magical solutions in family law matters that did not exist in real life. I had finished my Masters in Cognitive Behaviour Therapy and with three degrees and a diploma was earning nothing. Every week I went around the country visiting the three offices and kept appointments. In 2012 I decided to call it a day. The funding was allocated for one year and did not get renewed.

Not much has changed except I have decided to give myself a second chance. I have started in private practice and get paid. Thus far my clients are happy and I am working on a project for the common good and our children's future while pursuing a PhD. I am also qualified and certified as a Mediator in conflict resolution by the Mediator's Institute of Ireland.

But 'Fatherhood' is what I cherish most. Life is good for now and I do not ask for more but wish for a helluva lot. I am not a victim as much as the system has tried to victimise me. In fact I am grateful that it gave me the strength to scare the living daylights out of the incompetent and the uncaring. I am neither battered nor bruised. I have lost nothing but the most precious thing that has ever existed in my life, my daughter Aisha's unconditional love.

Rihana is still there dealing with her demons while trying to be a good sister and a loving daughter. I am always there for both of them, twenty four hours a day and seven days a week. I have retained my self respect and dignity and no one can take that away from me, no matter what. I am who I am, what I am and what I choose to be, forever trying to be a decent human being. Sometime, somehow, some day soon I hope to achieve my objective.

For now, I feel content.